HORROR

Horror cinema is a hugely successful, but at the same time culturally illicit, genre that spans the history of cinema. It continues to flourish with recent cycles of supernatural horror and torture porn that span the full range of horror styles and aesthetics. It is enjoyed by audiences everywhere, but also seen as a malign influence by others.

Brigid Cherry provides a comprehensive overview of the horror film and explores how the genre works. Examining the way horror films create images of gore and the uncanny through film technology and effects, Cherry provides an account of the way cinematic and stylistic devices create responses of terror and disgustin the viewer.

Horror further explores the role of horror cinema in society and culture, looking at how it represents various identity groups and engages with social anxieties, and examining the way horror sees, and is seen by, society. A range of national cinemas both historical and recent are discussed, including canonical films such as:

- *The Curse of Frankenstein*
- *Night of the Living Dead*
- *Ginger Snaps*
- *Suspiria*
- *Halloween*

- *The Evil Dead*
- *Candyman*
- *Saw*
- *Ringu*
- *Nosferatu*

Brigid Cherry is a senior lecturer at St Mary's University College where she teaches courses on film and popular culture. Her research into horror film audiences and fan canons has been recently published, alongside articles on *Candyman*, *Hellraiser*, and *Interview with the Vampire*.

Routledge Film Guidebooks

The Routledge Film Guidebooks offer a clear introduction to and overview of the work of key filmmakers, movements or genres. Each guidebook contains an introduction, including a brief history; defining characteristics and major films; a chronology; key debates surrounding the filmmaker, movement or genre; and pivotal scenes, focusing on narrative structure, camera work and production quality.

Bollywood: a Guidebook to Popular Hindi Cinema
Tejaswini Ganti

James Cameron
Alexandra Keller

Jane Campion
Deb Verhoeven

HORROR

BRIGID CHERRY

Routledge
Taylor & Francis Group

LONDON AND NEW YORK

First published 2009
by Routledge
2 Park Square, Milton Park, Abingdon, Oxon OX14 4RN

Simultaneously published in the USA and Canada
by Routledge
711 Third Avenue, New York, NY 10017 (8th Floor)

Routledge is an imprint of the Taylor & Francis Group, an informa business

Typeset in Joanna and Akzidenz by Taylor & Francis Books

British Library Cataloguing in Publication Data
A catalogue record for this book is available from the British Library

Library of Congress Cataloging in Publication Data
Cherry, Brigid, 1957-
   Horror / Brigid Cherry.
      p. cm. – (Routledge film guidebooks)
   Includes bibliographical references and index.
   1. Horror films–History and criticism. I. Title.
   PN1995.9.H6C44 2009
   791.43'6164–dc22
   2008034974

ISBN 13: 978-0-415-45667-8 (hbk)
ISBN 13: 978-0-415-45668-5 (pbk)
ISBN 13: 978-0-203-88218-4 (ebk)

ISBN 10: 0-415-45667-3 (hbk)
ISBN 10: 0-415-45668-1 (pbk)
ISBN 10: 0-203-88218-0 (ebk)

For Brian, who always knows the right movies to watch

CONTENTS

Figures and tables   viii
Acknowledgements   x

1. The horror genre: form and function   1

2. Horror aesthetics and affect   52

3. Horror cinema and its pleasures   94

4. Horror and the cultural moment   167

Filmography   212
Notes   219
Bibliography   225
Index   235

FIGURES AND TABLES

FIGURES

1.1	The *Shaun of the Dead* poster signposts the film's generic hybridity.	20
1.2	Laurie, the resourceful final girl of *Halloween*.	28
2.1	Expressionist shadows in *Nosferatu*.	64
2.2	Sam Raimi's use of Dutch angles used for over-the-top effect in *The Evil Dead*.	67
2.3	Anticipation before the shock of the reveal in Hammer's *The Curse of Frankenstein*.	78
2.4	Sharing the tactile sensation of disgust in *Suspiria*.	81
2.5	Make-up and prosthetic effects create the skinless Frank in *Hellraiser*.	83
3.1	Brigitte watches as Ginger transforms in *Ginger Snaps*.	114
3.2	Ana at the centre of the action in *Dawn of the Dead*.	130
3.3	Helen's gaze is highlighted in *Candyman*.	146
3.4	The alluring monster of *Candyman*.	148
4.1	Ben's body is thrown on the fire under the end credits of *Night of the Living Dead*.	180

4.2 The burning corpse of William Brown (28 September 1919,
     Omaha, Nebraska).   180
4.3 The gay male family in *Interview with the Vampire*.   184
4.4 Marketing and fictional world collide in the search for the
     missing students of *The Blair Witch Project*.   187
4.5 The on-camera confessional of *The Blair Witch Project*. 191
4.6 Technology is the conduit for horror in *Ringu*.   195
4.7 Sadako: an incarnation of the vengeful female ghost in *Ringu*. 197
4.8 Torture is the game in *Saw*.   201

TABLES

1.1 Categories of cinematic horror   5

ACKNOWLEDGEMENTS

The author of a book is never alone when they are writing and there will invariably be too many individuals to thank each by name. Over and above the usual thanks to colleagues and family (you know who you are), I would also like to acknowledge all the students who have taken courses on horror cinema with me over the years, whether at university, at the BFI or at the Filmhouse cinema in Edinburgh. I can honestly say that each and every one of them has been a delight to teach. Their interest, inquiring minds, lively discussion and love of horror have shaped this book.

1

THE HORROR GENRE: FORM AND FUNCTION

A hoard of shambling, decaying corpses hammer at the glass doors of a shopping mall. Three student filmmakers get lost in the woods searching for evidence of witchcraft. A teenage couple are slashed to death after sex. A man chokes on his dinner, writhing in pain as a creature tears its way out of his stomach. A woman's eyelids flutter in a state of ecstasy as an undead aristocrat punctures her neck with his fangs and drains her of blood. A scientist mutates into a disgusting half human-half fly creature after he teleports himself in a careless experiment. A journalist watches the ghostly images on a videotape and is doomed to die in seven days. A doctor saws off his own foot in an attempt to escape from a maniacal torturer. A vampire tells a journalist about his life of existential angst. A gigantic, lizard-like, alien creature rampages through Manhattan. A rape victim castrates one of the men who assaulted her.

All these very different scenes come from films that have at one time or other been labelled as prime examples of the 'horror genre'. Given that film genres are intended to be descriptive categories based on shared common traits, how can so many different scenes of horror be usefully contained by either popular or academic conceptions of genre? Surely, it should be easy to define a genre by its distinctive set of characteristics, formulaic plots and identifiable visual style? Yet this is not quite so true of horror, as evidenced by the sheer variety of characters, narrative events and styles in the above examples.[1] Some are set in the past, many in the present, one or two in the future. Several contain impossible supernatural monsters, others merely all-too-human killers, a small number improbable – yet physically possible – extra-terrestrial creatures, the odd exception may not – or may after all (hesitation being the key) – even contain a monster. A fair number are extremely violent and/or gory, others rely on a creepy atmosphere. Some show the horror in explicit, close-up detail, a few show very, very little or merely hint at a horrible sight before cutting away. Many tell a story from the point of view of the victims, others from that of the monster. Some are about revenge, several feature the struggle to survive, a few embrace death. It is not simply that there is a range of conventions that offers some degree of variation on a coherent, formulaic theme (as there are with other genres such as westerns or action films), but that this genre is marked by a sheer diversity of conventions, plots and styles.

One explanation for the variation may lie in the fact that genres are never fixed. In fact, the whole concept of genre is problematic, and this is especially true when it comes to the horror genre. Individual films may be shoehorned into marketable categories that can be sold to audiences, but those films may not exactly 'fit' the formula. Genres evolve, transforming and hybridizing over time in order to offer their viewers variations on a theme. Here perhaps is a key to the horror genre's sheer diversity: it has endured for so long, from the earliest years of cinema to the present day, and derives from so many different sources[2] that it has fragmented into an extremely diverse set of sub-genres. Horror cinema's longevity (it is now well over 100 years old, not to mention the fact that horror stories are themselves as old as mankind), means that the genre has evolved and developed many branches and offshoots. Deciding on a classification as to what film (or kind of film) is (or isn't) a horror film may not therefore be straightforward: what might be classed as the essential conventions of horror to one generation may be very different to the next, and what one person considers to be the defining features of a horror film may be in total disagreement with another's classification (Jancovich 2002b: 152). How, then, is it possible to discuss the horror genre as a coherent group of films? This book approaches that question by addressing its aesthetics, affects and audiences, and organizes this discussion around four further questions. First, in this chapter, what is horror? This looks at the traits and characteristics of the films that comprise horror cinema. Second, in the next chapter, how does horror work? This considers the way technology has been used historically to create its affects and audience responses. In the third chapter, the question of why horror is pleasurable is considered in the context of a range of theoretical approaches. Fourth, in the final chapter, the question of where and when is addressed to look at the ways horror sees and is seen by society.

In his discussion of Giallo,[3] Gary Needham (2002) suggests that these Italian mystery, crime and psychological thrillers are less a genre than 'a conceptual category with highly moveable and permeable boundaries that shift around from year to year'. The same could well be said of the horror genre. So rather than thinking of it as a distinct, unified set of films with shared conventions, the genre should perhaps be more accurately thought of as an overlapping and evolving set of 'conceptual categories' that are in a constant state of flux. Put more simply, horror is not one genre, but several; furthermore, as those various sub-genres – which Stephen Neale defines as specific traditions or groupings within genres (2000: 9) – change, so the boundaries of the genre as a whole shift. It is therefore perhaps better to think of the horror genre as a collection of related, but often very different, categories. These can include:

- sub-genres that divide the whole along lines of plots, subject matter or types of monster;
- cycles, defined by Neale as groups of films made within a limited period of time which exploit the characteristics of a commercially successful film (2000: 9), that mean one type of film is extremely popular for a short time, giving rise to many sequels and copies;
- hybrids – defined by Rick Altman (1999: 43) as the cross-pollination that occurs between genres to produce recombinant forms – borrowing

conventions from one or more different genre(s) and mixing them up with horror genre conventions;

- styles associated with particular film studios (Universal in the USA in the 1930s, RKO again in the USA in the 1940s and Hammer in the UK in the 1960s) or filmmakers (the films of Canadian filmmaker David Cronenberg made in the 1980s were collectively labelled 'body horror'[4]).

In addition, the diversity that arises from the large number of national horror cinemas can be considered. These have developed styles and varieties of their own based on their particular cultural histories (while many genre critics focus on Hollywood cinema, genres are also fundamental units of other national cinemas). The function of horror – to scare, shock, revolt or otherwise horrify the viewer – also means that filmmakers are constantly pushing at the boundaries in order to invent new ways of arousing these emotions in their audiences (who over time will naturally learn what to expect from a specific type of horror, a process that may well lead to viewers becoming used to or even bored with the formula) and thus keep the scares coming. In all these ways, notions of what the horror genre might be – or should be – are constantly shifting, creating new conceptual categories in order to keep on scaring the audience. We might, therefore, want to think about horror as an umbrella term encompassing several different sub-categories of horror film, all united by their capacity to horrify. This, the principal responses that a horror film is designed to exploit, is thus a more crucial defining trait of the horror genre than any set of conventions, tropes or styles. Nevertheless, it is worth thinking about those different conceptual categories that make up the horror genre. Some of the primary sub-categories or sub-genres of horror are presented in Table 1.1.

These sub-genre categories illustrate that a range of different forms can be identified within the genre (this taxonomy is merely intended as examples rather than a definitive list of sub-genres – they could be broken down further, or other categories could be added). The descriptions in this table are also kept to a minimum, and are intended merely to suggest

Table 1.1 Categories of cinematic horror

The Gothic

Films based on classic tales of horror, often adapting pre-existing horror monsters or horrifying creatures from novels and mythology

Dracula, Frankenstein, The Mummy (and all subsequent versions of these), I Walked with a Zombie and other traditional voodoo zombies, Masque of the Red Death, Near Dark, Interview with the Vampire

Supernatural, occult and ghost films

Films that involve interventions of spirits, ghosts, witchcraft, the devil, and other entities into the real world, often featuring uncanny elements

The Haunting, Rosemary's Baby, Kwaidan, The Exorcist, The Amityville Horror, Suspiria, The Sixth Sense, The Others, Ringu, The Grudge, The Eye, The Blair Witch Project

Psychological horror

Films that explore psychological states and psychoses, including criminality and serial killers

Cat People, Psycho, Peeping Tom, Eyes Without a Face, Repulsion, Carrie, The Hand That Rocks the Cradle, The Silence of the Lambs

Monster movies

Films that feature invasions of the everyday world by natural and secular[a] creatures leading to death and destruction

Godzilla, The Birds, The Thing from Another World, Alien, The Host, Cloverfield

Slashers

Films portraying groups of teenagers menaced by a stalker, set in domestic and suburban spaces frequented by young people, the only survivor a female who (in the early cycles) has not participated in underage sex

The Texas Chain Saw Massacre, Halloween, Friday the 13th, A Nightmare on Elm Street, Scream, I Know What You Did Last Summer, Cherry Falls, The Faculty

Body horror, splatter and gore films (including postmodern zombies)

Films that explore abjection and disgust of the human body, often involving mutation, disease, or aberrant and fetishistic behaviour (for example cannibalism or sado-masochism)

The Brood, Videodrome, The Fly (and other films by David Cronenberg), The Thing, Tetsuo, Night of the Living Dead, Evil Dead, Hellraiser, Dawn of the Dead, Shaun of the Dead, Resident Evil, The Howling

Exploitation cinema, video nasties or other forms of explicitly violent films

Films focused on extreme or taboo subjects, including violence and torture, other controversial subject matter such as Nazi death camps, rape and other sexual assaults upon women

I Spit on Your Grave, Last House on the Left, Henry: Portrait of a Serial Killer, Man Bites Dog, Hostel, Saw, Audition, Ichi the Killer, The Devil's Rejects, Irréversible

[a] Andrew Tudor (1989: 8) uses the term to distinguish creatures which are feasible according to the laws of nature (extra-terrestrial life may well be possible, even if we consider it unlikely) from supernatural creatures which we know cannot exist within the natural order (such as vampires, zombies and ghosts).

major conventions or plot directions, in order to avoid setting out pre-scriptive lists of conventions and thus ensure that these groupings remain relatively open and flexible. The same reservation applies to the examples of films given; these are suggestions rather than definitive lists. These categories are presented in order to illustrate the ways in which con-ceptions of the horror genre change or ways in which the boundaries shift. Looking at the examples given, it can be seen that some forms of horror might be more popular at certain times (for example, the classic Gothic horrors were more prevalent in the 1930s, whereas slasher films were dominant in the 1980s), some might be refreshed with a new cycle after a period of decline (the Gothic's resurgence in Hammer films from the UK in the 1950s and 1960s or the reworking of the teen horror films in the neo-slashers of the 1990s), some might be representative of different national cinemas (the supernatural has been a strong form in Japanese horror since the 1950s), and a few might be linked with horror by association rather than definitive style (psychological thrillers and some of the video nasties). On top of this, elements of horror might also be present in films that are not marketed as horror – Steven Schneider (2004a) employs the useful term 'cinematic horror'. Such instances of cinematic horror might allow viewers who are not usually addressed by horror cinema (since many horror films are aimed at the 18–24-year-old demographic and the typical horror fan is represented as male, this might include female, older, and high-brow audience seg-ments) with a similar viewing experience (being scared) without them having to make overt their taste for horror. Furthermore, categories may overlap – Carrie might just as easily be placed in the supernatural/occult category and The Others or The Blair Witch Project classed as Gothic, and films may also be generic hybrids (Alien is a science fiction-horror cross, which in some respects is an old dark house movie set in space; there are also any number of horror-comedies such as Shaun of the Dead, horror-westerns such as Near Dark, and Resident Evil has elements from science fiction but might also be classed as a computer game movie, and so forth).

What is clear from this is that the longevity of horror cinema, the sheer diversity of horror film subgenres and styles, the large numbers of generic hybrids, and the various national horror film cycles that have developed mean that horror is an extremely complex genre. Any attempt at producing a thorough overview of the genre covering all the styles in all of the historical and national cycles that have emerged since the beginnings of cinema would result in an extremely lengthy and convoluted account. This means it is nigh on impossible to provide a brief, comprehensive, and inclusive capsule definition of the genre that includes all the forms of horror that have arisen throughout its long history. Falling back on an overly-generalized or reductive set of generic conventions would exclude too many films or cycles which might in fact be widely considered to belong to the category 'horror'. On the other hand, trying to include every single generic characteristic would soon lead to over-complexity and potential contradictions. What is required, is a loose, rather than a concrete, definition of horror cinema. Nevertheless, before discussing horror cinema further, it is useful to engage with accounts of what is commonly considered as horror, even though we might want to put such accounts to one side in the long run. Engaging with genre theory in this way is only intended to serve as a broad introduction to horror cinema and a context for further discussion of particular subgenres or styles.

To begin, it is appropriate to consider why genres are important to the film industry and why the horror genre in particular has been so prevalent and popular. Horror is highly profitable for both the mainstream and the independent, low-budget or cult sectors of the industry. A few examples illustrate the economic significance of horror films.[5] *The Exorcist* (the leading film in the cycle of 1970s mainstream occult cinema) is among the most successful of all horror films. It was made for $12 million in 1973 and took $193 million from its domestic box office on initial release. With several re-releases, it has taken a worldwide lifetime gross of over $441 million. More recently, *Scream 2* (with a production budget of $24 million) took $33 million in its opening weekend in 1992, at that point, the highest for a December release. In total to date, *Scream 2* has taken over $101 million in domestic and over $172 million in worldwide lifetime grosses. In the independent, low-budget sector, *The Evil Dead* cost an estimated $350,000 to make, and grossed over $2 million in the USA on its initial release in 1983. After a re-release in 2005, *The Evil Dead* has taken $11 million worldwide. Another low-budget horror film, *The Blair Witch Project* was made for $60,000 (although quoted figures vary according to whether the costs of the marketing website are included, see Highley and Weinstock 2004: 16) and has taken a total of almost $141 million in domestic sales and almost $249 million internationally. Of course, there are horror films that are not as successful in terms of box office takings or indeed have flopped, but these examples illustrate that horror films are lucrative economic units for studios and independent filmmakers alike.

Genres are also, by their very nature, fundamental to the mainstream film industries (within Hollywood and without); they are units around which production and exhibition are organized. Barry Keith Grant (1986: ix) defines genre movies as 'those commercial feature films which, through repetition and variation, tell familiar stories with familiar characters in familiar situations'. Such films, he says, 'have been exceptionally significant in establishing the popular sense of cinema as a cultural and economic institution'. According to Grant, genre cinema is thus created by 'an industrial model based on mass production'. Production practices within the mainstream film industry (especially in the classical Hollywood era) tend to be centred around specializations, with studios, filmmakers, effects technicians and actors all becoming associated with particular types of film. At the consumption end of the industrial process, viewers tend to have particular tastes and want to see the kinds of films that they know they will enjoy, so genres have become a major selling point in the marketing and exhibition of films. However, such specialization in terms of production practice is common across genres, and there is no reason why this alone would explain horror's endurance. As much as there are large audiences for horror, it is not the only genre in which the general public is interested. Production and consumption contexts are central to the development of genres in general, not for any one genre in particular. In any case, horror has tended to be regarded as somewhat disreputable and it is often independent filmmakers and the smaller or less powerful studios that have specialized in horror. This does, in effect, mean that horror is successful outwith the mainstream film industry to a greater or lesser extent at different times. There ought therefore to be other more specific reasons that can help explain why horror – as one of several popular genres that have become essential economic units to many national film industries – has endured.

Other productive and well-loved genres have waxed and waned according to public preferences and cultural trends; genres that were once well established (westerns and musicals, for example) have declined to be replaced by others (action films and teen comedies, for instance) that better suit contemporary tastes. In contrast, despite periods of threatened (or media proclaimed) stagnation and decline, horror cinema has invariably been revitalized by new forms of the horror film, or variations on existing forms of horror cinema, sometimes combined with elements of other genres, often provided by low-budget, independent or international crossover hits. Drawing on the Russian Formalists theory of genre development, Neale (2000: 213) explains that these kinds of displacements in the genre occur through the acceptance (or 'canonisation') of a 'junior branch' that contributes, via some new artistic direction, to the process by which genres are contested and changed. On this level of course, horror's longevity is then simply explained by the artistic expansion of the conceptual categories. If horror cinema is a collection of evolving sub-genres and cycles, new forms can simply be added into the whole without destabilizing the genre as a whole. The many different forms of horror (sub-genres, cycles and hybrids) can also satisfy the tastes and preferences of various audience segments, thus increasing the range of horror films on offer and increasing audiences overall. But the question still remains, why should horror be an exception in defying its often-prophesied decline and continuing to flourish (even if on the fringes of or outside of the mainstream film industry)?

All films to a greater or lesser extent reflect the conditions existing at the time and place in which they were made. Genre films, because they are made as economic 'units' that rely on formulaic narratives that are especially vulnerable to reflecting a dominant ideology, are more likely to be barometers of the cultural moment. They meaningfully address contemporary issues and reflect cultural, social or political trends. By way of illustration, this is an argument that can be used to explain the decline of the western – the ideologies that were encoded in westerns reflected myths about the taming of the American wilderness and the role of the lone hero in those myths. As America moved into the postmodern period after the Second World War, the need for that myth declined – and so did the genre. Successful westerns that were made after this time were more likely to reflect the rewriting of those myths to incorporate the histories of the Mexicans (*A Fistful of Dollars*), Native Americans (*Dances with Wolves*), African-Americans (*Posse*), and women (*The Ballad of Little Jo*), or reconceptualize the traditional cowboy (*Unforgiven*), though the latter examples tend to be standalone films rather than becoming a junior branch which revitalizes the genre.

Horror cinema, on the other hand, has always appeared to be rather more flexible and adaptable in its encompassing of the cultural moment, giving scope for filmmakers to encode changing socio-cultural concerns with ease. In fact, since fear is central to horror cinema, issues such as social upheaval, anxieties about natural and manmade disasters, conflicts and wars, crime and violence, can all contribute to the genre's continuation. Since horror films tap into the cultural moment by encoding the anxieties of the moment into their depictions of monstrosity, there is an endless flow of material to 'inspire' horror filmmakers. Horror is thus a genre that is always ready to address the fears of the audience, these being fuelled by events and concerns on an international and national level. In this way, horror cinema is extremely flexible, and able to adapt easily to various periods of cultural change and differences across national boundaries. This can also explain historical forms of horror cinema, for example, the science fiction-horror hybrids of the 1950s (which encoded the oppositional politics of the Cold War), the slasher film cycle (reflecting social policies, class and the failure of social responsibility in the era of Reaganomics), and postmodern zombie films (social and political alienation in the consumer society). Such films are thus cathartic, allowing for these anxieties and other negative emotions towards the world or the society one inhabits to be released safely (a 'bounded experience of terror' according to Pinedo 1997: 41). And, of course, horror cinema can also represent more personal fears and phobias, which are ever present, and thus act to confront or release those fears on a psychological as well as a social level. We can thus see horror cinema as fulfilling a basic human need – for society and for the individual.

Yet if horror cinema is ideally suited to address issues of anxiety, the fact that it represents these anxieties as monstrous entities that commit acts of violence or disrupt the social order also imbues it with a taboo status. A further aspect of the genre's longevity may, then, be due to the fact that the depiction of such horrors is often regarded as being – at worst – dangerous and – at best – somewhat disreputable. Horror cinema's 'outsider' status derives largely from the fact that (unlike many genres which are designed as pleasurable escapist entertainment) it is designed to elicit negative emotions from its viewers – something that does put many people off. While its viewers do love to watch horror cinema and enjoy being vicariously scared in the safety of the cinema or living room, many people are put off or find such films distasteful. While there are horror fans who love the more extreme forms of horror, these films do often gain a lot of negative publicity – which further reinforces the low cultural standing of horror cinema generally. And if in terms of reflecting the cultural moment, horror films deal on an unconscious level with fears of violence by depicting acts of violence, might they not be easily misjudged for influencing their viewers and contributing to the violence in society? This is obviously a difficult question to answer, tied up as it is with the mass media effects debate: do horror and other violent films merely reflect violence in society or do they trigger it? Whatever the points in this debate are, the whole genre is potentially tainted. It has therefore been denigrated or ignored, never quite wholly acceptable, and relegated to areas of low budget, independent production – and even when it is embraced by the mainstream (clearly it is a profitable genre and since profit is the main driving force of the mainstream film industry, big budget, mainstream horror films are produced), it can never quite be 'tamed' and it continues to exist on the margins when it has gone out of fashion (where it is freer to confront taboos or contentious issues). As some sort of cultural 'other', horror flourishes thanks to its status as 'forbidden fruit'. This is not an inconsequential point, considering that horror films are particularly popular among younger audiences and underage teens are very likely to regard seeing a higher rated horror film as a rite of passage. Horror cinema's continued success therefore depends to some extent on it remaining taboo.

In these different ways, horror cinema acquires cultural longevity both within mainstream cinema and as cult, low-brow or trash cinema on the fringes of film culture. In the wider popular culture, horror also has strong and long-established traditions in the fields of the arts and entertainment. It is a productive and persistent genre within television, literature, comic books and the theatre. For example, horror novels and short stories are, and have been for some considerable time, an extremely popular literary genre (since the eighteenth century at least, but more recently with writers such as Stephen King, Clive Barker, Anne Rice and Joyce Carol Oates). Horror has also been a significant form of television drama from the early days of *The Twilight Zone* and *Quatermass* serials through to *The X-Files*, *Buffy the Vampire Slayer* and *Supernatural* in recent years. Horror cinema is thus often 'presold' by dint of its popularity and common cultural currency in other forms (fans of horror film are also likely to consume it in these other media). And since horror itself has a basis in older forms of storytelling such as myth and folklore, it is apparent that horror fiction generally (in whatever medium) might fulfill some necessary psychological or social function, being an essential dimension, for many individuals, of the 'human condition'. The logical conclusion, then, is that this human need is also key to explaining the genre's enduring qualities. Despite the fact that horror is variously depicted as trash culture, suitable viewing only for hormone-ridden teens, or as a dangerous social problem inciting viewers to acts of actual violence, filmmakers have continued to be attracted to the genre across the globe and audiences have flocked to their films to be – by choice – scared, grossed out, transfixed, amused and even sexually aroused.

In the light of this success (the genre's popularity, reach, complexity and economic viability, as well as its ability to reflect the anxieties of the cultural moment), it seems that horror cinema is an important context for studying genre theory as well as cinematic horror in its own right.

GENRE THEORY AND THE COMPLEXITIES OF HORROR CINEMA

Having established that horror cinema is an extremely heterogeneous collection of films, it seems appropriate to consider what the terms 'genre' and 'horror genre' might mean, not simply in terms of locating films within a genre, but also in terms of what the methodological and theoretical contexts of the classification process itself might imply about such terms. Underlying this question, of course, is what is meant by the term 'genre' itself within the contexts of film production, marketing, consumption and reception, as well as academic analysis and film criticism. The term is an easy enough one to grasp (it simply means type), but the notions of what distinguishes one genre from another or what the functions of genres might be (particularly as it has been widely considered within academic debate) is more complex. The precise nature of genre is slippery. Some genres – like westerns – are rather more homogenous and have somewhat more distinct conventions and boundaries than horror, but regardless of whether any single genre is more or less homogenous or markedly heterogeneous, the concept of genre as a taxonomy is not as straightforward as might at first appear.

Take the seemingly straightforward question of classification for example. The very term 'genre' suggests that there are groups of films that have a typology in common. The relatively straightforward approach of a typology suggests that generic conventions such as iconography (characters, costumes, props, settings), narrative (plots, subject matter, themes), or style (cinematographic features, musical cues) can be analysed in order to identify a film as belonging to a particular genre. Most viewers, media critics and film industry personnel refer to the horror genre, or to a film as being a horror film, in a relatively straightforward way. Despite horror cinema being a set of subgenres within shifting boundaries, it is still apparently easy enough to recognize a horror film when one sees one, regardless of whether it is a slasher, zombie, or supernatural film. It may seem intuitive, but at the same time this apparent ease in applying a label may mask the fact that people are not always clear about what types of films they categorize as horror or what features they might be basing such a categorization on. Certainly there will not always be any clear consensus on this. Applying a label to a film may involve subjective decisions, possibly based on prior opinion or expectations, and this complicates the whole notion of genres as distinct categories. Disagreements may well arise as to whether a film can be considered a horror film. As Mark Jancovich (2002b) has outlined, differences of opinion certainly exist over whether *The Silence of the Lambs* can be classed as a horror film, with different groups of viewers making contradictory classifications. Indeed, opinions can sometimes be very strong: on the bloodydisgusting.com forum one post reads '*Silence of the Lambs* is a thriller, you dickheads!' in response to the suggestion that it is an example of a horror film winning mainstream film awards (it won five Academy Awards in 1992).

Differences of opinion in classifying a film may also arise depending on whether a film 'works' as horror (that is, is it scary and therefore worthy of the label?). Is *Bram Stoker's Dracula*, for example, a horror film, or is it perhaps a Gothic Romance with a Byronic monster who is conflicted rather than wholly evil and who is sexually appealing to female characters and female audience members alike? Can it even be classed as a horror film, when in many people's opinions it is not a *scary* film? As Joyce Woolridge reminds us when discussing Coppola's film[6]: 'the sensitive lover that Dracula had been for most of the film in his velvet jackets and blue spectacles would terrify no one'. Yet the film still fits a typology of horror: a supernatural monster, female victims, ineffectual male characters, a final girl, and the religious and sexual iconography associated with vampire films including crosses, holy water, garlic, and stakes. In particular, the linking of sex and death may well instil typically horror-related responses in some viewers, suggesting perhaps that different conceptions of the horror genre exist amongst different sections of the audience (or indeed, as Jancovich's discussion suggests, between audiences and academics). Such instances of divergent classifications illustrate that there are other factors besides typological conventions involved in making genre classifications. With respect to the horror genre, one factor involved in defining the genre should perhaps be the way the films work on their audiences to create particular emotional responses. Thus, any film that shocked, scared, frightened, terrified, horrified, sickened, or disgusted, or which made the viewer shiver, get the goosebumps, shudder, tremble, jump, gasp or scream in fear could be classified as horror. Yet this then raises a further question about what this means when a film that is clearly not a horror film is horrifying in ways that make the audience experience one or more of these responses, at least for a particular audience segment. Examples of horrifying non-horror films could be *Blue Velvet*, *Fatal Attraction*, *The Wizard of Oz*, or even *The War Game*, a documentary about the results of a nuclear war (all of which are included in Channel 4's 100 Scary Moments list[7]). Accounts of genre should not just engage with film form, then, but with function and intended audience as well (and in this respect the marketing of films and the construction of audience expectations, together with the receptions of genre films, as well as aspects of the texts themselves, are all important considerations in analyzing the horror genre).

It is worthwhile exploring some of the theoretical approaches to genre in order to further illustrate how the whole notion of a horror genre might be interrogated. Stam (2000: 14) sums up some of the questions that concern genre theorists:

> Are genres really 'out there' in the world, or are they merely the constructions of analysts? Is there a finite taxonomy of genres or are they

in principle infinite? Are genres timeless Platonic essences or ephemeral, time-bound entities? Are genres culture-bound or trans-cultural? Does the term 'melodrama' have the same meaning in Britain, France, Egypt, and Mexico? Should genre analysis be descriptive or proscriptive?

To take Stam's final question first, a descriptive analysis would tell us what a horror film is. Yet being a heterogeneous collection of conceptual categories, no easy description is forthcoming. A proscriptive analysis would tell us what it is not. But defining a distinct and sharp boundary to the genre is not helpful either as the boundary is likely to shift. Both analytical approaches are thus problematical, but it is nevertheless worth exploring the way theorists have attempted to resolve this question.

Edward Buscombe (1970) engages with the idea that genre films have certain aesthetic characteristics – an iconography, in other words, a set of visual conventions comprising the common objects, figures and actions in the films. Indeed this idea has been widely applied in introductions to genre theory. It is true that some genres are easily described and thus recognizable by their narrative and stylistic conventions, as well as their iconographies. The western for example, appears to be identifiable quite clearly by a very specific locale or setting (in terms of landscape and historical period), as well as a fairly well-defined range of characters, props and costumes, and a distinctive set of narrative characteristics and themes. Gangster films and war films are somewhat similar to this in their (seemingly) well-defined and fairly static iconographies, even when set in different time periods or locales. This seeming ease of descriptive analysis may well be one of the main reasons why westerns and gangster films formed the subject of early engagements in genre theory such as those by Buscombe, Will Wright (1975) and Thomas Schatz (1981). But the approaches made in these accounts raise a number of concerns. Having described a genre, what happens when that genre evolves? Schatz, for example, discusses (1981: 15) what he calls the static elements of the genre (the generally agreed-upon traits such as images and themes), but also emphasizes that genres must in addition have dynamic elements (they must also contain innovation) – though these must be balanced in order to keep meeting audience expectations for the genre.

However, since no genre is ever completely static for any significant period of time (a horror film from the 1930s bears few points of resemblance to a horror film from the 1940s – let alone the 1980s), the notion of a typology is thus problematized by the way genres shift over time. As Christine Gledhill (2007: 64) points out genres are not discrete systems with a fixed list of characteristics. It must also be noted that not all genres are easily defined by iconography alone (as is clear with horror cinema). Other generic groupings, as David Bordwell (1989: 148) lists them, might be identified by mode (animation, documentary), style (film noir, German Expressionism) or audience (teen comedies, family films). Some genres are typified by the emotions they seek to create (comedy, thrillers, horror), or by format including the placing of set pieces or spectacles within the plot – this can be song and dance routines in the musical, or action and special effects sequences in the action film or disaster movie. What is interesting here in terms of problematizing genre, is that many of these groupings contain films that might also be accepted as horror: The Rocky Horror Picture Show (musical), The Mummy (action), Vampire Hunter D (animation), Nosferatu (German Expressionism), for example.

These points link to the reservations Stam raises regarding the taxonomy of genres being finite or infinite. If there are many overlaps between genres, leading to hybridity and exchange, and new variations are constantly being produced, how can the taxonomy of genres be finite? Aren't there a potentially infinite number of genres and generic crossovers? And since generic hybridity is so pervasive, any number of films that can ostensibly be classed as horror can be situated in terms of their specific combinations of genres. Near Dark is a modern-day western with vampires, for example. Alien is an old-dark house movie set in space; Resident Evil a computer game adaptation that combines gameplay-style cut scenes with conventions of science fiction and horror. Shaun of the Dead is in the tradition of British comedy but is also a proficient zombie film, as it says on the poster (Figure 1.1) that otherwise contains all the signifiers of the postmodern zombie with the grabbing hands of the zombie hoard and besieged heroes with improvised weapons: 'A Romantic Comedy. With Zombies'. And these films are not at all unusual in their mixing of generic features. In fact, genre hybrids have always been a factor in the evolution and transformation of genres, and John Hill (1998: 100) lists generic hybridity as one of the key features of postmodern cinema – so we might expect genre hybrids to be widespread. This would also suggest that genres are changeable. Although the horror genre appears to be timeless, the conceptual categories that make up the genre are linked very much to a particular historical moment and can indeed be ephemeral. Certainly some genres do go through peaks and troughs (the rise and decline of musicals and westerns for example that for a time fill a socio-political niche and then decline as the moment passes). There may well be links with the peaks and troughs of different kinds of horror film in response to social anxieties about violence, family breakdown, the war on terror, climate change, and so forth.

PROBLEMS WITH GENRE AND THE SLASHER CYCLE

Stam raises other questions that genre theory engages with, but these will be considered later. Before then, it is worth considering the changing nature of the horror genre and the difficulties in defining it. The examples in this discussion are drawn from the original cycle of slasher films; there is no particular reason for choosing the slasher except that the original cycle consists of a relatively contained set of films produced over a short period of time. Dika (1990) delineates the peak of the slasher film to be the period between 1978 and 1981, though it is perhaps worth extending that to the mid-1980s (the cycle has a long tail with seemingly endless sequels through to the 1990s and a resurgence in the wake of *Scream*, of course, but it is the main cycle when the subgenre

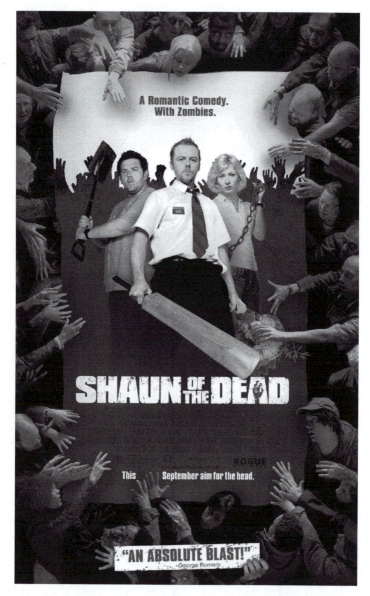

Figure 1 The *Shaun of the Dead* poster signposts the film's generic hybridity.

flourished that is considered here). The exercise can – and certainly should – be repeated with other subgenres of horror.

In writing an account of the slasher film in terms of early genre theory (this is merely meant to illustrate the concerns, it is not to advocate the method), one approach would be to include all the possible slasher films in the definition without question. However, it might be simpler to only discuss the canonical slasher films – *Halloween, Friday the 13th*, and *A Nightmare on Elm Street*, along with one or two others such as *Prom Night* perhaps. The criteria for canonical status would – for the sake of this argument – be the most high-profile examples, but other criteria for selection might be applied (the films with the strongest cult standing – perhaps the films considered so-bad-they-are-good or those that are the subject of cult status for the very fact that they do play with the conventions, for example). A definition based on an analysis of these other films might then lead to a different set of core conventions. Andrew Tudor (quoted in Langford 2005: 13) sums this problem up when he states that:

> To take a genre such as the 'western', analyse it, and list its principal characteristics, is to beg the question that we must first isolate the body of films which are 'westerns'. But they can only be isolated on the basis of the 'principal characteristics' which can only be discovered from the films themselves after they have been isolated.

Tudor calls this the 'empiricist dilemma' (essentially the same conundrum as whether the chicken or the egg came first). If we replace western with horror in the above quote, it can quickly be seen that the set of conceptual categories making up 'horror' simply makes the problem worse. Thinking of a genre as a categorical type with distinctive characteristics is not always helpful. Such an approach to genre has at its core the contradictory notions of on the one hand identifying the key characteristics or essential features of the genre drawn from typical films belonging to that genre and on the other of typing films so as to place them into particular genres. Those films often taken as prime examples of a genre give rise to a certain set of characteristics then taken as defining the genre (a cyclical process which can become self-defeating). In this way, a genre can become a self-defining entity – a definition can be selective, excluding films that are too dissimilar to a pre-supposed definition, or it can be so wide that the definition becomes too unwieldy or ambiguous. As we can see from the above example of the slasher film, this begs the question of how earlier precursors such as *Psycho*, *The Texas Chain Saw Massacre* or *Black Christmas* and later neo-slashers such as *Scream*, *I Know What You Did Last Summer* and *Cherry Falls* might be included, as well as variations such as *When a Stranger Calls* in which the killer returns to stalk the adult he previously attacked as a teenager or *Silent Night, Deadly Night* which tells the story from the narrative point of view of the killer.

As Altman points out (1999: 89–90), in populist terms a genre might be thought of as 'inclusive' – comprising all the films that met a straightforward definition, but on the other hand early academic genre analysis would focus on a much smaller 'exclusive' list of films (usually those considered to be 'canonical' in that they were good examples of the 'essential' generic conventions). It is already clear that horror cinema is extremely varied in terms of its narrative and iconographic conventions, not only in the wide variation between different subgenres or cycles, but within subgenres and cycles too. An inclusive list of films in the horror genre would quite obviously be unwieldy. An exclusive definition, of course, could easily be contradictory. Under this approach, if the canonical horror films of the 1980s are taken to be slasher films, say (and many members of their teen audience would no doubt agree), then definitions of the horror genre are centred on slasher conventions. Of course, the slasher film with (at least superficially) an easily definable cast of characters and limited range of locations (American teens being stalked by a serial killer in a suburban locale) has a very different set of conventions, styles and narrative approaches from Gothic vampire films (bourgeois or middle-class characters in historical and often European settings having their ordered lives disrupted by an aristocratic monster) or body horror (when monstrosity erupts from within and graphically transforms the body of the contemporary, usually urban character into something disgusting). And even if the slasher film is taken as the defining style of the late 1970s and early 1980s alone, then the derived conventions are likely to exclude the large numbers of exploitation, splatterpunk and gore films which were also in circulation at the time. Many of these were from Italy and Spain – films such as *Anthropophagus*, *Macabro* and *City of the Living Dead* which feature zombies and cannibals, suggesting cultural or national differences. This period also saw the flourishing of horror cinema in Korea, Hong Kong and Japan and these often took different forms than the American slashers in featuring superstition, demons, ghosts, and revenge – films such as *Demon Pond*, *House of the Lute*, and *Bloody Smile*. Nor does it consider Brazilian horror films of the period such as *A Deusa de Mármore* – a horror-cum-sexploitation film – or the Gothic horrors of *A Virgem da Colina* and *As Filhas do Fogo*. These examples of different national horror cinemas hark back to Stam's questions about the cultural nature of genres.

One point that Andrew Tudor (1974: 132) makes relates to how early models of genre sought to identify a 'factor X', or single defining characteristic of a genre. But Tudor himself points out the problem with this in *Monsters and Mad Scientists* (1989). Under such a model the factor X of the horror film might be taken as being a supernatural monster, say. Any film that contained such a monster would be a horror film, and any film that did not would not belong to the genre. Noel Carroll (1990) takes this argument further and suggests that horror films must contain a frightening and disgusting monster. Carroll claims (1990: 39–40) that since the monster (Brundlefly) retains the sympathy of the heroine even when he has become a monstrous revolting half human-half fly creature that therefore by this definition *The Fly* is not a horror film. This is only one possible factor X but it does illustrate that it can be very difficult to identify a single defining trait. In which case, how is it possible to draw up a meaningful descriptive account of the horror genre? Tudor (1989) suggests that the attention should be moved away from the films themselves onto the classification systems that are used. In this case, to talk about horror films is to talk about a set of meanings common to the culture (1989: 6). The boundaries of a genre may well be blurred (or shift as they do with horror), but the members of the culture still know a horror film when they see one. So to describe a film as a horror film is not therefore to say that it has features X, Y and Z, but that the culture recognizes it as such. Genre, Tudor says (1989: 7) is 'what we collectively believe it to be'. Altman refers to something very similar to factor X, what he calls 'essences' (1999: 2). However, Altman is doubtful whether any cultural consensus on what a genre is can ever be agreed on. This is illustrated by the fact that different audience segments might well have different ideas of what horror is or should be. There might be divergences between fans and casual viewers for example.

Carroll relates these different audiences to co-existentialist and integrationist models (1990: 191–92). The integrationist viewers are those he deems to be 'specialist' viewers (we might think of them as hard-core horror fans or gorehounds) who enjoy graphic examples of horror, who enjoy experiencing the disgust and other negative emotions of horror, and want to see the most explicitly gory effects displayed on screen. Such specialist viewers (as a fan culture) might well conceive of horror cinema as defined by gore and other explicit effects. On the other hand, Carroll argues that most viewers are co-existentialist, or average viewers (his term for more casual viewers). He argues that viewers in this group will put up with the emotions of disgust and horror, in order to have their curiosity about unnatural monsters satisfied. For this audience, satisfaction may come just as much from watching films that could be placed in other genres such as fantasy. In these co-existentialist terms, the viewers might well recognize much less explicit films as horror. As Altman suggests, collective agreement may not be forthcoming between these two groups, and as he asserts the term 'horror genre' may be used for different purposes and in different ways by different user groups (1999: 123–24). As Mark Jancovich (2002c: 470) concludes, this means that 'genre terms are therefore fundamentally unstable and ambiguous and resistant to any essential definition'.

Exactly how resistant to definition genre terms are is illustrated by the peak slasher cycle of the late-1970s and early-1980s. The slasher formula is often taken to be something along the lines of 'a killer returns to the scene of his or her earlier crimes and kills a group of people one by one, before finally being killed by a female survivor'. However, even films within the same cycle quickly evolve beyond the basics. The three most significant films in the original slasher cycle are *Halloween, Friday the 13th* and *A Nightmare on Elm Street*, each having initiated a long series of sequels and each having a monstrous killer who has become a horror icon (Michael Myers, Jason Voorhees and Freddy Kruger). Yet each of these films shows significant variations from a basic slasher formula. In *Halloween*, the final girl does not 'kill' the monster alone: Michael is also shot by Dr Loomis. In *Friday the 13th* – as viewers of *Scream* should know, even if prior to this they had made the same mistake as Casey – the killer was the mother of Jason, masquerading as her son who only became the monster in subsequent films. *A Nightmare on Elm Street* introduces a much stronger supernatural theme into the formula in the shape of a monster who can invade and kill through dreams (rather than stalking his victims in real life). Since *Halloween* and *Friday the 13th* were made very early in the slasher cycle, a formula was not yet firmly established. The fact that *A Nightmare on Elm Street* was made late in the cycle, demonstrates the way filmmakers innovate within genres.

Other films in the slasher cycle also vary the elements. *Slumber Party Massacre* is an overtly feminist critique of the slasher film (it was directed by Amy Jones from a screenplay by feminist writer and gay and civil rights activist Rita Mae Brown) and allows several final girls to assist in killing the stalker. *My Bloody Valentine*, apart from presenting a spate of murders on a special occasion (Valentine's Day, of course) as is typical of slasher films, diverges from the rest of the formula almost entirely. The film moves the setting from suburbia to an industrial mining town, the characters are not teens but adults in their 20s, and as opposed to teenage sex, the plot centres on a love triangle, the male rivals of which are forced to co-operate when they believe the woman to be in danger. Nor does the film open with the events in the past that are coming back to haunt the present (this comes later in a flashback), and there is no final girl as such. Of course, there were other films in the cycle – *Prom*

Night or *Sleepaway Camp*, for example – that did follow the formula fairly closely, but others similarly varied it – *Happy Birthday to Me*, *When a Stranger Calls*, or *Silent Night, Deadly Night*. Not only would a proscriptive definition clearly have to exclude some of these films, but where should the line be drawn and who should draw it? What percentage of the formula is essential, how many elements can be varied – and by how much – for a film to still be classed as a slasher, and at what point might a film stop being a slasher and fall outside the genre? What would it be labelled then? Even if these questions had meaningful answers, they wouldn't necessarily address the issues of how the culture or audiences conceive of the genre, how viewers respond, or what the films tell us about production and consumption contexts. These films also illustrate the way that a genre definition might vary according to whether we include all the films that might have some similarity to the key slasher films, or only those that are close to the formula established by these same films. Clearly, to return to Altman's and Tudor's points, these films are all recognized as slashers by their teen audiences, horror fans (who might reject or disparage them, but still regard them as such), media critics, and academics.

A more important factor in discussing horror cinema and its sub-genres or cycles, then, is to engage with what these films 'say' rather than what they 'are'. Altman (1999: 207–10) defines the debate about 'inclusive' and 'exclusive' definitions as a semiotic or structuralist one. In undertaking a structuralist analysis of genre, the inclusive (semantic) approach advocates a study of all the films that appear to share the common elements (characters, locations, shooting style, etc.), whereas the exclusive (syntactic) approach analyzes the relationships between these elements and how they are structured within narratives. Altman uses the linguistic terms semantic and syntactic since they refer, respectively, to the building blocks and the structures into which those blocks are built. However, Altman notes that the semantic approach can provide a useful description of a genre, but it is limited in that it does not explore the social significance of the genre. Applying this to horror, and returning again to the slasher cycle, the semantic approach would identify the constituent elements (teenagers, a killer returning to the scene of earlier crimes, a final girl who overcomes the killer), whereas the syntactic approach (such as that of the western by Jim Kitses 2004 in which he sets out the narrative oppositions of garden and wilderness) would identify themes such as the warning against underage sex.

In several slasher films the sexually active teenagers are killed and the final girl is either literally a virgin or not interested in boys. In *Halloween* it is not spelt out that Laurie (Figure 1.2) is a virgin, but she is represented as being academically bright and focused on her school work (which makes her unattractive to the boys). Virginity/purity versus sexual activity/impurity thus becomes a key organizing syntax in these slasher films (though in the neo-slasher cycle *Cherry Falls* varies the trope with a killer who selects virgins, meaning the teenagers are encouraged to have sex). In this respect it is also interesting to note that other socially unacceptable behaviour results in death in the slasher film: in *Friday the 13th* for example Jack is killed after smoking cannabis. Other horror subgenres might be organized around ideologies of the family and women's independence, say, or the larger overarching themes of narrative oppositions such as good and evil, or life and death. These themes are organized in such a way as to bring stable, coherent meanings to the genre. The syntactic approach is thus intended to produce an explanation, to bring deeper ideological meanings to the fore, but there is a tendency to ignore those films that do not contain the social meaning that the analyst has chosen to focus on. Altman originally proposed therefore that a dual approach (the semantic/syntactic approach) was necessary in order to identify the full significance of a genre. Altman (1999: 221) points out that in this respect it can be seen that 'not all genre films relate to their genre in the same way or to the same extent'. So certain slasher films might then exhibit different semantic/syntactic patterns: *The Silence of the Lambs* employs several visual and narrative patterns of the thriller, but is about the rite of passage of a final girl; *Alien* (Carol Clover 1992 includes Ripley in her list of final girls) is a combination of the mise-en-scène of a science fiction film with the psycho-sexual themes of horror.

Figure 1.2 Laurie, the resourceful final girl of *Halloween*.

Altman's dual approach therefore engages with inter-generic connections and generic hybridity, as he says (1999: 221) 'numerous films [...] innovate by combining the syntax of one genre with the semantics of another'. Schatz (2004: 691) suggests that since a genre cannot be productively discussed as either a single film or all films, genre analysis should instead address 'a *system* of conventions which identifies [a genre's] films as such'. Furthermore, this illustrates that some conventions are shared between genres, but might be used to create different meanings in different genres. As Stephen Neale points out, the horror film and the gangster film both foreground violence. Neale (1980) renegotiated genre theory by examining the parameters of genre cinema from a post-structuralist perspective. He addressed the question of how the categories (conventions) used in the definition of specific genres could be used in formulating a model of genre. He recognized that particular elements were capable of 'performing different and distinct functions' (1980: 16) in different genres. (Guns, for example, are an integral part of the iconography of both the gangster film and the western, yet in each genre having very different roles and conveying very different meanings.)

Neale examines theoretical categories of genre cinema and with respect to narrative he considers the 'process of transformation' (1980: 20) of the various elements involved. Genres, he proposes, are modes of the Hollywood narrative system: 'Particular genres function simultaneously to exploit and contain the diversity of mainstream narrative' (1980: 20). For instance, violence in westerns, gangster films and detective films is physical and serves to disrupt the equilibrium. It is signified in terms of Law. However, other genres deploy 'figurations of violence' (1980: 21) in different ways. Violence also marks the horror film, but in the horror genre it is not the violence per sé which is a characteristic of the genre but its 'conjunction with images and definitions of monstrosity' (1980: 21). It is the monster's body in conjunction with violence, and not the violence alone, which is the focus of the narrative disruption. So whereas in gangster films the 'discursive disjunctions' (1980: 22) are related to law and order, the legal system, crime and justice, etc., the disruptions in the horror film are between the natural and the unnatural (or supernatural). Hence (1980: 22):

> The narrative process in the horror film tends to be marked by a search for that discourse, that specialized form of knowledge which will enable the human characters to comprehend and so control that which simultaneously embodies and causes its 'trouble'.

In the horror film, this knowledge is metaphysical. However, there is no clear universal set of monstrosity and metaphysical knowledge at work within horror. Different forms, cycles and subgenres produce different reworkings of the basic pattern. In a film such as *Psycho*, the monster is a psychologically disturbed individual and the metaphysical element is scientific (a psychiatrist is called on to explain Norman Bates's delusion), whereas in the Gothic forms of horror, for example, adaptations of *Dracula* or *Frankenstein*, the monster is clearly beyond human and the metaphysical element has a religious aspect.

Neale argues that darkness is another important element in both the thriller and the horror film. In the thriller, 'darkness is the edge between presence (that which it conceals) and absence (that which it is)' (1980: 43). Darkness, Neale claims, does not quite belong to the narrative world, but nor is it simply a signifier (in a semiotic sense). It oscillates between the two. Shadow plays a similar role in the horror film, frequently in those moments of suspense that centre on the appearance of the monster. Neale's account suggests that genre analysis should focus on the way the conventions and common elements are structured within the text. The vast majority of horror films do follow some of the conventions of the genre, and as such they are situated in a generic context. It is this context that is perhaps more important than the exact combination of generic conventions that the films employ.

In that respect, particularly since the approaches to genre discussed above do not wholly account for how genres work in practice, it is also helpful to focus on other, pragmatic as Altman calls them (1999: 208), properties of genre. According to James Naremore (1995: 14), these might be commercial strategies or aesthetic ideologies, for example. As Kendall Phillips (2005: 5) puts it: 'if we talk about a film as if it is a horror film – market it that way, respond to it that way, interpret it as one – then it is, effectively, part of the horror genre'. Altman (1999: 210) similarly states that the semantic/syntactic approach is lacking because it leaves out considerations of the audience and institution. In pragmatic terms, the labelling of a genre film is more likely to be intuitive rather than based on a specific definition of any kind (which may be subjective in the case of inter-generic or hybrid films in any case). Stam's reminder about whether genres really exist or are the creation of analysts is important here. Who exactly is it who determines the genre of a film – the filmmaker, the marketing department, the media critic, members of the audience? What if the purpose of the genre label as applied by any of these groups is different? In what contexts does such labelling matter, if at all?

The pragmatic approach Altman suggests would, for example, ask questions intended to determine exactly how filmmakers conceive of genres or film cycles. While it is important to note that even though a typology derives as much from standardized industrial production practices (particularly the specialization by Hollywood studies during the classical Hollywood era) as from anywhere else, what is subsequently thought of as a genre is not necessarily defined by the industry. In fact, as Jane Feuer (1992) points out, genres are synthetic rather than organic in terms of their conception. They are artificial creations, and as such genres are often 'created' after the fact. Filmmakers may create texts, but they do not create genres. Though a few filmmakers may create innovative approaches (which others then emulate in order to cash in on a successful formula), film theorists or critics (or even fans) are often the people who invent labels for groups of films.

The term 'slasher' for example only became a popular label for the horror films of the period in the early 1980s – two or three years after *Halloween* and long after *Psycho*, or even *The Texas Chain Saw Massacre* and *Black Christmas*. Reviews for films in the early 1980s often referred to them variously as 'mad slasher movies', 'knife-kill flicks' or 'dead teenager pictures' (though the term slasher has stuck, whereas the others did not). The popular film critics Siskel and Ebert used the term 'mad slasher' in their television and newspaper reviews, thus lending it popular cachet. Though Siskel and Ebert may not have been the first to use the term slasher in reference to this group of films, they did bring it to public attention – before this, slasher had occasionally been used to refer to so-called snuff movies or was used in the stalk-and-slash label, particularly in reference to the Italian Giallo. In the context of Altman's approaches to genre, it is useful to note the way these labels are being taken up by particular audience groups. Terms such as stalk-and-slash and mad slasher may be in circulation among fan cultures, and where films cross over to more mainstream appeal, the term may also make a cultural transition from cult to mainstream. As Tudor (1986: 7) asserts, 'notions of genre are not critics' classifications made for special purposes; they are sets of cultural conventions'.

In terms of such cultural consumption, Tom Ryall (2000: 27–28) usefully defines genre as 'patterns/forms/styles/structures which transcend individual films, and which supervise both their construction by the filmmaker and their reading by the audience'. Once a film genre has been named and linked with certain successful or notable films, only then does it become an organizing structure which other filmmakers aspire to and audiences latch on to. There are clearly examples of the slasher subgenre that were made before *Halloween* (*Black Christmas*), but it was only after the success in the marketplace of such films as *Halloween* that the cycle gained a label that stuck. And having been thus linked to a generic type, the label 'imposes expectations on the viewer' (Fowler 1989: 215). It is interesting to note that in labelling these kinds of films, critics coined terms that indicated the kinds of horrific acts depicted in the film: thus 'knife-kill', 'slasher', 'stalker' or 'stalk-and-slash'. The supposition here is that they were simply letting the potential viewer know what to expect from the film. It is the focus on such acts of violence that therefore supervises the production and consumption of further films in the cycle.

Genre thus becomes bound into the way the film industry is organized (particularly within the mainstream Hollywood system). Genre conventions act as a kind of contract between the producers of films (be they studios or filmmakers) and their audiences. There is thus an acceptance of certain artificialities in the specific contexts of genre film production. This unspoken agreement results in an organized system of film production that is based on sameness rather than innovation, and produces entertainment rather than art. In the case of the slasher film (and by extension, horror cinema as a whole), this feeds into the idea that the horror film belongs to low culture rather than art, resulting in the debasing of horror generally. There is a strong suggestion that it is fit only for teenagers who have not developed the critical faculties to appreciate more refined forms of entertainment. During the early 1980s slasher cycle, the critics who applied the term mad slasher to these horror filmmakers did so in the context of disparaging the genre. Gene Siskel, for example, wrote[8] that *Looker* was 'nothing more than a … mad-slasher film'. There are clearly implications related to notions of high/elite and low/trash culture. Genre labels might then indicate value judgements: films labelled splatter, slasher, gore and so on, along with exploitation or video nasty,[9] are linked to low culture, whereas films that are labelled psychological thrillers can be positioned in the mainstream (middlebrow if not exactly high culture). This is one reason why a film such as *The Silence of the Lambs*, which Jancovich (2002b) reminds us is considered horror by some audiences, can be nominated for and win several Academy Awards.

In general terms, industrial practice and the collaborative nature of filmmaking lead to the production of standardized units (in this case the genre films themselves). However, the underlying notion that genres tend towards the formulaic does not mean that genres are either static or lacking in artistic value. Box office success might lead to further similar films being made in order to cash in on that success, but staying too close to the formula of past success can lead to stagnation and rejection by the audience. Indeed, some degree of variation is required in order to keep the interest of the audience, and filmmakers strive to produce novel or distinctive work by which they can be recognized while remaining within a marketable category. A good example of this is *A Nightmare on Elm Street*. For Wes Craven, the film was an opportunity to innovate: thematically the film represents the culmination of his interest in the world of dreams; in avoiding the cliché of the knife as the weapon of choice in the slasher film he came up with Freddy's razor-fingered gardening glove, and he also wanted to humanize the monster and gave Freddy Kruger rather more of a personality than some other slasher villains (see Robb 1998: 62–63). Craven's experience in making *A Nightmare on Elm Street* also illustrates the struggles that filmmakers sometimes experience during production. Brian J. Robb (1998: 65) reports that the script was rejected by all the major studios it was submitted to because it was difficult to categorize: neither a formulaic slasher film, nor a traditional horror movie, and nor was it in the style Craven was at that point known for. It was only the then independent company New Line that would take a risk on the film.

Horror filmmakers frequently push against the boundaries of the genre in this way. While some films might be extremely formulaic, the best (often these are most enduring) examples of the genre frequently break the rules: some films are genuinely innovative, while others introduce variation, perhaps by taking elements from other genres and thus creating genre hybrids. In fact, horror cinema is an extremely adaptable genre in this way, overlapping the Gothic romance, melodrama, fantasy, film noir, the psychological thriller and science fiction in addition to the range of genre hybrids that have been produced from the horror-western to the horror-comedy. Many of these attempts to break out of the formula have led to new cycles within the genre. This is true of all genres to a greater or lesser extent but since horror tends to be produced on the margins of the mainstream (as Craven was forced to do with the 'unclassifiable' *A Nightmare on Elm Street* or because the genre is regarded as somewhat disreputable), low-budget filmmakers often have more freedom to push against the boundaries. In terms of economics, since many horror films are produced at the low budget end of the scale, filmmakers are forced by circumstance to be innovative or inventive with what little resources they do have access to, often making a virtue out of a necessity. And since depictions of cinematic horror depend to a large extent upon special effects technologies, technological developments are also frequently exploited to introduce new themes and trends.

At other times, horror can sometimes be accorded a much more central position (as in the Hollywood occult cinema of the 1970s), again leading to further variation as the genre's features are merged with more mainstream film forms. The filmmaker's intent is – as Altman has proposed – frequently key to understanding the role of genre in production and consumption. With *Slumber Party Massacre*, Brown's feminist approach to the slasher formula resulted in a film that was parodic in its intent to expose the sexist nature of the cycle. While there are clearly elements which foreground (and thus poke fun at) the psychosexual nature of horror (one of the final girls in the film uses a large machete to cut off first the excessively long rotating drill bit of the killer's power tool weapon, and then – in case anyone in the audience failed to spot the castration symbolism – his hand, before he is finally decapitated), some young male horror fans report having sought the film out for the female nudity – as fan-critic Michael Saunier[10] writes:

> Back in the 7th grade my best friend and I rented a flick that he assured me featured FULL frontal nudity, or as he so elegantly put it 'bush'. The promise of seeing a woman in all of her glory was all it took to get my hormones into a feeding frenzy and we took *Slumber Party Massacre* home for the next three days. [It] did not have the full frontal as promised by my liar of a friend, but there was a cornucopia of breasts and quality horror to more than make up for his betrayal.

Feminist responses to the film were different again; Justin Kerswell[11] recalls that:

> Many feminists at the time clearly didn't get the joke and were reportedly outraged by the picture and felt betrayed. Jones however, in a televised interview, said that she felt that the protesters were taking the movie and its violence much too seriously.

As this illustrates, audience responses and readings can be a vital element of how genre works in practice.

AUDIENCES AND THE AFFECTIVE NATURE OF HORROR

Despite the difficulties with genre classification (and the problems with some aspects of genre theory itself), the horror film is one of the few generic types widely regarded – that is, by audiences, the industry and the popular media – as a distinctive film genre, even if it is not easily definable. Crucially, the horror genre is seen in a unique light in respect of its audience. As Robin Wood (1986: 77) states:

> The horror film has consistently been one of the most popular and, at the same time, the most disreputable of Hollywood genres. The popularity itself has an unusual dimension that sets the horror film apart from other genres: it has an audience that is restricted to fans and others who wholly embrace the genre, while amongst the rest of the population there is almost total rejection; people either love or hate the genre, tending to watch horror films either enthusiastically or not at all.

The horror film, then, might be expected to have a discrete and strongly loyal audience, the vast majority of people either showing a strong liking for the genre or a total dislike, with little feeling in between these extremes. In the vast majority of cases this comes down to whether the individual embraces the negative emotions of horror film viewing (that is, enjoys being vicariously scared) or feels uncomfortable and upset by being made to experience disturbing or displeasurable emotions in this way. My own research into the horror film audience (Cherry 1999) illustrates that being scared is not an entirely negative experience and, especially when it is linked to a fascination with violence, supernatural entities, or the dark side, some viewers undoubtedly enjoy the emotional affects of horror cinema. As most fans will probably agree, being scared can in itself become the main pleasure of watching horror films, and not the particular films themselves.

In this way it is the emotional or physiological responses that are as (if not more) important than any specific narrative or thematic characteristics of the genre. This can be taken to explain the broad definition of what constitutes the genre for some fans: they expand the boundaries to include any film with effectively scary content (Cherry 2008: 206). In respect of this liking for being scared, it can be something which stems from the childhood or early teen years for many fans (Cherry 1999: 196), and it may be related to Joanne Cantor and Mary Beth Oliver's (1996: 75) finding that 'coping with media-induced fears' is linked to 'the presence of a caring adult and discussion with a parent', both of which 'are potent fear reducers for children'. The response of the care-giver in a case where a child has been frightened by something she watched is, according to Cantor and Oliver, crucially important to how well the child learns to deal with his or her fears. This suggests that it is possible to learn how to be safely scared in response to scary images in fiction.

In other words, all viewers experience the same emotional responses, but some people are able to handle – and therefore accept and take pleasure in – the films that engender these emotions more easily than others. It is also likely that some people who have difficulty dealing with their emotional responses to horror films are nevertheless curious about the way they feel and might want to explore horror films further – and it is possible that once they start viewing horror, they then 'learn' to deal with the emotions or become accustomed to them. This would suggest that it is not only a matter of taste per se that divides the audience, but cultural competencies (which can be taken to include learning to understand horror cinema and how it functions or works to create emotional responses) and the acquired ability to handle the emotions that horror films engender that comes through such competencies.[12] Dolf Zillman and James Weaver (1996: 86) recognize in this respect that since frequent horror film viewers become habituated, then the responses one observes at horror film screenings (audience members screaming, jumping in fright, clinging onto their friends, averting their look at the screen, even shouting warnings at the characters or laughing) are to a large degree play-acting or pretence. It is a performance that is expected, if not demanded by the construction of the horror film itself.

According to Zillman and Weaver (1996), horror films – and they are particularly concerned with slashers and other teen horror films – represent a safe means for adolescents to learn and practise the gender roles that they will shortly be expected to as adults. Their model of the genre suggests that it is designed to allow adolescent males to demonstrate to their peers that they can stand up to the frights and shocks offered by horror films and offer comfort and protection to their girlfriends, while adolescent females can demonstrate their sensitivity and need for protection. Attendance at horror films for adolescents is thus part of the teenage dating ritual. Zillman and Weaver (1996: 82) maintain that this process derives from ancient rites of passage characterized by 'strong gender segregation along protector-protectee lines'. In contemporary society, watching horror films with one's friends provides a social context that stands in for formal rituals which mark the passage into adulthood. Horror films are particularly appropriate for this ritual since they allow males to demonstrate their fearlessness, bravado and protectiveness towards women, while females are able to show their dependence on men and demonstrate their emotional reactions.

This rite of passage depends on habituation, especially for adolescent males – as Zillman and Weaver state (1996: 86):

> With repeated consumption of horror films ... even squeamish boys should soon be able not to express any residual distress. Eventually, they should not experience distress and be at ease signalling protective competence. Girls should analogously experience a lessening of distress reactions. Their task of exhibiting dismay and helplessness may prove difficult after habituation, and demands on play-acting may ultimately be greater on them than on boys.

This would seem to be suggesting that the horror film audience is more likely to be comprised of those individuals who learnt to cope with their emotional responses to fictional events in early childhood or those who are practising some sort of peer-group ritual, but learning to cope with being scared by fictional horror and learning the responses that are required by the films may be 'skills' acquired at any time of life (the horror film audience obviously has a wider demographic spread than teenagers and younger adults alone). What is clear is that regardless of age, gender or other demographic grouping, the responses – and the modes of affect that create those responses – are central to the genre itself.

Given that the audience is constructed around the genre in this way, and that responses to horrific material in films are integral in this, it is important to incorporate considerations of audiences and audience responses as significant factors in any model of the horror genre. There are two aspects worth considering further here. The first of these is related to who exactly horror film viewers are: what demographic groups make up the audience, what specific tastes and preferences they have in terms of different types or styles of horror, and what the relative proportions of each are (that is, how important each audience segment might be in economic terms to the industry and how high profile the segment might be in influencing what types of horror films get made). The second is how horror cinema depends upon specific intended responses in its construction, and in particular how it plays on these in the production, marketing and exhibition of different conceptual categories of horror.

CONCEPTIONS OF THE AUDIENCE

In the first instance, the horror film audience is often thought of as consisting of younger people in their teens and early twenties. With the preponderance of the teen slasher films since the late 1970s dominating the genre, the horror film audience has been widely regarded as consisting primarily of those under the age of 24. As Vera Dika (1990: 87) states:

> The audience for the stalker film, as is typical of the horror genre, is overwhelmingly young: these R-rated films (no one under seventeen admitted without a parent or guardian) were frequented by adolescents between the ages of twelve and seventeen.

Obviously, this refers specifically to the American audience, but a similar profile can be found in other countries where slasher films are popular. James Twitchell's observations of horror film audiences (1985: 70) lead him to the conclusion that 'most of the audience are in their early to mid-teens'. Carol Clover (1992: 6) claims that 'the proportions vary somewhat from subgenre to subgenre and from movie to movie [...], but the preponderance of young males appears constant'. Charles Derry (1987: 163) describes teenagers as 'the major audience for horror films', Morris Dickstein (1980: 69) finds that 'those who submit to (horror films) are generally young', and Evans (1984: 54, my emphasis) finds horror movies to be 'uniquely tailored to the psyches of troubled adolescents, *whatever their age*'. Evans seems to be suggesting here that some adults may like horror films, but he implies that they do so only because they retain the mindset of adolescence. This may well be an important reason why some older individuals retain their liking for horror films beyond their teens, but other factors may apply; the continued liking for horror may also be attributable to a love of the dark side or a fascination with appealing monsters such as vampires that may have very little to do with adolescent psychosexual issues (although there may well be an element of erotic appeal in the case of vampire cinema). Overall, however, the assumption is that young males predominate. Underlying these assumptions is the further supposition that the young female viewers in the audience are present as the dates of the young males (and furthermore are cowering viewers). These quotes reflect the perception of the contemporary horror film spectator as a young male in his teens or early twenties.[13]

Some media perceptions of the horror film audience also denigrate the audience members as somehow unintelligent or dangerous. A review of Hammer's The Curse of Frankenstein in the Financial Times in 1957 called the audience 'the saddest of simpletons' (quoted in Hutchings 1993a: 7–8). The media frequently suggests that horror film viewers are somehow disreputable or dangerous. In the June 1992 edition of the woman's magazine *Cosmopolitan*, for example, an article by E. Lederman entitled 'The Best Places to Meet Good Men' (quoted in Crane 1994: 18) warned its readership against starting up a conversation with a man looking for horror films in the local videomart since such men have 'questionable feelings about women'. Lederman goes on to state that 'Whether buried deep within him or overtly expressed in his words and actions, his misogynistic tendencies make him a man to avoid'. Often, criminal cases where horror films are cited or blamed are widely covered in the media.

One recent example is that of a man who slashed a friend after they had been drinking with his replica of a Freddie Krueger glove: the judge in the case described the defendant as 'an extremely dangerous man' who 'was obsessed with […] *Nightmare on Elm Street*'. An investigating police officer made a statement that declared 'it is obvious these films influence the way people act. It gives us some concern, and unfortunately we have to pick up the pieces afterwards'.[14] While horror fans would not hesitate in condemning acts of violence in real life, these attitudes illustrate that the horror film audience has always been regarded as a somewhat dubious other, the fans dismissed as 'them' in contrast to the normal 'us'. These are clear examples of the way in which horror films and their fans are demonized. This may well work to marginalize older viewers and non-fans who do not wish to be aligned with such negative stereotyping. Furthermore, the view that the horror film audience is primarily male persists in many areas of the film industry. In part, this may be because the Hollywood-based film industry sees its primary target audience as a whole as males between the ages of 16 and 24 and consequently aims most of its big budget films and blockbusters – and accordingly much of its marketing and publicity – at this demographic group (Kramer 1998).

However, it should not be assumed that the wider interest in horror and the desire to view horrific material is restricted only to (unintelligent) males in this age group. As my own research has shown there are many older horror film viewers over the age of 24 and many female fans (Cherry 1999). In her account of horror film marketing, Rhona Berenstein (1996) also sets out to confront the ideas that the horror film audience is predominantly male, that female viewers if they do exist cower in fear at the horrific sights on screen, and that horror films construct a sadistic, male ideal viewer. She also questions whether the monstrous heterosexual desire at the centre of the narrative depends on the terror and suffering of the passive female victim/heroine at all. In confronting these assumptions head on, she notes that press reviews of classic Hollywood horror films could be contradictory, for example in the way that some coverage regarded the horror film audience as homogenous and ungendered, while other coverage pointed out with surprise that horror films were as popular with women as with men.

Such surprise seems to be a perennial occurrence – more recent press coverage of horror in films and other media such as computer games has taken a similar tone. As the president of Miramax Mark Gill (interviewed by Andrew Hindes for *Variety*[15]) says when expressing surprise that audiences for *Scream 2* were more than 50% female: 'Horror film audiences used to be heavily male. If they could drag their girlfriends along you were lucky'. Even if this supposition is true (and it is not at all clear that it is), viewers not in the younger male demographic may be a hidden audience viewing horror films in their own homes on DVD or television broadcast. It may take films like the *Scream* series to bring the female horror film audience into the cinema. It can be seen therefore that not only are there different audience segments (teens, hardcore fans, female fans, and others – perhaps the co-existentialist viewers that Carroll discusses), but as Jancovich (1996: 10) points out, 'the differential distribution of cultural competencies and dispositions means that different audiences have different senses of how genres are defined and where the boundaries between them lie'. This argument suggests that audiences might well be significant in constructing definitions of the genre (harking back to the assertion that genres are cultural artefacts, and what we believe them to be). As Kim

Newman (1992: 16) recognizes, the fan audience tends to have a high level of generic competence: 'Few areas of cinema depend so much on the loyalty and inside knowledge of their audiences'.

The (often independent or low budget sectors of the) industry market their films accordingly, but more significantly the loyalty and knowledge are recognized in the horror press. Horror films are written about in great detail and are the subject of enthusiastic coverage and critically balanced (though not always highly positive) discussions and reviews in specialist magazines (many published and/or written by fans themselves), while by contrast mainstream press reviews often apply the term 'horror' to films in a pejorative manner in order to pass over a film or depict it as low-brow entertainment (as in Siskel and Ebert's remarks about mad slasher films). Fan discourses about horror (and this may be in the many online e-zines and discussion forums, as well as the traditional print media) may then construct a genre definition very different from that of popular consensus.

Since genre categories as defined by fans, or by teens and other demographic segments of the audience, may be different from popular perceptions or even some academic accounts, and may indeed be vague and indefinite in some cases, Jancovich (2002a: 11) states that 'the genre distinctions which usually dominate within film studies seem almost irrelevant'. In focusing on the audience rather than the text, any definition based on generic conventions is bound to be less relevant not least since different audience groups will undoubtedly have their own ideas of what films constitute the boundaries of horror (or, indeed, what is horrific). In this respect, a potentially useful engagement with horror (and one which seems to be used by many of the fans themselves in their own subjective ideas about what horror is) is where emotional and physiological responses rather than generic conventions become the focal point of the definition. As Twitchell (1985: 8) states: 'Horror art is not, strictly speaking, a genre: it is rather a collection of motifs in a usually predictable sequence that gives us a specific physiological effect – the shivers'. Twitchell (1985: 11) describes what he calls the shiver sensation as first and foremost a physiological response – for example, the goosebumps; it is not purely emotional – there is some kind of physical response as well (this could also be jumping in fright, feeling that one's skin is crawling or having a physical sensation of nausea, perhaps even fainting).

The horror film does not have sole ownership of images or narratives that inspire or are centred on fear and other related emotions. According to S. S. Prawer (1980), for example, the works of the surrealists and their successors (the work of David Lynch can be included in this category) are closely related to the horror film in their intent to create unease in the audience. However, horror fans and viewers frequently rely on such affect in their own categorization of films as horror and, although a reliance solely on emotional responses to films as a basis for the classification of horror could be misleading on an individual level (if a viewer is responding to what they personally find horrific), it can – and does – reflect a cultural consensus in fan cultures or interpretive communities related to connoisseurship (see Matt Hills 2004: 71–90). While it might be theoretically advisable to take into account, as Twitchell indicates, the narrative and generic motifs of the films as well as emotional responses when defining horror as a genre, it is also necessary to acknowledge what elements audiences themselves consider to be indicative of the genre. In addition, Tudor (1989: 3–6) states that: 'a popular genre is significantly constituted by the conceptions of it held by its audience as well as by the texts that instantiate it' and further that:

A genre is a special kind of subculture, a set of conventions of narrative, setting, characterisation, motive, imagery, iconography and so on, which exists in the practical consciousness of those fluent in its 'language'.

As he goes on to say (1989: 6), a genre is thus a social construction; it is subject to 'variable understanding by different users at different times and in different contexts'. Waller (1987: 6) also observes that: ' … given the diversity of the genre since 1968, it is impossible, I think, to define once and for all the essence of modern horror'. Given such an impossibility, the responses constructed by the films may well be the only linking feature.

MODES OF EMOTIONAL AFFECT

It should be clear from the preceding discussion that the key factors in the way genres are conceptualized are different for different genres. In this respect horror cinema is particularly centered on its spectacle (images of cinematic horror) and the responses such spectacles are intended to create in the viewer (feelings of fear and revulsion). Prawer engages with a model of genre that is extremely fluid (1980: 17) in that it is closely tied to 'sensations of safely terrifying shock' (1980: 9). In his account of what he calls the 'fantastic terror film', he suggests (1980: 7) that there are two denotations of the word horror. The first, which he terms 'horrific', is defined as 'an emotion compounded of fear and loathing'. The second he describes as a 'feeling of awe and imaginative fear', and he gives this the label 'uncanny'. In this way, Prawer does not define the horror film, or the 'cinematic tale of terror' as he calls it, in terms of a set of narrative or aesthetic characteristics, but rather links his definition to how the horror film works on its audience. He suggests that such films:

- are receptacles for theological transfigurations;
- play on fears of invasion of privacy;
- appeal to fears that base instincts may emerge;
- articulate terrors of everyday life/social concerns;
- exploit fears of the consequences of science or aspirations of 'alchemists';
- lure viewers into half-willing complicity with evil or madness;
- connect with the spirit of place;
- appeal to fear of what we do not know.

This is an extremely important idea since in this model (whether the key features of horror cinema are restricted to Prawer's categories or not) the content of a horror film primarily serves to create emotional responses. These emotions are either ones related to the uncanny (the shivers or goosebumps) or those related to the horrific (revulsion and disgust), though it is of course worth noting that any single horror film might provoke both.

This idea has been developed further by Neale (1980) in his post-structuralist analysis of genre. Neale suggests that the relationships between films within and across generic categories can be theorized in terms of modes of emotional affect. In this respect it is appropriate to ask what function(s) a horror film has. The generic label – horror – is perhaps the best clue here: like the thriller or the weepie, the genre is named for the emotional or physiological response it is expected to produce in the viewer. Just as the thriller is expected to have the viewer sitting on the edge of their seat in intense excitement (from the 'thrilling of intelligibility' as Barthes 1966 calls it) or the weepie to bring them to the point of tears, so the horror film should horrify or scare the viewer. In fact, the term 'horror' is related to the scientific term 'horripilation' (referring to the effect when one's hairs stand on end, colloquially referred to as 'the goosebumps'). For Carroll (1990), however, shocks and jumps – the scare tactics of certain kinds of horror film – are not emotion, but rather they are reflexes. Such responses, he points out, are also a feature of mysteries, thrillers and suspense. He is much more concerned with an emotional state he calls art-horror. This emotion is 'some non-ordinary physical state of agitation' created/caused by 'the thought of a monster ... which ... is threatening and impure' (1990: 35). Regardless of this more nuanced approach, it is the responses to depictions of horror onscreen – be they emotional, physiological or physical reflexes – that are key. Linda Williams (2003) gives an interesting account of the affective nature of horror that is rather more focused on how films function than on their specific forms. She locates horror, melodrama and pornography in one larger grouping of genres that she calls 'body genres'.

Films belonging to these body genres elicit strong physical responses in their viewers and focus on the corporeal: for melodrama this is shedding tears (weeping), for pornography it is sexual arousal (orgasms), and for horror it is fear (violence). Indeed, she suggests that the stronger the physical response, the better an example of the genre the film is judged to be by its viewers who use the level of affect as a determining factor of 'quality'. In the horror film this takes the form of violations of the body, as for example in the slasher film in which the bodies of the slaughtered teens are stabbed, slashed and opened up (a violation that is also perhaps a symbolic rape as the knife of the killer penetrates the body). Williams recognizes that all three of the genres she analyzes are marginal in that they are designed to elicit base (or lower) emotions (she calls this the 'jerk effect' in that they are literally tear-jerkers and fear-jerkers in the case of melodramas and horror films, or in the case of pornography – jerk-off movies). She calls these types of film body genres since they all feature bodily excess (and it is important that the excessive body is most often gendered female) and the films rely on the spectacle of the body undergoing intense uncontrollable emotions. Obviously, these spectacles of emotion are intended to be mirrored in the spectator. In the horror film, this is in the 'portrayal of violence and terror' in which the body is out of control, 'beside itself' with fear (2003: 144). Williams suggests that the aesthetic of the horror film is designed to bring about intense sensations of fear, in other words to provoke affective experiences around depictions of violence. What is important here is the way the responses of the viewer are contained within – and thus key features of – the narrative and stylistic components of the horror film.

MARKETING AND AFFECT

The privileging of these different modes of emotional affect clearly do differ over time or subgenre, and the marketing of various films reflects this. In particular the way in which gore films (privileging revulsion and disgust), slashers (privileging shock and dread) and the supernatural (privileging the shiver sensation) take precedence at different times in the evolution of horror cinema is significant. This does not necessarily mean that only those types of horror film are in circulation at that time, but that the predominant forms of horror effects are exploited within a range of films. For example, the supernatural film has undergone something of a regeneration since the late-1990s (in the wake of the cross-over success of Japanese horror films such as *Ringu* in English-speaking territories), but while the intended affects of films such as *The Sixth Sense* and *The Others* are primarily based on the shiver sensation, others incorporate a substantial level of gore resulting in feelings of disgust alongside the shivers. One such example of this mixing of emotional affects is *Malèfique*, which in its narrative of prisoners seeking to escape from jail by locating the caballist knowledge hidden in the prison cell combines an uncanny, eerie atmosphere with excessive violence and moments of extreme body horror.

One question that remains is how expectations are raised (and thus how audiences are primed to respond to such films). Obviously, marketing plays a key part in this, informing the potential audience whether a film is uncanny and suggestive, or gory and violent – thus allowing the individual to select their viewing material according to their own tastes in horror. Berenstein's study (1996) of horror film advertising (this includes media reviews and marketing stunts such as having medical staff or ambulances on standby should viewers be overcome by the onscreen horrors) from the 1930s points out that posters, trailers and other marketing promotions for horror films were often designed in a way that 'trained' the audience in how they were expected to respond. Berenstein finds it significant that this often circumscribed horror as an ideal site for the performance of socially constructed gender roles (including heterosexual dating rituals). Horror films such as Universal's *Dracula* were presented in their posters not as horror films, but as frightening thrillers and romances in order to attract both male and female audiences, respectively (the thriller being seen as a masculine genre and romance feminine).

This does not mean that the male audience is not interested in romance, though it may be socially difficult for men to admit to such, whereas a taste for thrillers and for horror is socially acceptable. Nor – more importantly – does it mean the female audience is only interested in romance per se, simply that at that time (and to some extent this situation is still true for some women, though the situation has changed significantly post-feminism) it was socially unacceptable for women to be seen to enjoy horror. If a horror film was marketed as being in a genre that was seen as socially acceptable for women to consume, women were free to enjoy horror films/thrillers. To a degree, this means that the romance label was a pretence to make horror acceptable for different audience groups, hiding the fact that women enjoyed watching horror films. Clearly this confronts preconceptions about the demographic makeup of the audience as well as the way films are categorized. Further highlighting the confusion of genre labels, Berenstein also points out that marketing practice between 1931 and 1936 (the period with which she is concerned) grouped hypnosis films (including vampires, zombies and mummies), mad-doctor movies, and jungle-horror films under the label horror (again illustrating the shifting boundaries and conceptual categories of horror cinema).

Horror film posters of the period typically depicted displays of fear – both male and female. On one of the posters for *Dracula*, for example, the top half contains an image of Dracula gazing intently at his female victim, his hand on her throat, her head thrown slightly back and her eyes closed in a kind of ecstatic trance (just perhaps as Bela Lugosi's female fans might imagine themselves to be[16]). By contrast the bottom half of the poster, divided off by the title of the film, shows the three male characters huddled in the lower left corner, the one at the front of the group holding out his hands to ward off Dracula who is descending a staircase on the right. Just as the image of the female character on the poster might be a reflection of the female viewers' responses as they might be swooning over Dracula/Lugosi, this image of the male characters might too reflect a male response, giving permission for the male viewers to experience fear of the monster, which at the same time can be held at bay.

On the other hand, promotional gimmicks of the time revolved around personifying 'fear' as feminine. These were based on gender expectations that women scream and cower during horror films, while men display their mastery of emotions as bravery (though this might simply mask their own fear since there is a danger this could be seen as feminine and thus emasculating). If the studios marketed films in this way, and the exhibitors went along with it, the films themselves also relied on these assumed gender roles in the representation of male and female characters. Berenstein claims that it is therefore likely that audiences too played along with these roles in a 'performative' sense; this is supported by Zillman and Weaver's social psychological research into gender socialization for the teen audience of the slasher film (1996). However, it must be noted that this also opens up spaces for audience members, particularly women, to react in oppositional and contradictory ways (to the socially prescribed norms of gender behaviour) – effectively meaning that women can enjoy the thrills, scares and shocks of horror cinema just as much as male viewers. Similar cross-categorization of horror films has taken place in other periods of horror cinema. Examples of new Gothic horror cinema made during the revisiting of the traditional horror monsters during the 1990s – *Bram Stoker's Dracula* and *Interview with the Vampire*, for example – were marketed as romance (recognizing a female audience demographic).

The advertising campaigns for these new Gothic horror films are markedly different to the campaigns for other films of the time such as *Se7en* (with its poster and trailer focusing on the murders with the tagline 'Seven deadly sins. Seven ways to die.'), *Candyman* (with the image of a bee crawling into an eye on the poster, and the playing up of the urban legend – 'We dare you to say his name five times' in the tagline), or *From Dusk Till Dawn* (for which the trailer focuses on the slaughter – 'It's going to be one hell of a night'). The campaigns for *Bram Stoker's Dracula*, *The Crow*, *Mary Shelley's Frankenstein*, *Wolf* and *Interview with the Vampire*, on the other hand, all played up the Gothic romance. Notable are posters for *Bram Stoker's Dracula* with the line 'Love never dies', a soft focus portrait of the stars of *Interview with the Vampire* under the phrase 'The sexiest bloodsuckers in town', *The Crow*'s image of a haunted goth-styled anti-hero under the tag line 'Believe in angels' and the scribed lettering of the film title over the image of a crow made up from eyes and moth-like wings, and *Wolf*'s moody sepia-toned poster (with the exception of Nicholson's glowing yellow eye, not unlike a photographic image from a Haagan-Daz advertisement) of lead actors Jack Nicholson and Michelle Pfeiffer which hints at the sexual overtones to the werewolf transformation with the line 'The animal is out.' Again this does not necessarily mean that female horror fans do not respond pleasurably to depictions of horror onscreen, nor that they might not enjoy films like *Se7en*, *Candyman* and *From Dusk Till Dawn* (and all these films have significant elements that might appeal to women). What it does indicate, however, is that there are culturally sanctioned forms of horror-romance that allow more casual female audiences (the co-existentialist viewers) to watch and enjoy horror films without calling the prescribed gender roles into question.

It seems, then, that there are a number of reasons why the term 'horror genre' itself needs to be challenged (and not least because the concept of genre is problematical in its own right). First, as we have seen, cinematic horror spans almost the entire history of film without ever seeming to go out of favour, and throughout history – in literature, theatre, folk stories, and mythology – horror-themed tales and monstrous entities have been widespread. Second, horror cinema has constantly evolved, taking on many different forms throughout its long history, being adapted by each new generation of filmmakers in response to the cultural moment and reflecting the anxieties of the age, the tastes of the audience, and the technologies available at the time. Third, the horror film has featured significantly in a large number of national cinemas, and while these have often achieved popularity in overseas markets – particularly among the core horror fan audiences, these productions often reflect national or cultural themes and local tastes. All these factors, together with the genre hybridization that gives us sci-fi horrors, horror westerns, horror-comedies, and many other fertile combinations, mean that the genre is complex, sprawling and heterogeneous. This means that any attempt to consider horror cinema as a distinct and clearly definable group of films is fraught with difficulties. However, if the audience and modes of emotional affect are central to conceptions of the genre, it is important to be clear how the aesthetics of horror cinema are used to construct modes of emotional affect or other responses.

2

HORROR AESTHETICS AND AFFECT

As outlined, horror cinema has taken many different forms, and its characteristics have changed (and do still vary widely) across a range of subgenres or styles – from the supernatural and the Gothic, through stalkers, slashers and serial killers, to the gore film, body horror and torture porn. Yet as explored in the previous section, in defining the horror genre perhaps its most important characteristics are the modes of affect that horror films are intended to create in their audiences. It is these emotional and physiological responses that remain constant while other characteristics and generic conventions evolve. Any consideration of the range of responses involved in watching a horror film (and this is a wide range consisting of: fear, terror, fright, dread or anxiety; being scared, shocked or made to jump; to shiver, feel one's skin is crawling or get the chills; to feel disgust, nausea or revulsion; to experience fascination, sexual or morbid curiosity, empathy, relief, and even laughter) must address how this works in practice. That is, how the technical codes of cinema are manipulated in order to bring these responses about. How do films actually create these intended affects?

The technical and formal features of cinema include editing, montage and pacing, camera work, framing and other aspects of cinematography and mise-en-scène such as lighting, sound and costuming, together with plot, dialogue, narrative and audience point of view, narrative structure and representations of characters. These cinematic codes have been developed and refined by horror filmmakers in order to depict horrific material visually and aurally. The aesthetic features that are frequently used by horror filmmakers to create strong emotions such as shock, fear and revulsion commonly include point-of-view camera shots and framing, dark or chiaroscuro lighting, jump cuts and variations in pacing, visual (and often violent) spectacles that employ make-up, prosthetic, animatronic, digital and other special effects, and discordant or otherwise unsettling musical cues and other sound effects. Such techniques have been used, albeit with variations depending upon local and historical technological developments and trends, throughout the genre.

If horror cinema's primary mode of emotional affect is fear, how that fear is constructed is key to our understanding of the genre. For the viewer, pleasure – or displeasure – can of course arise from different factors (including narrative themes) but the triggers are often aesthetic. Horror films by their very nature are designed to disturb the viewer, they have a 'negative aesthetic aim' (Freeland 2000: 5). With this in mind, horror cinema can be defined in terms of the viewing experience. It is common for fans and critics to speak of the horror film viewing experience as being like a rollercoaster ride. This implies a wild swing between slowly building expectations of something terrifying or dreadful, and the climactic moment of terror at the height of this anticipation, as well as an escalation of terror, anxiety, excitement and thrills in the aftermath. The cycle is generally repeated in a series of steps that heighten the emotions at each stage until the final climactic sequence (often also followed by a twist or hook right at the end to leave the viewer in a state of heightened emotion). This clearly suggests that a mix of emotion must be present, and that these are also dependent on the fight or flight responses of the adrenalin flow in addition to the shiver sensation and revulsion common to horror. One of the best ways to begin to determine how these affects are created is to focus on the aesthetics of horror – the horror genre having clearly established sets of aesthetic traits which serve to heighten the emotional responses of the viewer.

In terms of the modes of emotional affect of horror cinema, what is actually horrifying, scary or terrifying can be extremely personal and what will scare one person may leave another indifferent. There are also films that seem to fall outside the category of horror, but which do create feelings of horror (at least within some members of the audience) – and crucially these films may be using the same aesthetic devices as horror cinema. Conversely, there are also films that clearly do employ the conventions of the horror genre, but which are not effective in creating the desired horror responses (for whatever reason – and this can be because they are badly made, or they are older films that now appear quite 'tame' to contemporary eyes). Nonetheless, the intended responses are invariably indentifiable regardless of whether they are effective or not, and even these films can be analyzed in order to link the technical codes of cinema (mise-en-scène and cinematography) and aspects of narrative directly to modes of affect.

For Prawer (1980: 50), discussing 1920s films, horror is ideally suited to the medium of cinema because:

> There is something potentially frightening in the cinematic image itself, and in the audiences' relation to it. The image we see on the screen is a kind of spectral double, the simulacrum of landscapes and town-scapes filled with human beings that seem to live, to breath, to talk, and yet are present only through their absence.

Cinema at this time used black and white film stock; although films did use colour (frames or strips of film would be tinted), the monochromatic images are 'ghostly' in appearance. Horror is thus inherently linked with the aesthetics of cinema itself. The images created by plays of light and shadow on the cinema screen (or the cathode ray tube or digital screen of the television) are ghostly (and thus uncanny or horrific) in and of themselves. Thus the very technology of film uniquely lends itself to the creation of cinematic horror. Many of the principal signifying conventions of the horror genre – and certainly the key conventions contributing to instant recognition (and therefore linked to 'performative' or 'learnt' responses) for most viewers – are visual and aural ones. These include: lighting codes used in order to create darkness, shadows and obscurity; discordant or unsettling sound effects and musical cues to enhance feelings of suspense, moments of shock or general feelings of unease; monster make-up and other special effects used to depict death and the destruction of the body; editing techniques and cuts which again create suspense or jump moments; and certain camera shots and angles (not least the point-of-view shot) to suggest danger. In this way, engaging with aesthetics illustrates how different forms of horror 'work'. Consider the following extracts from media coverage and reviews of recent horror films:

Feverish '28 Days' will give you chills: If SARS and monkeypox terrify you, you might want to avoid *28 Days Later*. But those with strong stomachs will likely find themselves riveted by this post-apocalyptic scare-fest that features a horrifying epidemic. The title gives little clue about the movie's spooky power. Bleeding eyeballs, ferocious growls and unstoppable aggression are its worst symptoms. The look of the film, shot on digital video, is haunting and gritty. The cleaner, prettier look of 35mm would have detracted from the immediacy and sense of foreboding created in this artful blend of sci-fi and pseudo-realism. A sense of dread permeates the film from its earliest scenes. But, amid the nightmarish images and gore, this grim tale does have moments of humour and hope. Mostly, it's an edge-of-your-seat scary movie that startles and chills.[1]

Pitching tent in audience psyche: Crucial to the film's eeriness is the use of natural sound. We're desperately listening inside that tent for those kiddie yelps and the crescendo of broken branches and crushed leaves with the same freaked-out paranoia as Heather, Josh and Mike. The forest has always been an anti-Walden dystopia for horror, from the *Deliverance* rapists to goalie-masked summer-camp psycho Jason. But *Blair Witch* forgoes a literal boogeyman in favor of the unseen, which, in this case, is as scarily bone-chilling as anything they could show you.[2]

Old-school exercise in shock and gore, with scary ideas and unblinking splatter: Not to cause any reader distress, but if you've seen *Audition*, all it takes is one simple word to retrigger the nausea: ankles. So, in anticipation of anybody going to see *Hostel* and rereading this review, here's one for the memories: yolky eye. Crossing your stomach yet?? Eli (*Cabin Fever*) Roth's new movie is a 'squirmer', one of a growing crowd of sado-horrors à la *Saw* where audiences are sausage-machined through a series of unimaginably ghastly scenarios and come out the other side feeling like they've been riding the ghost train on a dentist's chair. This isn't jumpy-scary pulp. This is extreme test-your-nerve pulp. But it's still pulp, and deeply proud of it.[3]

Film fans faint at *Saw III* show: Staff at a UK cinema have had to call emergency services three times in one night because of a spate of people passing out during horror film *Saw III*. One woman was taken to hospital and two other adults were treated by medics after fainting in Stevenage, Herts. And in a separate case, a man collapsed at a cinema in Peterborough, Cambs, 'due to the film's content'. 'If you know you're squeamish, don't go', warned a spokesman for the East of England Ambulance Service.[4]

These reviews emphasize both the range of horror aesthetics (the technical and narrative cinematic codes) that are employed within the genre, and the affects (emotional and physiological responses) that cinematic horror is intended to create in the viewer. The first extract, from a review of 28 *Days Later*, illustrates that horror is very often dependent upon visceral special effects: the reviewer points out the moments of gore (bleeding eyeballs) and violence (unstoppable aggression) in the film, elements that any postmodern horror film might be expected to contain in excess. Alongside this, attention is drawn to the kinds of responses that will be created by these aesthetics – chills, terror, scares, foreboding, dread, humour, hope, 'edge-of-your-seat' tension, and startles. These affects, some inciting physical responses such as being made to jump, shiver, tense up or hold one's breath, others creating emotional states which cause various uncomfortable and disturbing feelings in the viewer, are linked quite specifically to the aesthetics of the film: the haunting, gritty look of digital video, the 'ferocious growls' of the soundtrack, as well as the make-up and other effects used to create the host of infected victims in the film.

The writer of the second extract points out that the aesthetic style of *The Blair Witch Project* is much less graphic, it is suggestive rather than gory and thus less explicit in its use of visceral effects. In this case, technical codes such as sound are of vital importance in creating the emotional affects of horror cinema. Again it is the emotions that are created by this aesthetic that are highlighted: desperation, paranoia, scares and chills. It is worth noting that while some of the physical reactions such as being made to jump are quite short-lived, emotional responses related to the uncanny or chilling aspects of a film can persist for some time, even after the end of the film. It is also interesting that the headline for each of these reviews also suggest a link with nightmares and the unconscious: *28 Days Later* is 'feverish', thus suggesting some sort of hallucinatory experience, while *The Blair Witch Project* is camped out in the 'audience psyche', implying that the viewing experience taps into unconscious fears and phobias.

The review of *Hostel* places the emphasis on the gore and graphic aesthetic of the film and how this will create feelings of disgust. It especially highlights the stomach churning nature of the visual and make-up effects – it is a 'squirmer' that will have the viewer 'crossing their stomach'. In fact, it suggests that even recalling some of this imagery to mind after having seen the film will instantly recreate the response, it teases the reader with a reminder of the 'yolky eye' that will 'retrigger the nausea'. It is the kind of film that is designed to test the nerve of the viewer by exposing them to a series of images that are 'unimaginably ghastly', in other words they are not the kind of images that the viewer would want to see even in their imagination. The review connects these images to emotional experiences that together constitute a rollercoaster ride (or being put through a 'sausage machine') – the real-life anxieties and potential pain of a dental appointment, together with the frivolous and possibly kitsch sensations of a funfair ghost train ride. This is emphasized in the summary of the review that links a scary narrative and splatter aesthetic: shock and gore. It is not insignificant that this plays on 'shock and awe' (the American military's tactic of making a spectacular display of force that is intended to overwhelm the enemy), suggesting that the viewer of *Hostel* is similarly going to be bombarded and overwhelmed with graphic imagery.

Reviews such as these, which are typical of recent successful horror films, illustrate that the aesthetics and affects of cinematic horror are keys to understanding the genre and its audience. That horror is intended to create such extreme reactions that are both emotional and physiological is further illustrated by the fourth extract, taken from a BBC news report on *Saw III*. We might take this kind of coverage to reflect the idea that horror cinema is expected to create such intense scares (indeed a horror film is often regarded as unsuccessful by its audience if it doesn't incite strong responses): what more could any self-respecting horror fan ask for than a film whose content makes people faint and require the cinema to call for an ambulance.[5] The history of the genre is littered with similar sensational coverage of audiences being overcome and even, on occasion, breaking into mass hysteria. Cinemagoers at screenings of *The Exorcist* in 1973 were said to have screamed, vomited and fainted (Kermode 1998: 84–85). It was widely reported that one man broke his jaw on the seat in front when he passed out and subsequently sued Warner Brothers. In other news coverage, one man in Berkeley is said to have thrown himself at the cinema screen in an attempt to get rid of the demon, and in Toronto four women were said to be so traumatized they required psychiatric treatment. In addition to pointing the way towards the critical importance of analyzing the aesthetics and audience responses of such 'events' as a means to exploring and understanding the genre, there is a further key aspect of horror raised by this report. It draws attention to the fact that although horror is considered to be a problem in some quarters, and not just in terms of warnings needing to be issued by the ambulance service to 'squeamish' viewers, the affects of horror can undoubtedly be pleasurable for fans (and this can include the more extreme and negative affects such as outright nausea and revulsion as well as those which might seem easier to cope with such as scares, shivers, shocks and laughter).

As these extracts from media reviews of horror films also illustrate, the horror genre is varied and heterogenous in both its forms and its functions, offering something for every type of fan, casual or curious viewer in its range of competing styles, cycles and subgenres. As they suggest, Hostel primarily incites feelings of revulsion, The Blair Witch Project shivers, and 28 Days Later tension. There are many different kinds of people who enjoy horror films, and there are just as many varied and different reasons why people choose to watch horror films, and indeed enjoy them. It can therefore be concluded that each viewer will choose the particular styles that create the particular affects they prefer. It can also be assumed that those film critics who write reviews like those above do so – at least in part – in order to communicate to the reader what kind of experience they might have if they choose to watch that film. Similarly, the creators of trailers and posters will play up the intended affects of the film. It is therefore important to consider how the range of desired affects are generated and directed by the stylistics of the films. Such accounts of horror cinema will draw on mise-en-scène, cinematography, special effects, music and sound effects as the organizing structure of the films.

TECHNOLOGY AND PRODUCTION FACTORS

The aesthetics of horror cinema have been shaped by developments in film technology and production practices. The history of horror cinema is in one respect a history of the technological developments and innovations in film. If one of the key criteria of horror cinema is scaring its audience, then how a film achieves this is dependent upon the cinematic tools at the disposal of the filmmakers. Filmmakers can be seen as artists exploiting the tools of their trade, but nevertheless they are required to work with the available technological resources (as well as the limits of budgets and personnel). Horror films frequently set out to create the sights and sounds of things that do not and never have existed in reality (monsters and creatures of various kinds, and supernatural events), or which are not normally seen or acknowledged in everyday life (the internal organs, the traumatized, injured, disfigured or dead – and mouldering – body, and images of the abject including blood, pus, excrement and vomit). Given that such material is created by teams of technicians working in the areas of sound effects, prosthetics and make-up, and animation and computer-generated imagery, the history of horror is also the history of special effects. The aesthetics of horror cinema are thus closely tied to the technologies available at any one time to any one filmmaker or group of technicians. Examples of aesthetic developments include:

Early innovation

While special effects are sometimes erroneously considered to be a recent technological development with gore film prosthetics and computer imagery, special effects have been used in cinema since its very earliest days. One of the pioneers of cinema was the trick photographer Georges Méliès and he used mostly in-camera effects and some post-production (multiple exposures, stopping and starting or slowing down and speeding up the film, early forms of pixillated animation where props or actors were moved between fames exposures, and imaginative set and costume design, and filmstrip colourization) to create horror- and science fiction-style fantasies (Ezra 2000). In the main, Méliès's films are silent, short (no longer than 3 or 4 minutes) comedies which may look obvious or naive to today's viewers, but they are technically impressive for the way they imaginatively exploited the available technology of the time and demonstrate what can be achieved with little more than some simple techniques based on locking off the camera, stopping the film and rearranging props, or rewinding the film and re-exposing it with an actor (often Méliès himself) in a different position – a form of early stop-motion animation. Although these films are not what might be thought of – then or now – as outright horror, they featured characters and events that would become horror film staples: people tormented by devils, imps, vampires, and giant insects, people being eaten alive by giant alien creatures, skeletons that come alive and dance, and all manner of 'poltergeist' activity involving haunted houses and objects.

In creating this material, Méliès was certainly one of the first film-makers to design films that were intended to surprise or shock and perhaps also terrify the audience, and he often did so in quite sophisticated ways. His film *The Devil's Mansion* made in 1896,[6] for example, is very likely the first film vampire. This film depicts a bat flying into a Gothic castle, a number of white-clad spectral forms and the 'devil' who is eventually driven off with a crucifix. Although not particularly horrific, film at this time did produce reactions of shock and amazement in viewers, and Méliès films were hugely successful. It is also intriguing to note in reports of the time that film was linked to death and the afterlife; a report in the French newspaper *La Poste* on 30 December 1895 reports[7] that thanks to film the dead will live on and 'death will no longer be absolute'. In fact, Méliès referred to his special effects as 'spirit photography' (Abbott 2004: 11–12). Méliès remains an influential filmmaker within the wider boundaries of horror and fantasy media: his work or style has been referenced in *Futurama*, *The Mighty Boosh*, the films of Tim Burton and Guy Maddin, and The Smashing Pumpkins video for *Tonight, Tonight*, for example.

In the early decades of cinema, and certainly during the silent era, the idea that cinema itself was spectral meant that film was seen as an ideal medium for the Gothic and horror stories popular in novels and plays. It is hardly surprising then that what is often deemed to be the genre's first notable cycle is that of the horror-themed films made during the 1920s in Germany, several of which are noted for their Expressionist style. These films include *The Cabinet of Dr Caligari*, *The Golem*, *Destiny* and *Nosferatu*.

Lighting and set design

As with any new technology, cinema developed very quickly, allowing for longer, technologically more sophisticated films with more complex narratives. Filmmakers continued to embrace and exploit these technologies to scare and horrify their audiences. Fuelled by the flourishing of modernist art movements throughout Europe after the First World War, some of the most innovative uses of film design took place in Expressionist cinema. In a similar vein to the Surrealists who made sense of the chaos of the world through theories of the unconscious, Freudian dream imagery and automatic writing, the German Expressionist artists and writers sought to find meaning in the essence of things. For this group, the works produced reflected a highly subjective expression of the world; if the world or a person seemed metaphorically twisted, this was how they would appear physically and literally. If there were very few parallel lines or right angles in the landscape in a painting, or that the lighting was extremely un-naturalistic in a stage play, this was because it was a comment on the state of the world or the psyche of the individual. The theatre quickly adopted the Expressionist style in the subject matter of its plays and its designs. Many of those who worked in Expressionist theatre moved over to film production, and the style flourished in German cinema of the 1920s.

With developments in cameras, lighting and studio set-ups, film was a medium that could be productively exploited by these Expressionists and their work was radical, innovative and extremely popular. Ted Perry notes (2006: 57) that: 'The style of German Expressionism allowed the filmmakers to experiment with filmic technology and special effects and to explore the twisted realm of repressed desires, unconscious fears, and deranged fixations'. Most notably these filmmakers developed the use of the chiaroscuro style of lighting that exploited extremes of light and shadow. Lotte Eisner (2008: 17) succinctly describes this as 'pools of light falling from a high window into a dark interior'. In the way that this is combined with the stark black and white of the sets, costume and make-up, not to mention the extremely un-naturalistic angles of the sets and props, there is a resulting abstract quality to the films. *The*

Cabinet of Dr Caligari and *Nosferatu* are good examples of the way in which the art design lends the films an aura of horror that enhances their gloomy settings, doomed characters, and all-pervasive themes of madness and death. These films may not originally have been intended as part of a horror cinema per se, but their use of aesthetics has created such a strong impression of horror that they are widely regarded as the first main cycle of horror cinema.

The Cabinet of Dr Caligari takes place in a town where the streets are steeply angled and the buildings crooked with windows and doors at oblique angles, and walls teeter precariously over the characters. The sets are all painted flats and the sharply angled shadows are painted on the walls and floors. This lends the narrative an otherworldly or dreamlike quality that is further enhanced by the make-up and mannered acting style (at this time film acting emulated stage performances), together with often disorientating camera angles. Cesare, the somnambulist controlled by the demonic Caligari, is zombie-like with dark shadows around his eyes created by make-up and lighting his face from below; Caligari even keeps him in a coffin-like box. During his first nocturnal excursions the murder of the young man is suggested via shadows on the wall, which are particularly affecting in their depiction of clawed hands and the falling knife. In one of the most reproduced sequences of the film, Cesare is shown carrying the heroine away up a steeply inclined zig-zag-shaped rooftop, an image that takes on a terror that is as exaggerated as the set itself. Madness, the theme of the film, is literally made visible in the visual aesthetic. *Nosferatu* and *The Cabinet of Dr Caligari* differ in their aesthetic primarily because *Caligari* was filmed on stage sets, which allowed the design to exploit Expressionist aesthetic to its extreme, whereas *Nosferatu* (unusually for a film of this cycle) was shot on location. It was given an Expressionist mood through lighting (Figure 2.1). This meant that the monster, Count Orlok, was strongly linked to the world of shadow, which through editing, created moments of shock as the monster approached.

In *Nosferatu*, pale faces of both victim and vampire loom out of darkened backgrounds, a cross-fade seems to bring Orlok from the distance

Figure 2.1 Expressionist shadows in *Nosferatu*.

into close-up as though he had moved preternaturally, a double expo-
sure makes a ghostly presence haunting the delirious sailor, his shadow
with clawed hands raised looms over the sleeping Hutter and proceeds
him up the staircase as he comes to attack Ellen, when it is his shadow
hand that clutches at her breast. While the angles of the film overall are
relatively naturalistic, sequences are rendered uncanny by unnaturalistic
camera movements and angles, such as that when Hutter first sees
Orlok in his coffin – the shot is divided at one angle by the stairs
behind Hutter and at another by the edge of the coffin in which Orlok
sleeps, and later on the ship when Orlok rises ramrod straight from his
coffin – the angles of the other boxes of soil similarly dissect the shot.
Stacey Abbott (2004: 5) describes cinema at the time of *Nosferatu* as a
form of 'technological necromancy' which highlights 'the ambiguity
between the living and the dead, the scientific and the fantastic' (p. 5).
By this she means that this early cinema had a spectral quality, using

dissolves and the negative image, equating the vampire with an artificially produced shadowy world, Orlok's castle is a shadow of the real world and Orlok himself a shadow of humanity. The fact that Orlok melts away as the sun's rays hit him in just the same way as the image on an over-exposed film would fade into nothingness, leads Abbott to conclude that the vampire has similar properties to film. Furthermore, in its use of location shooting instead of Expressionistic sets, Abbott suggests (2004: 13) that *Nosferatu* 'evokes its horror through the eruption of the fantastic from within a realistic setting'. Even in these early films, then, we see aesthetics being used to evoke psychological states of mind and being.

These Expressionist films are not only important in their own right (many accounts of horror begin with these films), but in their influence on the genre once it was established in Hollywood. The Expressionist aesthetic – particularly the lighting – was used in the Universal horror films, one of the first major horror cycles in the sound era, but was also employed by Orson Welles in *Citizen Kane*, translated into the film noirs of the 1940s, and can still be seen extending its influential reach more recently in the work of Tim Burton in films such as *Edward Scissorhands* and *The Nightmare Before Christmas*. Many horror films still employ Expressionistic camera angles and lighting to convey moments of horror or unease. Although the sets may not explicitly employ Expressionistic angles, Dutch angles where the camera is tilted to the side so that the resulting shot is skewed at an angle and the floor or horizon is off the horizontal, have been used in many horror films to convey disorientation or psychological unease, including states such as shock or madness.[8] Dutch angles were used in *The Evil Dead* to suggest the unseen demonic force and have also been employed in films such as *The Blair Witch Project* and *Cloverfield* where the film is ostensibly found footage from hand-held cameras. In the final sequence of *The Blair Witch Project* as Heather and Mike enter the house, the image sways disorientatingly from one side to the other and up and down, frequently off the horizontal (the image is also blurred during frequent fast pans). In the final shots Mike appears to be standing slightly off-kilter as the camera shakes in Heather's hands (we also hear her screaming continually) and after she falls the final image is at a complete right angle (horizontal and vertical are reversed). This disconcerting image accompanies the realization that the characters are in all probability dead.

In *The Evil Dead* films camera tilts are used to indicate when characters are possessed or to indicate the point of view of the entity. The sequence in *The Evil Dead* when Ash is alone in the cabin is an exercise in the excessive use of the camera tilt for both disturbing and comic effect. As Ash climbs the stairs from the cellar, a classic Dutch angle is used as he reaches the top (Figure 2.2). Ash is shown at a 45° angle emerging from the bottom left of the screen, and as he turns towards the sound of the clock chiming, the shot reverses so he is seen at a similar angle but from the bottom right. After another cut to a shot that reverses the tilt back again, the camera straightens, but then cuts to a shot that tilts the camera through 180° so he appears to hang down from the top of the screen. The camera then passes right over his head so that he again appears to be standing upright, but after a further cut the camera angle is looking up from between his feet. Further tilts follow as the camera pans around the cabin while the entity attacks. Together with the hand-held camera style and the use of the Raimi-cam (a camera strapped to a board which was held by two people low to the ground as they ran with it to film the sequences where the entity appears to be rushing towards the cabin) this creates a very subjective horrifying experience (which also, given the excess with which it is used, adds to the blackly comic tone of the films).

Increasingly, lightweight cameras allow filmmakers to create a range of effects to suggest horror. *Pi*, for example, employs a range of cinematographic effects to create the character's state of mind. When Max walks the streets, the camera is attached to the actor (the Snorricam). These juddering images, together with subtle changes in the film speed, separate Max from his environment and depict his isolation and alienation. A similar kind of subjective shot is the zoom-in and pull-back technique (also know as a dolly zoom) that Alfred Hitchcock first devised for *Vertigo* and which has the effect of depicting a moment of

Figure 2.2 Sam Raimi's use of Dutch angles used for over-the-top effect in *The Evil Dead*.

sudden shock. This shot creates the effect of the character moving forward, while the background seems to recede. An example can be seen in *Poltergeist* when the mother Diane is trying to save her son Robbie from being sucked into the other dimension. She runs down the hallway and as she runs the door seems to recede away from her giving the effect that she has further and further to run. This creates a nightmare scenario that again raises tension and dread in the viewer. Similar shots have been used frequently in the slasher subgenre, as well as in *Jaws*. In general, shots such as Dutch angles and dolly zooms are used to heighten moments of excessive emotion or psychological trauma.

Hitchcock and sound cinema

The German Expressionist films did not of course employ sound effects to convey horror, although the accompanying live music would certainly do so. Robert Sherwood, a film critic of the time (quoted in Eyman 1997: 39–40), reported of *The Cabinet of Dr Caligari* that: 'At the moment when the heroine woke up suddenly and gazed into the fiendish countenance of the maniacal somnambulist, the clarinet player in the […] orchestra emitted a wild, piercing shriek'. This was effective enough for Sherwood to recall that 'Fear came through my ear then, all right. In fact, the gruesome sound of that clarinet terrifies me to this day … '. As well as music, some cinemas employed sound-effects specialists to sit behind the screen matching gunshots or the creaking of doors to the action on screen (Brownlow 1992: 338). Reports from the time suggest that audiences themselves would also supply their own sound effects for horror films, screaming and growling along with the action on screen when required. What this demonstrates is how important sound is to horror cinema. As soon as sound was technically feasible and widely available on the scale of Hollywood mass-production, horror filmmakers employed it in imaginative ways to create suspense and fear.

Sound cinema, the 'talkies', arrived in earnest in 1929. Sound technology existed before this point, but it was the success of *The Jazz Singer* that encouraged the industry and the cinemas to embrace it. Horror film, which aesthetically is as strongly dependent on sound as on the visuals, was no exception in this respect. Although it is considered a thriller rather than a horror film, Blackmail demonstrates how sound could be used to create subjective states and emotional affect. Alfred Hitchcock (now widely recognized as a master of suspense and a major contributor to the genre with Psycho and The Birds[9]) remade his then silent film Blackmail with full sound in order to exploit, and innovate, the technology. According to Elizabeth Weiss (1982: 29), Hitchcock manoeuvred the studio into re-shoots so the film could be exhibited with a full soundtrack. In the scene in which the guilty character Alice holds a bread knife at the dining table, the sound becomes increasingly subjective, so Alice hears just a murmur of indistinct conversation as it gradually fades until only the word 'knife' stands out loudly and clearly. 'Knife' is repeated again and again, until Alice (who has recently stabbed a man, killing him, when he sexually assaults her) cracks under the strain of hearing 'knife' again and again. This scene subjectively encapsulates just how much Alice is haunted by the guilt of her 'crime'. Weiss (1982: 44) writes that this is more than just 'an isolated gimmick, […] the knife sequence as a whole should be seen as the culmination of a larger movement to which Hitchcock has been building since the murder'. She also states (1982: 30) that this is 'the most often cited example in film history of the use of non-realistic sound in a narrative film'. She argues that Hitchcock's use of sound subtly manipulates the audience, something that is essential to horror cinema. This creation of such subjective states is why Hitchcock's later films (Psycho and The Birds, but Psycho especially) have been so influential on the postmodern, 'internal' horror film.

Psycho, of course, is renowned (and much emulated) for its screeching violins over the shower scene, but other notable elements of the sound design include the voice of 'mother', as well as the horror staples of creaking staircases and the sound of the knife puncturing flesh (for which a melon was substituted). Music in particular can create sensations of tension, alarm and anxiety in the viewer, and horror film music can often be discordant, pulsing with the rhythm of a heartbeat. With long eerie sequences that culminate in a sudden orchestral or operatic climax, such music operates in conjunction with the images of cinematic horror: just as each screech of the violin strings in the shower scene of Psycho corresponds to the stabbing action of the knife. Stephen Rebello, writing about Bernard Hermann's score for Psycho (1999: 139), states that:

> The score would prove to be a summation of all of Hermann's previous scores for Hitchcock's films, conveying as it did the sense of the abyss that is the human psyche, dread, longing, regret: in short, the wellsprings of the Hitchcock universe.

This perfectly illustrates just how important sound design and the musical score can be to horror cinema, representing subjective states of mind or encroaching horror, and creating desired emotional affects in the audience. Music using harmonic intervals in the range of the major second, minor second and diminished fifth can create moods of anticipation, anxiety and malevolence, respectively (Sonnenschein 2001: 121). Certain musical cues have thus become tropes of the genre, and are thus subconsciously recognized by the audience, creating certain feelings of horror and expectations of dread. Long, deep notes can create states of tension, staccato rhythms indicate a raising in anxiety levels: John William's Jaws theme indicating the imminent presence of the shark, or the simple yet effective theme tune for Halloween immediately setting the listener on edge. Horror film music can be orchestral or adopt a rock soundtrack (often using tracks from alternative genres such as goth or metal which already have dark or downbeat associations, the use of Nick Cave and the Bad Seed's Red Right Hand in Scream or the Portishead tracks in Nadja being good examples of this). But whatever its source, the music is often dark and brooding, although American Psycho uses music that is ironically dissonant with the images (Bateman kills one victim to the accompaniment of Huey Lewis and the News's Hip to be Square), and An American Werewolf in London employs musical pastiche by selecting popular songs with 'moon' in the title (*Blue Moon, Bad Moon Rising* and *Moondance*).

Developments in horror film sound design have also been enabled by digital editing technologies,[10] and this can be extremely important in the ambient sound of a film. As with *Psycho*, this can include all sorts of sound effects to create an atmosphere of horror, and in addition to creaking houses and knives puncturing flesh, this can include human sounds such as heart beats, breathing and screams. In addition, an absence of sound can be used to create effect, often contrasted with sudden loud noises or a cacophony of sounds. In *Dead Silence* (2007), James Wan (also the director of *Saw*) effectively employs a soundscape that signals an attack by a puppet possessed by the spirit of ventriloquist Mary Shaw. Shaw is taking revenge from beyond the grave on the family of a boy who once heckled her on stage because he could see her lips moving; after the boy disappears, his family murder Shaw, forcing her to scream and cutting out her tongue. The motif of sound is central to the film, not only in the notion of 'throwing one's voice', but in the image of a forefinger being held to the lips that is used in the publicity material. Shaw's modus operandi is that the victim has their tongue torn out when they scream. This effectively conveys a sense of dread, the potential victim must not scream – or they will die – but the atmosphere becomes such that they cannot but scream, it becomes impossible not to. They must stay silent to survive, but the scream is involuntary. The breaking of the silence thus becomes the moment of death, evoked in the title of the film. Sound is thus a vital part of the film (in fact, as many reviewers note it is the most significant aspect of the film). In the moments before the ventriloquist's dummy/Shaw is about to strike, much of the diegetic sound in the scene diminishes, to be replaced by a hush, an absence of sound, which is broken (and emphasized) only by the sound of the victim's breathing or footsteps (and this could well be taken as subjective, the victim, finding themselves in silence, becomes aware of the sounds of their own body).

At the beginning of the film the first attack takes place when Jamie leaves Lisa to get a Chinese takeaway. She sets Billy the dummy up on the bed as a surprise for Jamie, but as she moves around the flat the ambient sounds drop out one by one – the music playing on the music system slows down to a standstill, the ticking of the clock is first amplified and then ceases when the pendulum stops swinging, to be replaced by the whistle of the boiling kettle which then also fades to silence. In the resulting absence of ambient sound, there is a momentary faint laugh before Lisa's breathing and creaking floor boards dominate, followed by a short piece of tense high-pitched extra-diegetic music as Lisa approaches the dummy propped on the bed. As she reaches out to pull away the sheet with which she had covered the dummy, the music ceases and there is a moment of silence before the level of the sound rises to a cacophony of noise that includes the flapping of the sheet, Lisa's grunts and the metallic sound of a knife penetrating flesh. Orchestral music then accompanies Lisa's scream as she is pulled across the floor, and this forms a sound bridge as the film cuts to Jamie coming in the front door: the scream becomes the sound of a car horn in the evening traffic. The sound effects create a build-up of tension, but also create uncanny sensations in their own right. The use of sound also suggests the presence of Shaw's spirit in other ways, her ventriloquist's talent being used to throw the voices of the dead and to lure further victims by emulating the voices of other people known to the victim. When Jamie returns home to find his wife dead, he hears her voice calling to him.

Wan aimed to make a film that was macabre and creepy, and not effects driven. He stated[11] that:

> We wanted to make a film […] similar to those from the 1950s and 1960s, like the British Hammer and the Italian horror films made by Mario Bava. These are films that don't rely on blood and guts but are more about an atmosphere dripping with dread.

This is created through sound and shock cuts, with the sound – and thus the sense of dread – often carrying over into the next scene. In the motel, the hum of the neon lighting winds down first, and then the dripping tap is amplified before it too stops. These sounds are replaced by the creaks of the wooden dummy as it moves to Jimmy's bed and hisses his name. The accompanying choral music is extremely eerie in its use of long drawn-out echoing vocalization. The music continues over into the next scene as the mortician Henry Walker goes to prepare Lisa's body, building anticipation to the point where he recognizes the signs of Mary Shaw left on Lisa's face. When he goes to reassure his disturbed wife, Marion, who has been hiding in the cellar, she incants a phrase 'The silent time is here, the silent time is here' several times.

These become repeated sound motifs signifying the horror throughout the film. In a later sequence, when the undertaker is lured to his death in his cellar, he enters because he hears a whimpering which he assumes to be Marion. When he is locked in he bangs on the doors and cries out, but these sounds become quieter before he is attacked by Shaw. And again, at the climax when Jamie returns to the mansion, there is a moment of complete silence when the clock stops ticking after which all that can be heard is creaking, and then there is a sudden burst of music and screams. As repeated motifs, these aspects of the sound design create tension, the viewer expects a gruesome murder to take place, and also jump moments cued by the sudden escalation in volume of the sound.

It is also interesting to note that just as sound is layered, with elements of the soundtrack dropping out at key moments with others being emphasized, the colour palette of the film follows a similar pattern. Colour throughout the film is subdued, which only serves to heighten the red of the blood during the gory murders as the victims' tongues are torn out, and thus the shock. Such colour contrasts can contribute to the emotional affects of the film, particularly those related to disgust and revulsion, and especially so when they are linked to other bodily fluids and the destruction of the body.

Colour

Like sound, colour film technologies were in existence from early in the development of cinema but were not economically viable or widely adopted by the industry until the late 1940s. This did not mean that horror filmmakers were not able to exploit colour, since various technologies prior to this time enabled tinting of the film stock itself. In early American horror cinema, for example, the special effects sequences in *The Phantom of the Opera* were machine-tinted in a three-colour system using stencils (Cook 2004: 351). However, initially colour was not deemed to be economic – black and white film stock being significantly cheaper both as a raw product and in the printing process. It was only in the 1950s when the expensive Technicolor monopoly was broken at around the same time as television was becoming widespread enough to offer significant competition to the cinema that colour film became the norm.

The first horror films shot in the early two-colour Technicolor process in the early 1930s were *Doctor X* and *Mystery of the Wax Museum*. Even in the 1940s, the use of colour had something of a novelty value (Hardy 1995: 57), as it was in *The Picture of Dorian Gray* for example in which colour is used solely for the reveal of the decrepit portrait at the climax of the film. There were occasional films in colour in the 1940s: for example, in a version of *The Phantom of the Opera* (though this was more of an operatic version than an outright horror film). Indeed, throughout the 1930s and 1940s (particularly in the Universal horror films and the Val Lewton-Jacques Tourneur films for RKO) atmospheric black and white film seemed – and often still does – an appropriate choice for depicting uncanny and psychological 'spectral' terrors.

Then in the 1950s alongside exploiting colour to draw audiences back to the cinema and away from their televisions, other gimmicks, including the development of 3-D cinema, were exploited in fantasy genres, particularly horror and science fiction. There were for example a number of 3-D horror films such as *House of Wax*, *Gorilla at Large*, *The Mad Magician* and *Phantom of the Rue Morgue*. William Castle famously employed gimmicks in films such as *The House on Haunted Hill* with Emergo – an inflatable skeleton which flew across the heads of the audience on wires as a skeleton rises from a vat of acid onscreen; *The Tingler* with Percepto – buzzers in cinema seats that would give viewers a buzz in order to get the audience screaming when Dr Chapin (played by Vincent Price) says

'Scream ... scream for your lives!'; and 13 *Ghosts* with Illusion-O – spectacles similar to those used for 3-D films which allowed viewers to choose whether to see the ghosts or not depending on how scared they were. These gimmicks did not add much to heighten the effects of the film (perhaps creating more laughs than scares), but they do indicate how filmmakers exploited the novelty value of such technological developments. With declining audiences in general and many Hollywood studios economically moribund (television was one factor, but other social change such as suburbanization also contributed to declining audiences), the niche teen audience was exploited throughout most of the 1950s. Teen movies came to the fore with films such as *I Was a Teenage Werewolf*, and the early Roger Corman films for AIP, including *A Bucket of Blood*, in addition to the William Castle and 3-D films mentioned above. These films were made quickly and cheaply – and colour film stock was expensive. Horror cinema continued in the main to rely on black and white cinematography – and it must be noted that in addition to the cult classics a few of these remain in the canon of horror cinema for their uncanny aesthetic, most notably the British film *Night of the Demon* and the French *Eyes Without a Face*, directed by the acclaimed filmmakers Jacques Tourneur and Georges Franju, respectively.

Notably too, the first horror films to significantly exploit colour were also European, namely those produced by the Hammer studio in the UK. Beginning with *The Curse of Frankenstein*, Hammer made a significant number of films very loosely based on the classic horror novels, revitalizing the Gothic with a blend of action and oversaturated colour. Hammer's horror films were immensely successful – so much so that they became a major British cultural export during the late 1950s and 1960s. Considering the fact that the competition were American teen horrors aimed at the drive-in audience or the science fiction-horror hybrids that Mark Jancovich discusses in *Rational Fears* (1996), it is perhaps surprising that Hammer's Gothic horror films would be so popular. It does appear though that the studio's signature use of colour (particularly well exploited in the posters and trailers which played up the colour with fluorescent titles and caption lettering) was a significant factor.

The Curse of Frankenstein was the first of three adaptations of classic horror monsters by Hammer at the end of the 1950s, the other two being Dracula and The Mummy. All three led to several further films with these monsters as well as others: the Wolfman, Jekyll and Hyde, and other vampire films based on Sheridan Le Fanu's Carmilla and the Blood Countess Erzebet Bathory, for example. Despite the fact that it could seem quite tame in comparison with many of today's horror films, it can be clearly seen that The Curse of Frankenstein is visually powerful (and it certainly shocked the media of the day and delighted audiences). In terms of colour, the palette for much of the film is rich and yet quite subdued, consisting of the blacks, greys, whites, aquas, greens and browns of the Gothic setting and Victorian props and costumes, reflecting the cold, clinical, sociopathic personality of the central figure, Baron Frankenstein. There are occasional spots of red in the early laboratory scenes when Frankenstein experiments on bringing a puppy back to life and decapitates a corpse. There is blood-red fluid in several flasks and jars, a red fire bucket hanging prominently on the wall, and the first use of blood as a motif are the smears of blood on Frankenstein's jacket and gloves and the cloth he uses to carry the head and a pair of hands as he begins to build the creature. The scene where Frankenstein returns and unwraps the hands is typical of the escalating level of graphic effects and the emphasis on blood: a cut to a close-up shot of the unwrapping shows the blood stained muslin being lifted to reveal the blood-spattered severed hands. The shot where Frankenstein buys a pair of eyes from the Municipal Charnal House is strangely framed such that only the hands, arms and torsos of the characters are shown, placing the emphasis firmly on the bloody, mucus-trailing eyes being unwrapped and tipped into a specimen jar. The coughing by the Charnal House attendant in this scene adds to the sensation of visceral horror. There are moments of violence too, as well as gore. The moment when Frankenstein pushes Professor Bernstein to his death off the landing (he has only invited him to the castle because he wants Bernstein's brain for his creature) is sudden, shocking, and brutal, revealing as it does the depths to which Frankenstein has sunk in an attempt to complete his experiment.

Outside of the use of body parts as props, the effects sequences themselves are not very detailed however. The removal of Bernstein's brain is not shown at all – it takes place behind the open coffin lid – nor are Frankenstein's operations to build the creature and later perform brain surgery (obviously the technology did not exist to produce convincing effects). The graphic aesthetic of the film builds after the creature is animated, though, and the colour is used more luridly as Frankenstein becomes more driven. More and more red is used, in the lighting of the laboratory during the lightning storm, in the lining of Frankenstein's surgical toolcase, in Krempe's dressing gown just before Frankenstein returns to the lab to find the creature walking around (Figure 2.3), the spilt blood on the floor when the creature escapes the lab, and the flames as the creature burns at the climax. This use of vivid colour allows the gore and violence to be graphically depicted in a way it could not be in black and white. The creature itself is also designed to create disgust. The reveal of the creature's face is again sudden and designed to shock: the camera zooms in fast and shakes slightly as the bandages are snatched away to show the hideous scars, disfigured skin and milky eyes in close up. There is a reverse shot of Frankenstein's shocked reaction, mirroring the audience's own, before another shot of the monster's green-white flesh and lurid red scars as he reaches out to grab Frankenstein. Such graphic material, including the stark contrasts in colour, had not been shown before (certainly it concerned the BBFC at the time[12] – see Johnson 1997: 182) and clearly the make-up is designed to elicit disgust. Heffernan (2004: 50) suggests that these contrasts in colour are a reflection of the contrasts between bourgeois class values and madness, death and decay, underscoring the narrative themes of the film. Certainly the colour was central to the success of the film, it grossed over $3 million worldwide within a year (Heffernan 2004: 44). The use of colour became a trademark through the 1960s and into the 1970s. As Hutchings has reported (2003: 35), Hammer's success with The Curse of Frankenstein and Dracula depended in part on their distinctive use of vivid colour. This characteristic colour cinematography became the staple aesthetic of British horror cinema, not just in the

Figure 2.3 Anticipation before the shock of the reveal in Hammer's *The Curse of Frankenstein*.

Hammer films but in those made by the Amicus studio and in some of the key horror films of the 1970s including *Witchfinder General* and *The Wicker Man*.

Leading cult horror filmmakers in the USA also began to make more use of colour in the wake of Hammer's success. They include William Castle who made *The Tingler* and *13 Ghosts* with colour sequences; Roger Corman who in collaboration with cinematographer Nic Roeg made noteworthy use of colour in *The Masque of the Red Death*; and Herschell Gordon Lewis who used colour to produce the early splatter aesthetic in *Blood Feast* and *Two Thousand Maniacs!* These films use colour in very different ways to create horror effects. *The Masque of the Red Death*, for example, contains some of the most accomplished examples of the colour aesthetic in horror cinema (and it should be noted that it was made in the UK). The film title itself plays on the idea of colour to signify disease and death and the film contains a sequence in which the various figures of death comparing notes on how many souls the black death, the yellow death and so on have taken, with the red death saying: 'I claimed many, only six remain' in the last shot of the film. The sequences in which characters move through a series of colour-coded rooms in Prospero's castle are also noteworthy. Hutchings (2000) suggests that the use of colour in this film is detached from Corman's usual psychologically expressive function (to reflect a character's state of mind) and instead:

> [It] takes on a non-representational, kinetic force – most impressively in the various camera tracks through a series of rooms, each of which has been decorated in a different colour – which is rarely seen in mainstream commercial productions and which anticipates moments of psychedelic abstraction in Corman's later 'drug-culture' film *The Trip*.

Lewis's films on the other hand rely on the trash aesthetic of 'so-bad-it's-good' cult cinema. *Blood Feast* is a film that offers an unremitting assault upon the female body and draws attention to the gore – amputations and eviscerations – with lurid colours, a dominant red and blue colour palette, dripping organs and blood-drenched bodies. The Italian horror film industry also began making significant contributions to the colour aesthetic in films such as *The Horrible Secret of Dr Hichcock* and *Black Sabbath*. However, many of the more mainstream horror films of the 1960s were still made in black and white: *Psycho*, *The Innocents*, *The Haunting*, *Whatever Happened to Baby Jane?*, *Onibaba* and *Repulsion*, for example. Even *Night of the Living Dead* as late as 1968 still employed black and white (for George Romero this was a matter of economics more than anything else). Although the choice may in some instances be as much pragmatic as artistic, clearly there are very different aesthetics at work in colour and black and white film, and this can be seen in the choice of black and white for films such as *Eraserhead* and *Pi*. Both of these films create an eerie, nightmare world in the use of black and white cinematography. In *Eraserhead*, David Lynch's use of light and shadow creates a grim, industrial gothic landscape that is heightened by the ethereal quality of the soundtrack. In *Pi*, Darren Aronofsky similarly uses black and white to create a subjective world, this time reflecting the paranoia and intense physical pain of the migraines that the mathematician Max suffers from.

In the main, though, bold use of colour followed in films of the 1970s and beyond, distinctive examples – though there are many others equally representative – including *The Exorcist* (typified by the image of Regan, strapped to the bed during the exorcism scenes, spitting 'pea soup' vomit at Father Merrin), *Suspiria* (in the murder at the beginning of the film the victim crashes through a stained glass ceiling light, the bright primary colours – red, yellow and blue – of the panes of glass come crashing down onto the black, red and white mosaic of the floor below), *The Shining* (a deluge of blood pouring in waves from the lifts in Danny's vision of The Overlook Hotel, strongly contrasting with the pastel blue of the twins' dresses) and *Dead Ringers* (the elaborate pre-parations for surgery as Beverley Mantle dresses in blood red surgical gowns that resemble a priest's garments, and the subsequent scene in the operating theatre – everything and everyone draped in a similar blood red). The visceral quality of the colour in such films, especially in relation to the special effects and make-up, was thus a primary con-tributor to the modes of affect of post-1960s horror.

Special effects

In films that are largely psychological or supernatural, modes of effect can be created through suggestion, the use of lighting, sound effects and music. Graphic or explicit horror films such as Hammer's Gothics, body horror, splatterpunk, and slashers rely much more on visual special effects to create their principal modes of effect such as disgust. In fact, what is depicted on screen can (empathically perhaps as we feel for and with characters on screen) affect all the senses including touch, smell and taste, as well as the obvious sight and hearing. In *Deleuze and Horror Film* (2005), Anna Powell proposes a model of visceral horror based on the ideas of French philosopher Gilles Deleuze. Powell's arguments are useful here since they focus specifically on the aesthetics of horror cinema. She states (2005: 2) that: 'The genre has showcased strongly affective style from its outset. Excessive forms of cinematography, mise-en-scène, editing and sound are the pivotal tools of horror, used to arouse visceral sensations and to "horrify" the viewer'. Powell's argument emphasizes the way in which horror films make a space for and even celebrate the viewer's physical (she calls them corporeal) responses to the effects sequences in the films. It is the experience of sensory effect that is important in Powell's argument, and not any inherent meaning derived from the text. It is the sensory experience of watching horror that is critical: the way the viewer feels their skin itch as if an insect were crawling on them when they watch Helen almost kiss the *Candyman* with his mouth full of bees or feel their own skin being sliced open when they watch Sara being cut to shreds by the wire coils in *Suspiria*, or in the same film squirm in revulsion as maggots fall from the ceiling onto the pupils' hair and bare skin (Figure 2.4). These are tactile sensations (Powell refers to them as haptic) that can be aroused by watching horror films; she describes this as 'affective contamination' (2005: 4). 'As well as terrifying sights and sounds', she asserts (2005: 142), 'we perceive affective textures of a repellent nature, such as the wet stickiness of human blood or the slimy trail of a monster'.

The work of filmmakers such as David Cronenberg, Clive Barker and Dario Argento are particularly interesting in this respect. Powell points out (2005: 145) that in *Suspiria* the colour scheme (of blood red, scarlet flames and peacock blue), blends with the excess of the sound design

Figure 2.4 Sharing the tactile sensation of disgust in *Suspiria*.

and props of the film to create an extremely affective texture. In the final sequence, after Suzy discovers the blue iris that opens the secret door, the primary palette of strong blues, reds and golds heightens the palpable horror alongside Goblin's prog rock soundtrack and the crashing thunderclaps. In Cronenberg's body horror films the emphasis is on what is, in *Videodrome*, called 'the new flesh' – the metamorphosis and transformation of the body. In *Videodrome*, Max Renn 'becomes' a video machine when an orifice opens up in his torso into which a cassette is inserted and a gun that had also disappeared inside his body emerges to become fused with his hand. In *The Fly*, Brundle's genetic code is spliced with that of a housefly, but later he fuses with the inorganic material of the teleport pod. These mutations and meldings of organic and inorganic present images which have 'affective force' (Powell 2005: 80). In *Hellraiser*, Frank Cotton's body is torn apart by the Cenobyte's chains, he is literally dismembered. At the start of the film, the Cenobytes search amongst lumps of flesh to retrieve specific parts that they reassemble like a jigsaw into a face. When Frank is revived by his brother's spilt blood on the attic floor, he reassembles himself layer by layer from the inside out until all he needs is a surface. In his brother's stolen skin, he is torn apart once again. These 'virtually affective images of torture', Powell says (2005: 84), are 'designed to haptically induce physical agony […] in the spectator'. In other words, they can be a potentially painful tactile experience for the viewer.

These scenes are each created through elaborate special effects sequences that animate the mutated, transformed or dismembered body. Linda Ruth Williams (1999: 34) states that: 'contemporary horror has specialized in making the inside visible, opening it up and bringing it out and pushing the spectacle of interiority to the limit to find out what that limit is'. Special effects in contemporary horror cinema are designed to open up the body in the way that Williams proposes, to expose the internal organs and the mechanisms of the flesh, and indeed special effects technicians often rely on medical textbooks in their craft. The more realistic these recreations are, the more likely is the viewer to experience them viscerally (unrealistic effects – as

Figure 2.5 Make-up and prosthetic effects create the skinless Frank in *Hellraiser*.

in *The Evil Dead* for example where the possessed bodies decay into lurid foamy sludge – may make the viewer feel disgust but this is quite likely to give way to laughter). Certainly, the way in which horror fan culture foregrounds the work of special effects technicians suggests that how these post-modern visceral horrors are created is significant for the viewers in their own right. Freeland (2000: 256) calls the heightened spectacle and emotion of such special effects sequences 'numbers' to acknowledge the fact that they very often operate in the same way as song and dance numbers in the musical. Horror magazines such as *Fangoria*[13] and *Shivers*[14] focus on the work of effects artists in particular. Barker, for example, has talked about how important the creation of Frank (Figure 2.5) was to the overall success of *Hellraiser*, and how he and his effects team led by Bob Keen produced the effects[15]:

> I said 'We've got an interesting problem here, Bob'. Our monster has a lot of dialogue scenes with the girl. Generally speaking, there isn't a great deal of exposition through monsters and I wanted to do something different. I wanted to have scenes in which the monster explained himself, talked as a human being, lit cigarettes. One of my favourite moments is when he lights up, because here he is, he lacks

a skin but he still wants a good fag. So I told Bob that the special effects were going to be a much more integral part of the drama overall than a lot of such beasties who are going to appear and disappear very quickly. This monster is going to have to stand great scrutiny over a long period of time, in a lot of lighting conditions. We're going to watch him closely, we're going to see him have perfectly reasonable dialogue, he's going to make one or two jokes, he's even got a love scene. It's a perverse love scene, but he's got a love scene with Julia. There were probably greater risks taken over the special effects than for most pictures at this financial level. When you think of Jason, for instance, he takes off his hockey mask once at the end of each picture and I think there's a couple of pictures in which he isn't revealed at all. The body suit for Frank in his skinned state was a considerable challenge. The suit that Bob and his team have created for Frank is brilliant. I think in those middle sequences when he appears after the first murder and he has that dialogue he's perfectly believable. Obviously, it's not the same actor who plays Frank in the skin. He's an incredibly thin man, so that we could put all of this stuff on top of him and he'd still look gaunt. I think that really works very well.

Such examples illustrate the importance of special effects for horror cinema, and the way in which these are judged by audiences is an important aspects of what Linda Williams (2003) maintains is the mark of a successful horror film. As Jenkins (2007: 49) states: 'Such works pushed the current destabilization of our thinking about bodily transformations to its apocalyptic endpoint, creating images of bodies and identities stretched, mutated, ripped open, and stitched together again'. These effects clearly incite physiological responses in the audience – they are designed specifically to make the viewer gasp, retch or cringe, and sometimes even laugh (not just when the effects don't work and are 'laughable' but sometimes in a kind of painful reaction too). The problem with Williams's original model of body genres was that when she argued that the physical responses of the characters on-screen were reproduced in the viewer. She maintained (2003: 706) that the affective responses of the three genres of pornography, horror and melodrama were organized around 'the sexually ecstatic woman, the tortured woman, the weeping woman—and the accompanying presence of the sexual fluids, the blood and the tears that flow from her body and which are presumably mimicked by the spectators'. It can be assumed that sexual fluids and tears can quite readily flow from the viewer of pornography and melodramas, but it is not usual for blood to flow during horror film screenings. However, if horror film viewers do respond haptically (as Powell 2005 would have it) to these intensely graphic representations of violence and gore of splatter punk and other explicit forms of horror cinema, then it is quite likely that there is the release of a scream or a gasp or an audible intake of breath. Perhaps there is vocal outpouring rather than a physical one of blood to mimic the onscreen characters' responses to horror?

The shock cut

One further element of film technology that contributes to modes of effect in horror cinema is the cut. Horror films have been using cuts to create modes of effect from the very beginning of cinema (Méliès work was dependent on in-camera edits, for example, and they are used effectively in *Nosferatu* to suggest the approaching menace of the vampire). Cuts are used in many ways from the shot-reverse shot to show the response of the victim to the monster through to cuts away to objects that suggest a foreboding presence (as in a shot of the full moon in a werewolf film, for example). David Scott Diffrient (2004: 52) presents an interesting account of the way the shock cut is used in horror cinema to create 'a sudden, violent eruption or peak moment in a film narrative'. The shock cut is thus an editing device designed to emulate the actual, physical experience of a moment of shock. It can have a visceral or tactile effect in the sense that it is a 'single savage moment' that possesses force and velocity (2004: 52), and significantly can often make the viewer jump or create other 'physical disturbances or agitations' (2004: 53).

The shock cut is thus a 'startle effect' and it 'can be differentiated from a standard jump cut by its graphic imagery' (2004: 53). Diffrient dates the establishment of the shock cut as an essential element of horror to the unmasking of the disfigured musician in *The Phantom of the Opera*. In this sequence the first shot shows Christine reaching out to remove Erik's mask. There is then a shock cut onto his hideous face in close-up (emphasizing Lon Chaney's make-up with skeletal features and virtually no nose). Each of the deaths in *Final Destination* also contains a shock cut at the moment of death. One of the most startling is when Amanda walks away from Carter saying that she is going to move on and there is a shock cut to a bus mowing her down, leaving her friends shocked and covered in her blood.

Shock cuts depend on tone, pacing, speed and motion, and are frequently combined with dissolves, freeze frames, whip pans and crash zooms. They depend upon the general aesthetics of horror cinema – rapid visual movements, claustrophobic framing, sudden reaction shots and discordant sound modulations that highlight death, deformity and the collapse of the body. Furthermore, Diffrient claims (2004: 52) that few other aesthetic or narrative elements characterize a film as horror 'so explicitly or dynamically' as the shock cut. Indeed, it is used in the vast majority of horror films regardless of whether they rely on an explicit or suggestive aesthetic. The shock cut itself takes the form of a sudden, jarring cut between two shots and the effect can depend on other cinematic elements such as framing, the tempo of the editing and the action, movement within the frame, and sound effects such as screams, thunderclaps, the howls of wolves or music. The visceral impact of the shock cut is particularly enhanced both by sound effects and – in a point that is important for Diffrient – a 'visual articulation of violence' (2004: 55). It is the refusal of the horror film to cut away from acts of violence that distinguishes the horror genre from related genres such as thrillers, science fiction and disaster films. Horror films, he says (2004: 55), 'turn the sight and site of death into a spectacularly graphic touchstone'. These acts of violence do not necessarily have to be long drawn-out shots, they can be brief glimpses that nevertheless stay with the viewer and can be mentally recalled later. In this way they contribute to the lasting impression of a film as successful horror.

A good example of the shock cut comes at the very beginning of *The Texas Chain Saw Massacre*. The screen is entirely black, but the blackness is suddenly punctuated by a flash of light that illuminates a mouldering corpse. Diffrient suggests (2004: 55) that this disrupts the mise-en-scéne and thus the spectator's consciousness. The shock cut is thus unexpected and startling. Such a cut will often happen at the height of suspense or after a build-up of false expectation. In the latter case, the revelation that the build-up of tension was a bluff, the viewer will experience a moment of respite in the tension – and it is at this point that the shock cut will provide an effective jump. The classic example of this is in *Cat People* when Alice is walking in the underpass, followed by Irena whom it is suggested by the sound effects has transformed into a cat. As she comes out of the tunnel, nervously looking around, there is a shock cut accompanied by a screech – but it is merely a bus. Another false startle can be seen in *Alien*. Ripley, Brett and Parker are hunting the creature – this in itself builds tension, but the tension is heightened further when the motion detector suggests movement in the locker. As the characters prepare themselves and then open the locker, there is a shock cut to an extreme close-up of Jonesy the cat. Such moments rely on the startle (or false startle) effect. They are designed to add shots of adrenaline to the experience of watching a horror film; they add to the modes of affect by eliciting involuntary physical reactions (aversion reflexes). Shock cuts are also effective when they occur at the end of a very long take which is designed to make the viewer hold their breath or tense up with expectation (as in the final sequence in the escape pod in *Alien* – as Ripley goes about preparing for the journey to Earth tension is built towards the moment when the alien will reveal itself curled in the machinery – the sudden movement of its arm creating the startle). This is very much what horror film fans talk about when they refer to the genre as a rollercoaster ride. In fact, like the rollercoaster ride, Robert Baird (1997) suggests that the viewer jumps even when they are expecting the moment to arrive. Normal cognitive responses 'remind the conscious mind to apply itself to what is always potentially more significant: the consideration of immediate space and its ever-changing objects'. Regardless of whether the viewer is expecting the shock cut or not, in the immediacy of it occurring (and shock cuts are sudden and graphic) the viewer cannot stop the physical response. Hutchings (1993b: 87) describes this in terms of the technology of fear: 'a willing subjection to the "mechanical" effects of horror'. Horror films make us tense, then make us jump.

A NOTE ON AESTHETICS AND THE SUBLIME

In any single horror film, the predominant aesthetic can be set up from its earliest shots – priming the viewer for the effects to come. From the very first shots of The Texas Chain Saw Massacre, with the shock cuts that Diffrient (2004) describes, the gore aesthetics are foregrounded. After the initial setup scroll with voice over – which significantly emphasizes words like tragic, mad, macabre, and nightmare, the pre-credits sequence begins with a black screen accompanied by sounds of digging and laboured breathing. This is punctuated by occasional camera flashes revealing close-ups of parts of corpses. At first these are so brief and in such extreme close-up that it is not quite clear what they show but their disgusting nature is suggested by the orange–green colour of the decaying flesh peeling back from the bones. These become wider and wider shots – a succession of brief images of an eye, fingernails, a foot, a torso, mummified hands and a skull in both full-face and profile – until the full image fades up. The camera pulls back to reveal 'a grisly work of art' made out of corpses; the police report blames the work on grave-robbers from 'out of State'. After the titles the camera lingers on a close-up of a dead armadillo, with the pulling over of the van taking place blurred and almost entirely out of shot. When Franklin is helped out of the van and then blown off the verge by a passing truck, a radio report relays the details of a grisly murder involving dismemberment. This serves to create a foregrounding of death and the expectation that the film will incite the viewer to feel concomitant pain and disgust (the accompanying music screeches, crashes and vibrates in a way that is physically uncomfortable). As well as offering the sight of unpleasant images, this also begins a build-up of dread – the viewer is already primed about what to expect from the coming film.

A philosophical approach to horror would question this aesthetic: the viewers' relationship to such images is not unproblematical. It raises the question of why anyone would want to submit themselves to watching anything that was discomfiting in this way. To talk about aesthetics is thus to engage with philosophical theories of beauty. Yet can it be said that images of horror are beautiful in any sense? Obviously, many images of horror such as those in the opening sequence of *The Texas Chain Saw Massacre* are the very opposite of what might be thought of as appealing to the eye, but art has always held a place for the negative aspect of beauty. If images can be said to be beautiful, there are also those that can be described as ugly, grotesque or foul. This is also related to questions of taste. Images of horror (especially in genre cinema) do not tend to fit sociocultural notions of beauty. Any discussion of aesthetics thus involves judgements, and this is also linked to emotions and physical reactions. Furthermore, such judgements can be culturally conditioned. It might not be hard to imagine, then, that an object that can be described as hideous might also be described as exquisite under a different set of cultural judgement values. In the history of art criticism, the eighteenth-century philosopher Edmund Burke's ideas about the beautiful and the sublime have proved invaluable for Cynthia Freeland in her account of 'art-dread' in response to horror cinema (2004). Burke connects the sublime to pain rather than pleasure (which looking at a beautiful object produces). The sublime inspires feelings of awe, dread and horror. In the Burkean sense it can be connected to the feeling of shock that comes from the realization that the human being is such an insignificant figure in the landscape of nature, the cosmos or God. It can certainly be encapsulated within a confrontation with the darkness and decay found in horror art (this might include the works of the surrealists including Dali and Jan Svankmajer – both also filmmakers, and H. R. Giger – who has contributed art designs to a number of horror films). It is there in the opening sequences of *The Texas Chain Saw Massacre*.

The introduction of the main characters is undertaken via camera-work in an intimate fly-on-the-wall style. This gives an impression of actuality, sending a message to the audience that events are close to or could be based on reality, and emphasizes the opening caption that indicates the film was based on actual events. Their journey takes them to the cemetery (where they are checking on their grandfather's grave) and past the old slaughterhouse, and they pick up the hitchhiker who proceeds to unsettle and then attack them (his photographs of slaughtered cattle and talk of 'head cheese' are intended to disgust, and the shots in which he cuts himself and then Franklin are clearly intended to inflict pain on the viewer). This sequence is book-ended by Pam's reading of the horoscope that similarly emphasizes future misfortunes. The landscape through which the group is passing at this point is open and flat, much of the vegetation dry and brown, with large pens to house the cattle. When they stop to pick up the hitchhiker, the van is outlined against the open sky that takes up five-sixths of the screen – rural Texas in its vast openness is sublime. The characters are dwarfed by the sense of space as much as they are prefigured to be overwhelmed by death in the near future.

The idea of the sublime in *The Texas Chain Saw Massacre* can be contrasted to the reputation it has as a gore film. In his review of the film Roger Ebert states[16] that 'it is as violent and gruesome and blood-soaked as the title promises' and it was banned in the UK as one of the video nasties. As Williams (2003) argues, images of fear in horror cinema are used to create comparable vicarious fear in the viewer – as the victims in *The Texas Chain Saw Massacre* scream and squirm, for example, so too does the audience. Filmmakers do not have to rely on particularly detailed imagery to achieve this (this may be through enforced economies of scale as much as artistic choices – horror filmmakers often do what they can within the available budget). *The Texas Chain Saw Massacre* does not always show explicitly detailed acts of bodily penetration or dismemberment, nevertheless the aesthetic of the film merely has to suggest the gruesome events that are happening and the viewer responds by 'feeling' the attack in a moment of empathy with the onscreen characters. The graphic scenes in the film involve fast cutting, close-ups and tight angles, the screen is largely dark and the action takes place in pools of light in marked-off areas of the screen. In the sequences where Leatherface attacks the characters the film often relies heavily on the soundscape that is dominated by Leatherface's chainsaw.

Writing about the Hong Kong action film, David Bordwell (2001: 78) suggests that fast-cutting and chaotic action sequences can work effectively 'because the shots tend to be readable at a glance – fairly close, simply composed, and displaying only one or two trajectories of movement'. Further, he relates this readability to the affective nature of the action (2001: 90): 'Not only must the action be legible and expressively amplified, it must be *communicated*, ... it must be stamped on the spectator's senses'. In the sequence where Pam enters the house looking for Kirk, the viewer is assaulted with the subjective shots from her point of view of the uncanny mise-en-scène of the house's décor – a layer of fur, feather and other slaughterhouse detritus, and furniture made from bones, all of which symbolize death and are in themselves of the grave and therefore disgusting. Pam falls over in this decay and coughs and vomits in disgust (and clearly the viewer is intended to reciprocate). Nevertheless, these images – these objects – have their own strange beauty, a sublime aesthetic. As Pam tries to run from the house, Leatherface attacks and carries her off to the kitchen. The soundtrack is then dominated by her terrified screams (just as the audience might be expected to scream in terror). When she is hung up on the meat-hook, this is not shown penetrating her flesh but it is preceded by two close-up shots of the hook dominating the frame and then her screams of pain as she is left hanging. As she is forced to watch helplessly while Leatherface butchers Kirk's corpse, this is implied solely through Leatherface strutting around the body with his chainsaw raised. Although they are shot economically, the sequences are easily readable and thus create 'a piercing arousal of the spectator's senses and emotions' (Bordwell 2001: 90).

In this respect, it is appropriate to consider the ways in which films such as *The Texas Chain Saw Massacre* are as Freeland (2000: 243) calls them, examples of the 'perverse sublime'. These 'graphic horror movies with over-the-top excessive visual spectacles provide certain aesthetic pleasures to devoted fans of the genre'. Such specialized aesthetic pleasures, according to Freeland, celebrate not just evil, but the cosmic forces of creation and destruction. Freeland (2000) contrasts this with what she calls the antisublime – uncanny horror films like *Eraserhead* and *The Shining* that create aesthetic pleasures through moral negativity in the form of a superior force of evil that cannot be defeated. According to Freeland (2000: 271), both these forms, the antisublime and the perverse sublime, move away from the idea of the sublime as a magnificent, awesome force of nature that overwhelms yet elevates the viewer. In this way, they provide a mechanism for engaging with the aesthetic pleasures of horror cinema.

However, a question that concerns many writers in the field of horror film studies is why viewers would subject themselves to these effects in the first place. We might ask what pleasures there could possibly be in watching *The Texas Chain Saw Massacre* (though anyone who enjoys these kinds of films or has ever sat in an audience will know that viewers do not only squirm and cringe, they also clearly enjoy the experience). Having established *how* horror cinema sets up various modes of affect using technical and artistic codes, Freeland's account of the sublime aesthetic indicates that it is also necessary to think about *why* such shocking, gory, and unnerving material might appeal to audiences. Horror films will invariable draw on recognized and frequently used stylistic or narrative devices to create a sense of horror. Such stylistic or narrative devices will include sound effects and musical cues, arrangements of mise-en-scène or technical codes of cinematography that depend on the technologies and budgets available to the filmmaker. Repeated from film to film within a genre, these not only become established as generic conventions, but serve to direct the responses of the viewers already familiar with the forms and functions of horror cinema. Horror films, in common with other genres, raise certain expectations in the viewer that are thus exploited in multiple ways in any one film.

As suggested by Prawer's references (1980) to horrific and uncanny modes, it may well be that there is a division within tastes and preferences in both the genre and its audience in terms of effects. The differing aesthetics depending on different combinations of effect (the explicit forms primarily working to create feelings of disgust, repulsion, nausea and very often shock; the suggestive forms of creating emotional unease and a shiver sensation, horripilation or the goosebumps) can disturb the viewer in markedly different ways. Of course, the audience is not homogenous and may consist of different segments that may find certain aesthetics more appealing than others (this does not necessarily mean audiences are split only by demographic groupings, but according to personal tastes as well). This may partly account for the wide variety of horror subgenres and also why the boundaries are so diffuse with overlaps to many other genres. It is clear from this that these diverse aesthetic styles might produce very different kinds of affective experiences (though it is worth remembering that they might well also occur together in one film[17]). It is therefore important to further consider how these might be related to the pleasures of horror cinema for various audience's segments. The salient point here is not that horror films scare their audience (they clearly do), but that despite their intended modes of affect being 'displeasurable' they are none-the-less consumed as pleasurable entertainment by members of their audiences for several different reasons. Behind this notion lie philosophical and psychological questions about the nature of horror cinema and horror film viewing.

3

HORROR CINEMA AND ITS PLEASURES

Cynthia Freeland argues in *The Naked and the Undead* (2000: 273–74) that horror films have appeal because:

> [T]hey continue a lengthy tradition of art-making as they address human fears and limitations, forcing confrontations with monsters who overturn the natural order – of life and death, natural/supernatural, or human/non-human. They depict vivid threats to our values, concepts, and our very bodily and mental integrity. [...] Such films, like other cultural artifacts, engage many of our intertwined human abilities. Horror films may aim at producing gut-level reactions such as fear, revulsion, anxiety, or disgust, but they also stimulate more complex emotional and intellectual responses. They provide visions of a world where action may or may not have meaning, where a monster may or may not be sympathetic, where evil people may or may not win out in the end.

As Freeland's summary suggests, the appeals of horror are complex. Despite horror films being aesthetically designed to create a distinctive set of disturbing effects and responses in the audience, large numbers of people obviously do gain pleasure and entertainment from viewing a very wide range of horror cinema for many different reasons. Theoretical and critical attempts to explain that appeal are equally multi-faceted, and it can therefore be difficult to identify a straightforward explanation for the appeal of horror.

In this respect, there have been many attempts to explore the complex emotional and intellectual responses that Freeland mentions, and the large body of work within horror film theory suggests a number of potential explanations or answers to the question of why fictional horror in cinematic form is pleasurable (some of them seemingly contradictory). These theoretical accounts have a broad history. As Stephen Neale *et al.* argue in their introduction to the horror genre in *The Cinema Book* (Cook 2007: 191–208), it is important to contextualize the development of horror as a subject for study within film theory. According to Neale *et al.*'s outline, early accounts of horror film were of censorship and reports on harmful effects (for example, of Hammer films in the late 1950s). There were also accounts that considered the artistic and literary merits of the horror film, linking the genre to the fantastique and surrealism in France for example, and then in the late 1960s producing historical accounts of the horror film as a development in the long tradition of 'the art of terror' in literature. More importantly for theoretical explanations of cinematic horror and its pleasures, film journals started publishing articles on the psychology of the genre in the 1950s – though horror cinema was not put firmly on the agenda of film studies until the second half of the 1970s. The academic legitimacy of horror film studies was thus initiated through cultural and historical accounts, but was then opened up within apparatus and spectatorship theory by drawing on Freudian and other forms of psychoanalysis. By the 1970s psychological studies proliferated and, particularly with respect to the 1970s cycle of violence against women, feminist critiques of the genre began to appear (and these opened up the extremely important area of gender and horror cinema to debate). However, some critics rejected the psychoanalytical approaches (those based on Freudian models of the workings of the unconscious mind) in particular because of the fixed and non-negotiable model of the spectator that this presented.

While psychoanalytical film theory has provided the basis of many accounts of horror cinema and specific horror films or cycles, philosophical accounts have provided a lively intervention into discussions about the ways in which horror 'works'. A major debate between cognitivism (based on the ways in which people think about horror rather than any universal underlying unconscious processes) and psychoanalysis was initiated in the 1990s, and this further illustrates the complexities of attempting to offer a straightforward explanation for the pleasures of horror cinema. In other empirical approaches to the genre, the actual audience became the focus of research into how viewers responded to horror films. Explorations of horror fandom and studies of the fan audience sit alongside social-psychological research into the observed behaviours of the audience. Neale *et al.* conclude (2007: 208) that the critical approaches to the horror movie broadly fall into those offering psycho-sociological explanations of the genre – what it represents for its audiences – and those attempting to analyze the aesthetic effects offered to the audience by the play of the genre's conventions. This does not however give much idea of the complexity of the field with respect to gender, censorship and mass media effects, or different audience responses.

In his introduction to *Horror Film and Psychoanalysis* (2004b: 2), Steven Schneider lists horror film critics as coming from a very wide range of disciplines: psychoanalytic film theory, philosophy, film aesthetics, sociology, cultural theory, cognitive film theory, feminist film theory, and empirical psychology. Undoubtedly, there will be tensions between different theoretical approaches to the genre; as Schneider (2004b: 1–2) says 'those who defend a [particular] approach to horror cinema typically have pet applications of their own' and those who critique particular theories 'almost always have alternative, incompatible (or so it may seem) paradigms in mind'. As this implies, there is a level of theoretical complexity within the field that cannot be reduced to a straightforward account of cinematic horror. This introduction cannot fully reflect this flourishing and productive area of film studies, but it is designed to engage with the field in a way that can set the context for further reading. It is therefore focused on just some of the key theories of cinematic horror. By thinking about the kinds of questions that these approaches pose, how they seek to answer these questions and how useful these answers might be in explaining or exploring different aspects of horror cinema, some clear directions might be forthcoming, particularly in addressing the seemingly paradoxical pleasures of the genre. It is also useful in drawing links between the different approaches and highlighting where there might be conflicts or contradictions in order to position the wide range of other approaches that there is not the scope to discuss in depth here.

WHY HORROR?

Certain theoretical approaches can usefully contribute to understanding the role of horror cinema for its audience and why it might be so paradoxically pleasurable to watch horror films. The key approaches dealt with here are psychoanalytical accounts of the uncanny and abjection that address the way horror films tap into the unconscious, theories of spectatorship and identification which can explain the way viewers identify with characters, and particularly what this means in respect of gendered audience responses, and philosophical accounts of entity-based and event-based definitions of art-horror which address the emotional experiences of horror film viewing in terms of cognitive thought processes. There are two main questions around which discussion of these theoretical and critical approaches is organized. First, how does the fascination with horror films relate to the contradictions between the conscious and the unconscious mind? This concerns the application of psychoanalytic theory to cinematic horror, particularly as it has been outlined by Robin Wood in terms of the uncanny and the return of the repressed (which links to a critique of the social order) on the one hand and Barbara Creed's account of abjection in the representation of monstrosity and the monstrous-feminine on the other. The subjectivity of horror cinema is addressed in terms of Linda William's essay on the horror film gaze and Carol Clover's account of cross-gendered identification in the slasher film. Second, how does the audience make sense of horror? This relates to cognitive psychology, specifically in terms of Noel Carroll's co-existentialist model of art-horror which explains the pleasures of horror in terms of narrative curiosity, and Matt Hill's and Carol Freeland's discussions of the horror narrative based on events and art-dread.

Tudor (1997: 443) begins his essay by asking 'What is the appeal of horror?' and this is the central question of all these key theoretical approaches. He states:

> Various attempts have been made to answer this question, generally combining arguments about the nature of horror texts with arguments about the distinctive character of horror consumers. The most common attempts at general explanation are grounded in concepts drawn from psychoanalytic theory, some depending quite directly on Freud's 'return of the repressed' argument in his discussion of 'the uncanny', others utilizing the framework of 'structural psychoanalysis' to explore the ways in which the unconscious structures forms of representation.

It is these approaches that are considered first in respect of what answers they might give to the questions about the appeal of horror.

THE BLACK LAGOON OF THE UNCONSCIOUS

David Cronenberg has often talked about horror films, his own and others, in terms of exploring the unconscious mind. Discussing the nature of horror at the Toronto Festival of Festivals in 1983, he wrote (1984: 57) about one of his favourite movies:

> For me the imagery of *The Creature From The Black Lagoon* was always perfect because the Black Lagoon is the dark pool of the unconscious and of course there are creatures within it. The exercise

is to jump down into the Lagoon to see what is going on down there and to say 'hello' to the creature.

While this does suggest that it may be in a very knowing, conscious and overt way, it does indicate that horror filmmakers are drawing on notions of the unconscious in relation to the monsters and images of monstrosity that they create for their films. When discussing the monstrous transformations of the characters in his films *Videodrome* and *The Fly*, Cronenberg (quoted in Charney 1997: 164) has also discussed what he calls the black lagoon as 'our collective unconscious' that contains a creature 'that wants to come out'. At the very least this suggests that horror films might very well – and in fact do – incorporate elements that draw on the Freudian notion of repressed mental content. 'Monsters from the Id' is a term frequently applied to creatures in horror and fantasy films,[1] for example Hyde in *Dr Jekyll and Mr Hyde* or the invisible creature in *Forbidden Planet*. In an article of the same name, Margaret Tarratt (1986) argued that monsters in films such as *The Thing (from Another World)* and *The Creature from the Black Lagoon* represent repressed sexual desire. However, since there is a level of knowingness here (at least in the case of Cronenberg, though it can probably be assumed that he is not alone in this as *Forbidden Planet* and other films such as *Psycho* attest) care should perhaps be taken not to overemphasize evidence of 'hidden' meanings linked to unconscious processes without noting the awareness of the author (or at least not always). The fact that filmmakers such as Cronenberg are overt users of Freudian psychoanalysis does not mean that the films themselves are beyond such explanations, however, and psychoanalytic readings of horror films can still contribute to accounts of the pleasures and other responses experienced by the audience. The thing to bear in mind is that they are not necessarily the universal and ahistorical accounts that drawing on psychoanalysis might sometimes suggest they are.

Nonetheless, in the search for answers to questions about the appeal of horror, psychoanalysis may be useful when discussing the fact that elements of horror cinema represent the anxieties, fears, fantasies and desires that are (to quote Schneider 2004b: 2–3) 'relegated to the unconscious during childhood either because they are too unpleasurable in and of themselves or because they conflict with more acceptable/ appropriate mental content'. Sigmund Freud proposed a model of the mind in which the majority of the individual's emotions, feelings, impulses, desires and beliefs – the things that drive their actions and responses to situations – are not available at a conscious level, but are buried in the unconscious mind. What the person is aware of (the conscious together with any memories recalled from the subconscious) is only a very small part of the mind; most of what makes up the personality is inaccessible in the unconscious. Freud, in what is referred to as repression, suggested that experiences in early childhood that caused extreme anxiety were pushed down into the unconscious in order to 'get rid of them', but they can never be totally excluded from the mind. They remain in the unconscious and continue to have an impact on the personality. Freud related this to psychosexual development, for example in the Oedipus Complex where the child's desire for the mother and attendant fear or hatred of the father must be repressed in order for the boy to overcome his fear of castration, identify with the father (as male) and thus develop masculine personality characteristics. (Although not an aspect of the Freudian model – Freud saw the Oedipus Complex in girl's resulting penis envy which has to be repressed in order to identify with the mother/female, a similar Electra Complex explaining female psychosexual development was proposed by Carl Jung.)

For the purposes of exploring why viewing cinematic horror might give rise to the responses it does, the role of the unconscious in fears and anxieties can be discussed in a broader sense than just the psychosexual (although this may well play a part). If the unconscious contains things that were repressed in order to avoid anxiety, then perhaps the activities of monsters or the traumatic events that are played out in cinematic horror are a representation of all that which is contained within the unconscious. Horror cinema could thus work as a replaying of those events and result in a working through of similar feelings of anxiety in the viewer. This need not be without its own attendant pleasures, of course. As the quotes from Cronenberg also suggest, audiences might very well want to meet the creature (who itself wants to emerge). This suggests that although they are unpleasurable or unacceptable, these repressed thoughts and desires need an outlet (perhaps in a safe context) and therefore can give some sort of perverse pleasure when revisited through characters, images and events in horror films. Viewers (and indeed filmmakers) may not, though, always be able to articulate why this is the source of pleasure in being scared. Low-budget cult filmmaker Roger Corman demonstrates why unconscious processes might be important in horror cinema, though not always at a conscious level, when he says[2] that:

> It's hard to say how the concept of the unconscious plays out for the viewer. The filmgoer is probably not aware of exactly what is happening, but they're aware of the result. If you're playing with the filmgoers unconscious, they react to it without really knowing why they are reacting to it.

In other words, we don't always know why we enjoy being safely scared, but we know we like it. Exploring this via psychoanalytically based accounts of horror cinema therefore remains an important area of horror film studies, even though as a theory in its own right psychoanalysis is often disputed.

Psychoanalysis itself is one of the most keenly argued and possibly most widely applied developments within horror film theory. Despite being contested within the field of psychiatry in recent decades, Freudian psychoanalysis is nevertheless an application that still offers productive readings of various horror films and cycles. Since it is a complex area – and it is complex not least because psychoanalysis is such a broad body of work with many reworkings and counter-arguments to Freud's original model – care should be taken in this approach, as in others, not to think of it as a blanket answer in reply to questions about the paradoxical pleasures of horror film viewing. As Schneider illustrates (2004b: 2), there are not simply difficulties of relating theories of horror to each other, or even of drawing links between them, there are also contradictions within the same area. He illustrates just how complex a field psychoanalytic criticism of horror cinema is in his introduction to *Horror Film and Psychoanalysis*:

> Especially since the late 1970s, there has been a tremendous diversity of psychoanalytic approaches to the horror film. These approaches differ, and often conflict, in substantial ways.

There have been many psychoanalytical approaches to horror cinema, then, and as Schneider points out it can be difficult negotiating the diverse and sometimes contradictory arguments. It is more useful perhaps to apply key concepts carefully and selectively in order to explore the nuances of particular horror films or certain kinds of cinematic horror. This section therefore focuses on two aspects of psychoanalytic theory that are related to the unconscious and repression as they can be observed in horror cinema – the uncanny and abjection. Of course, no one (or even two) main concept from psychoanalytic theory can provide a universal account of horror, and there is also overlap between these concepts to take account of, but these particular approaches serve as a focus for useful analysis of responses to key horror films.

The uncanny

The psychoanalytical concept of the uncanny can be directly linked to modes of affect produced by images of cinematic horror. Freud (1919) himself discussed the uncanny in terms of aesthetics, not just as a theory of beauty but as related to 'qualities of feeling'. He unreservedly links the uncanny to what is frightening, specifically to things or events that arouse dread and horror. It is worth remembering, though, that the word is not always used – as Freud recognized – in an unambiguous way. It is also linked to fear in general. The term can be used to refer to the awareness of something disturbing as when we encounter a figure standing in the darkness only to realize that it is really a piece of furniture or coat hung in an unusual place, but it is also used to refer to the feeling that is created – it is a sense of unease. The uncanny is thus both a moment of perception and an emotion. In the essay where he discusses the uncanny in depth, Freud (1919: 148) describes a moment on a train where he is alone in a sleeper compartment:

> [A] more than usually violent jolt of the train swung back the door of the adjoining washing-cabinet, and an elderly gentleman in a dressing-gown and a travelling cap came in. I assumed that in leaving the washing-cabinet, which lay between the two compartments, he had taken the wrong direction and come into my compartment by mistake. Jumping up with the intention of putting him right, I at once realized to my dismay that the intruder was nothing but my own refection in the looking-glass on the open door.

This moment involves a shock and a feeling of dismay upon realization of the truth. What is uncanny is thus unnerving. It is an emotion experienced when something familiar returns to the conscious mind but is unrecognized. It is unfamiliar, yet at the same time strangely familiar – and in this respect can be frightening or disturbing as Freud's own reflection was and the coat in the dark might be.

The very term 'uncanny' can itself be slippery in this way. In his writings Freud used the German word 'unheimlich', which is only approximated by the term 'uncanny'. Unheimlich and its antonym heimlich have the approximate meaning of unhomely and homely (terms which do not exist with the same meaning in the English language). Uncanny and its opposite, canny, derive from the root word meaning to know (also related to the Scottish term 'to ken'). In English, uncanny is often used to describe something that is strange or creepy, but it can also be applied to something so surprisingly accurate that it seems eerie. While the term 'canny' has the meaning shrewd, it can also infer something that is crafty or sly. In this way Freud is discussing something that is both unhomely and homely. Or in its translation as uncanny, it is thus something which is unknown and yet once known. It is this very tension between feeling that something is simultaneously familiar and unfamiliar (like the unrecognized old man that is only one's own reflection or the home invader that is really only a coat) that creates an uncomfortable and frightening cognitive dissonance.

For Freud, the uncanny is directly related to repression. In this sense, what creates the uncanny feeling is not something which is unknown, but something which only *appears* to be unknown because it has long been forgotten (repressed). This is a process of the unconscious mind in that unwanted, painful, unpleasant, distressing or uncomfortable experiences, desires or thoughts are never entirely forgotten, but are 'submerged' and thus preserved – repressed – in the unconscious (and in this respect relate to the monsters from the id and the creatures from the black lagoon of horror cinema). In Freud's model, these unwanted experiences, desires and thoughts are constantly threatening to return to the conscious level of the mind – the 'return of the repressed'. This is why they are simultaneously familiar and unfamiliar – when they do return they seem frighteningly strange, but since they are repressed thoughts returning to consciousness, we recognize them too as disturbing moments from the past. In terms of mental processes, Freud suggested these repressed elements can return in the forms of parapraxes (slips of the tongue), phantasies, and dreams. In terms of clinical psychoanalysis, unresolved repression can also result in phobias and anxieties (what Freud called neuroses). It is in terms of critical analysis of the arts, though, that the uncanny and the return of the repressed are useful concepts, especially so for analysis of horror cinema that draws on feelings of dread and anxiety.

Freud himself analyzed literature in his essay *The Uncanny*. He drew on Ernest Jentsch's work in *The Psychology of the Uncanny* (written a decade before Freud's essay in 1906), in analyzing E. T. A Hoffman's stories, and the automaton in *The Sandman*[3] in particular. Jentsch described uncanny beings as those inanimate objects that appeared to be alive and animate objects whose apparent life was doubtful. This is pertinent, since there is often uncertainty about whether the monstrous creatures in horror cinema are alive or dead: undead horror figures such as vampires and zombies who rise from coffins and graves abound in the genre, and even the killers of the slasher genre who seem human keep getting up after they are slain, and often return from the dead in sequels (Freddy Kreuger is clearly signified as dead from the very start of *A Nightmare on Elm Street*). Jentsch's discussion of *The Sandman* also clearly applies to artificial creatures such as Ash in *Alien* and the Replicants in *Blade Runner*. Freud drew on Jentsch's essay to illustrate the link between these uncanny beings and the emotion of the uncanny. The emotion is incited by the underlying intellectual uncertainty that such a creature – because we are not sure if it is alive or dead in the case of a horror monster, or real life or artificial in the case of a science fiction android – creates.

Freud related this to the surmounting (or overthrowing) of childish beliefs, for example that the dead can come back. He suggested that we can never quite replace these old childish beliefs with our new adult certainties. In fiction and in cinema, vampires, zombies, serial killers who won't stay dead, and androids or other automata are uncanny because they make us doubt our adult beliefs. This 'reconfirmation of the surmounted' (a second class of the uncanny alongside the return of the repressed) is discussed by Schneider (1999) in relation to a typology of monsters that breaks down as:

- 'reincarnated monsters' (either 'zombies' that are 'non-natural' – including vampires, the living dead, and so on – or 'medico-scientific' – Frankenstein's creature, for example, and 'spirits' that can be 'disembodied' – ghosts – or 'embodied' – a person possessed by a demon);
- 'psychic monsters' ('telekinetics' – *Carrie* is a good example, and 'telepathics' – as in *Scanners*); and
- 'dyadic monsters' (which could be first in the group of 'replicas' – either 'doppelgangers' such as twins, clones or chameleons, or 'replicants' such as robots and cyborgs, or second in the group of 'psychos' – a group that can include 'schizos' such as Norman Bates who takes on the persona of his mother, 'shapeshifters' such as Jekyll

and Hyde and werewolves, 'projections' where the killer takes over another body as in *The Brood*, and 'serial killers' such as Hannibal Lecter).

Schneider, borrowing from cognitive linguist George Lakoff's idea of conceptual metaphors, neatly accounts for the whole range of horror film monsters as metaphorical representations of surmounted beliefs (without having to struggle with questions of supernatural or real world existence of the monstrous characters). In terms of why this might be satisfying for the audience, he argues that these metaphorical monsters 'are able to produce in many viewers that conflict of judgment necessary for a feeling of uncanniness'. Furthermore, they are all the more horrifying since 'the paradigmatic horror narratives such monsters metaphorically embody are likely to have a basis in reality'. And this works effectively to release the anxieties of the audience: in a similar way to tragedy, it 'promotes emotional catharsis', it offers the same 'escape from the tedium of everyday life' as fantasy, and like comedy, it provides 'a relatively safe (because relatively disguised/distorted) forum for the expression of socio-cultural fears'. This effectively links the uncanny – the feeling of dread created when something returns to the surface from the depths of the unconscious – with the satisfactions and pleasures of viewing cinematic horror on a number of levels: as a release valve for negative emotions, as a way of getting through the mundane, and as confrontation with issues of the day.

In Robin Wood's account of American horror (2002), the concept of repression (and thus the return of the repressed) is important in accounting for the paradoxical pleasures of horror film viewing because it also permits an expression of deep-seated psychosocial and psychosexual anxieties. Wood argues that the return of the repressed is central to the horror film narrative in the figure of the monster. The monster is an embodiment of that which is repressed, and further its appearance in the horror film narrative is symbolic of the return of the repressed. In this respect, it is useful to keep in mind that the monster of the horror film is frequently a figure from the past that returns to haunt new victims in the present. This applies as much to classic horror monsters such as Dracula and the mummy who return from the grave to 'possess' the heroine, as it does to the serial killers and stalkers of the slasher genre who return to the scene of their past crimes: Freddy Kreuger is a paedophile who preyed on an earlier cohort of local children, for example, and Michael Myers who returns to the community where he murdered his sister after witnessing a symbolic 'primal scene'.

These monstrous figures not only come out of the past to haunt the present (in a parallel to the repressed thoughts from the past that return to the surface conscious mind in the present), but are also coded in some way as 'the monstrous Other'. The concept of Othering is related to identity, both in terms of the self and of society. The Other is central to definitions of identity since it is anything that is outside of or different from the self or the society. Edward Said (2003), for example, explored how Western societies Othered the people of the 'Orient' in order to control and subjugate them. Jacques Lacan (1998) introduced the idea of the Other in his account of language and symbolic order. In very simple terms, the Other is that which is separated off from ourselves by subjectivity (we are only created as subjects in relation to the Other and for Lacan desire is always of/for/by the Other – so perhaps we can see why the monstrous Other of horror cinema is so fascinating). For Wood (2002: 25), the monster as an embodiment of the Other is linked to dominant ideology of Western/American society (what he calls 'bourgeois ideology'):

> Otherness represents that which bourgeois ideology cannot recognize or accept but must deal with ... in one of two ways: either by rejecting and if possible annihilating it, or by rendering it safe and assimilating it, converting it as far as possible into a replica of itself.

He thus lists the category of the Other as including:

- other people
- women

- the proletariat
- other cultures
- ethnic groups within the culture
- alternative ideologies and political systems
- deviations from sexual norms of the culture
- children

In the American horror film, normality comes into conflict with these subordinate groups in the form of the monster (and it is a very easy exercise to identify examples of horror film monsters in all of these categories). Wood has declared that his application of psychoanalysis to horror cinema was 'a valuable weapon that could be used politically' (2004: xiv) and his socio-political arguments are explored further in the final chapter.

This conflict between normality and the Other is what for Wood (2002: 32) 'constitutes the essential subject of the horror film': the monster represents the return of the repressed since 'in a society built on monogamy and the family there will be an enormous surplus of repressed sexual energy, and what is repressed must always strive to return'. This is why many monsters of the 1970s horror films that Wood was analyzing seek to seduce the heroine and kill the hero (who in an Oedipal sense represent the mother and father figures) or are demonic children seeking to kill their parents (he discusses films such as John Badham's *Dracula* and *The Omen*, for example). In this psycho-analytical sense, monsters are literally or figuratively children since children's polymorphously perverse infantile sexuality must be repressed by society and channelled into monogamous heterosexuality. In a more general sense, such monsters are an expression of Western society's fear of any sexuality that is not of the 'normative' mono-gamous heterosexual kind (these may be of the repressed unconscious kind, but they may well be conscious too). Women too are a particular focus of these horror films. Wood argues that femininity is repressed in a patriarchal society; it is not simply that women as a group are oppressed, but that men must repress their feminine side in order to adopt the normative masculine identity. In a patriarchal society, Wood says (2002: 27), men 'project their own innate, repressed femininity' onto women 'in order to disown it as inferior'. Again this emerges in horror cinema as violence against women. While this is common in the horror film (and a particular concern for feminist critics in general), Wood also analyzes films such as *Psycho* and *Dressed to Kill* in which gender identity is a root of monstrosity (both films are about male killers who dress as women when killing). These examples (of repressed fears about gender and sexuality) illustrate that horror films can be read as nightmares that allow repressed desires to emerge. As Wood says (2002: 32): 'Central to the effect and fascination of horror films is their fulfillment of our nightmare wish to smash the norms that oppress us and which our moral conditioning teaches us to revere'.

The paradoxical pleasures of horror film viewing thus arise from our attitudes towards social norms. This is directly related to repression, in that Western societies are based on the family unit (which requires bourgeois, heterosexual, monogamous, capitalist individuals to sustain both it and the society it exists within[4]). It is clear that the family has thus become the primary source of horror in films such *The Exorcist*, *The Stepfather* and *The Brood*. There has been a family breakdown in each of these examples that seems to be either the source of the horror or an entry point for the monster to invade. In *The Brood*, the mother is in a psychiatric institute where she has been encouraged to give physical form to her 'rage' (clearly a metaphor for the return of the repressed, especially since she was abused by her own mother and has similarly abused her daughter), and she gives 'birth' to unnatural children who act out her revenge on the family. In *The Exorcist*, Regan's parents are separated – making an absence in the family through which the devil can gain entry and possess her (the signs of Regan's possession are the giving into repressed urges as she swears, urinates in the living room in front of guests, makes sexual taunts and masturbates with a crucifix). In *The Stepfather*, single-parent families become prey to the monster when they cannot live up to his ideas of perfection (they are not sufficiently repressed and must be killed). The family is both the reason for and the means of repression, and it is therefore both threatened and a threat in the horror film.

Wood's underlying argument about horror cinema is based on the work of Marx and Marcuse, and is thus as much political as it is psychoanalytic. In thinking about repression in this way, it can be broken down into basic and surplus repression. According to this model, civilization in general could not have come into being without repression. Basic (animal) instincts and urges have to be overcome in order to develop the self-control, consideration of others and postponement of gratification that humans must have in order to exist successfully within groups or societies. Without this 'basic repression' there would be no human cultures, only states of individualistic anarchy. Particular cultures or societies may, however, require much greater degrees of repression (of sexuality in particular, but also of behaviours related to classes and ethnicities) and thus 'surplus repression' is more culturally specific. Since Western societies require such a high degree of surplus repression, the return of the repressed is an ever-present threat. Horror films are one way in which this can be represented and worked through (although comedies can also operate in this way). Two levels of repression can thus be identified in the horror film's images of monstrosity, though since there is an excess of surplus repression monstrosity is more likely to represent this form. In *The Exorcist*, for example, the possessed Regan may urinate on the living room carpet (basic repression), but it is in her pubescent sexuality (surplus repression) that she becomes most monstrous (after she masturbates with the crucifix she pushes her mother's face into her crotch, saying 'Lick me, lick me!').

While there are clearly Freudian interpretations here (the desire of the child to possess the mother sexually), Wood's arguments about basic and surplus repression are not solely Freudian. One of the criticisms of Wood's model is that it is overly general and gives a satisfactory account only of 1970s horror films that are progressive in that they represent the monster as emerging from the id to disrupt the social order and temporarily lift surplus repression. Wood himself addressed this issue in discussion of the 1980s slasher films by suggesting there had been a shift in cultural politics. Such horror films were not progressive, but reactionary. Their monsters were superego figures avenging themselves on 'liberated female sexuality or the sexual freedom of the young' (1986: 195). They were thus a backlash against the sexual revolution of the post-war period, rather than a resistance to the traditional family during a period of social change. The monsters of progressive horror films represent the oppressed and repressed, while those of reactionary films are simply evil and inhuman. This can explain some of the differences between different types of horror cinema, and it can certainly be used to explain why different audience segments might prefer different types of horror films – why the female fans in my own research (Cherry 1999) might dislike slasher films, for example. However, this does leave questions about why viewers might enjoy scenes of violence and gore, and it is here that a second related concept from psychoanalysis is useful.

Abjection

Since the uncanny in horror cinema gives rise to the uncomfortable experience of cognitive dissonance where something can be attractive and repulsive at the same time, it further suggests that the gross-out effect of explicit horror is crucial to this discussion. This is clear from *The Exorcist* with its scenes of excessive vomiting and head spinning, the abrupt outbursts of violence within *The Stepfather* which opens with the blood-drenched crime-scene after Jerry slaughters his previous family, and Nola's revelation of her external womb sac which she viscerally bites open with her teeth to release her sexless parthenogenic child. These moments might very well create revulsion in the viewer, but they are also compelling. This is especially true of *The Exorcist* and *The Brood*; while *The Stepfather*'s violence might be cathartic in the same way as tragedy, it is the visceral gore of the other two films that cause more of a problem in explaining why it might be pleasurable to view. While images of abject bodies can be found in all sorts of horror films, it is worth taking account of the fact that *The Exorcist* and *The Brood* are both centred around the female body and reproduction. Nola's body is clearly the site of excessive, abject reproduction with its external womb sacs, but *The Exorcist* can also be understood in these terms since Regan is the right age to be entering puberty and the blood when she masturbates could be read as menstrual blood from her first period (Carrie similarly begins exhibiting supernatural symptoms when she reaches menarche, as does Ginger in *Ginger Snaps*).

Barbara Creed (1993) develops this in terms of a psychoanalytical argument in her reading of the monstrous-feminine in horror cinema (both *The Exorcist* and *The Brood* contain representations of the monstrous-feminine that she analyzes in depth in her book). Creed argues that the monstrous-feminine is a form of transgressive femininity. The text of such horror films is not about the sexual repression of women or even their liberation from sexual repression, but about the failure of sexual repression to contain women (Lindsey 1996: 293). In her argument, Creed draws on the work of psychoanalyst Julia Kristeva, specifically Kristeva's model of abjection outlined in *Powers of Horror* (1982). In Kristeva's model, abjection is linked to an adverse reaction such as disgust, nausea or horror caused by being confronted with an object that threatens to disrupt the distinction between self and other (or subject and object in Lacanian terms). Thus to be in a state of abjection is to feel revulsion when confronted by objects that threaten to cross (or do cross) the boundary. Kristeva suggests that this causes a collapse of meaning which results in the feeling of revulsion. There are obvious links to intended affects of horror cinema here. Abjection clearly applies to the object that is on the boundary between life and death itself: the corpse, which is seen in all kinds of horror film monsters. The corpse is particularly abject because it is not just that part of the self which is expelled to become non-self, but is the disintegration of self entirely (literally out of life and into death, 'I' is eradicated since 'I' no longer exists). But meaning may also collapse (and thus disrupt the boundary between self and other) around things that confront the self with the trauma of one's own death: open wounds, blood, pus, vomit, faeces, and so on (again, all of which are repeated motifs in the horror film). Kristeva makes it clear that these things are not symbols of death (as the flatline on a heart monitor may be), but are threats of death itself.

In relation to repression, this can be linked very much to primal repression in terms of the border between human and animal (or between culture and that which preceded it). Such representations can be found in horror films where humans transform into bestial creatures, the werewolf film being a case in point. Scenes of transformation in werewolf films tend to be elaborate special effects sequences that explicitly and graphically depict the disintegration of the body's boundary as the animal emerges. These often depict the destruction of the male body (see Peirse forthcoming). After tearing off his clothes because he is burning up, David in *An American Werewolf in London* watches as his hand elongates (with bone crunching sound effects). Hair is shown sprouting from his back and his face distorts as it becomes a snout. Although there is no overt bursting out of the skin, there is a strong sense that the animal is breaking through the surface of the body. Immediately before he transforms into a werewolf in *The Howling*, Eddie digs into his head through a bullet hole in his skull and pulls out a piece of flesh or brain, saying 'I'm going to give you a piece of mind' to Karen as he does so. During the transformation the skin of his face bubbles and seethes as the werewolf's snout emerges and claws thrust up from the tips of his fingers, again showing the emergence of the animal from within the normal boundaries of the body. These examples demonstrate abjection in the form of bodies without stable boundaries (Creed 2000: 85) – they literally shift and distort before our eyes. In *Ginger Snaps* (Figure 3.1), Ginger's transformation is more gradual but she too sprouts excess hair, her vertebrae become more prominent and threaten to burst through the skin, her teeth become sharper and more protruding, and she grows talons and a tail. Several other moments of abjection occur. When Ginger attacks Norman the dog, she vomits copious amounts of blood (her face and hands are drenched) and after having unprotected sex with Jason, he too is infected as if lycanthropy is a sexually transmitted disease, signified when he urinates blood.

Figure 3.1 Brigitte watches as Ginger transforms in *Ginger Snaps*.

It is also significant that in *Ginger Snaps*, Ginger begins her transformation into a werewolf at the same time as she gets her first period and becomes attractive to boys – and interested in them. As the film progresses her body becomes more and more unclean, she is smeared in blood as she attempts to escape the bathroom where Brigitte has imprisoned her while she and Sam make the drug that will kill or cure Ginger, and then is surrounded by the bloody mess she has made first in Mr Wayne's office after she has killed him and second in the corridor when she kills the janitor. Each time, as the dialogue emphasizes, Brigitte has to clean up the mess. Cleanliness is something that recedes as Ginger becomes more monstrous, and by the time she is totally wolflike, Brigitte gives up and (having mingled her blood with Ginger's) laps Sam's blood alongside the wolf-Ginger, although having not yet reached menarche herself she can't and won't continue. Creed (1993: 71–72) lists the three ways in which horror films foreground abjection: with images of abjection, boundary crossing in the construction of the monster, and the construction of the maternal figure as abject. These can all be identified in *Ginger Snaps*, but moreover, as Bianca Nielson points out (2004), Ginger and Brigitte's mother Pamela is a frightening figure who does not want to let her daughters grow up or to relinquish control of them. As in *Carrie* and *The Exorcist*, the sexually mature, adult female body (fertile, menstruating, maternal, controlling, oppressive) is also coded as unclean and therefore abject.

In terms of psychosexual development, abjection is closely linked to femininity in that it is organized around the moment of separation from the mother (as in Freud's Oedipal complex) and awareness of the boundary between 'me' and '(m)other'. It is mother/other here and not simply other since it is linked to the concept of the archaic mother. Kristeva says that the first object of abjection is the pre-Oedipal mother who is lost when the child develops the awareness of self (Lacan's mirror stage). In this sense, abjection involves a lack (the loss of the mother). Although there is a desire to fill the lack (go back to when the child was one with the mother and had no sense of separate self), this also involves a threat since this would lead to disintegration of the self. This is why the border between self and other is the major focus of abjection, but it also means it is both a repulsive and a desired place (which of course mirrors responses to images of monstrosity in the horror film).

In terms of the archaic mother figure of the horror film, Creed finds it interesting that Freud found the womb uncanny. She notes (1993: 62), for example, that in *Alien* the female genitals and the womb are presented as 'horrific objects of dread and fascination'. The archaic mother (who reproduces via parthenogenesis as Nola does in *The Brood*) is a dark abyss in the mise-en-scène of the film: 'she is there in the images of birth, the representations of the primal scene, the womblike imagery' (Creed 1993: 50). The alien ship that the crew of the Nostromo investigate resembles a pair of legs spread apart with the entrance at the apex like female genitals as though the explorers were re-entering the womb, an impression which is reinforced since within this ship there is an egg chamber. However, this representation of the archaic mother is not based on lack, as the phallic woman would be, since it is not a form of castration anxiety (or defined in relation to the penis – parthenogenetic reproduction does not require a male partner). Instead, it represents sexual difference without reference to lack (the womb can connote fullness or emptiness but only on its own terms) and is thus outside of the patriarchal order entirely (this is why it can only be represented through mise-en-scène). It is the phallic mother that is represented in the film in form of the alien creature itself with its devouring toothed vagina – with its double set of jaws, one emerging from the other, the alien's mouth is both vagina and phallus. These representations are relevant here since art (in which we can include horror cinema) is one of two ways that Kristeva says the abject can be purified. The other is religion.

Abjection gives rise to rituals of cleanliness which are frequently found in religious codes of practice. These codes contain taboos and rites surrounding the elimination of waste and other biological processes (some religions, for example, prohibit contact with menstruating women). These rituals or prohibitions are intended to project the 'clean and proper body' (Creed 1993: 72). Anything (bodily wastes, blood, etc.) that crosses the boundaries of the body becomes non-self and therefore in order to keep the self 'clean and proper' it must be cast out. We see this in Carrie, for example, when she is in the shower frightened after discovering blood that she doesn't realize is her first period – the other girls throw tampons and sanitary towels at her yelling 'clean yourself up' and 'plug it up'. The state of abjection is further emphasized by the scene just prior to this when Carrie misses the ball in the volleyball game: Chris taunts her by saying 'You eat shit!' Religious and cultural taboos also centre around 'food loathings' in that certain things are deemed unfit to eat (abjection can thus involve ingestion as well as expulsion). While these taboos can involve foods such as shellfish or pork, the most abject forms of consumption are the eating of faeces (coprophagia) and of human flesh (cannibalism). Kristeva emphasizes 'orality' as signifying an important boundary of the self. Food, and the ingestion of food (crossing from the external Other to the internal self), thus signifies a transgression of the boundary. For Kristeva, this is tied up with the relationship between the child and the mother since it is the mother who offers the food to the child. She says (1982: 63–64) that food is 'the oral object (the abject) that sets up archaic relationships between the human being and the other, its mother'.

Again, many such examples can be found in the horror film. Coprophagia is relatively uncommon, but there is a whole subgenre of cannibal movies that includes Cannibal Holocaust – said even by hardcore horror fans to be one of the 'grossest movies ever made'[5] and 'the single least defensible film on the [video nasties] list'.[6] The film is about the search for and discovery of several cans of film, all that remains after a film crew recording material for a documentary on an Amazonian tribe go missing. The final sequences of Cannibal Holocaust are the revelation of the found footage – which involves explicit and prolonged scenes of rape, mutilation and cannibalism (which led to bans and charges of obscenity in several countries). The film deserves its bad reputation in many respects (even fans accept that its violence is unconscionable), but as a mockumentary, it also sets out to question the morality of manipulating events for entertainment or the titillation of audiences. Intriguingly, Professor Monroe – searching for the original film crew – is himself forced to consume human flesh with the cannibal tribe in order to win their trust so that they will hand over the cans of film left by the filmmakers. It is therefore significant that as a film crossing one of the last taboos in such explicit fashion, *Cannibal Holocaust* is one of the most prominent to come to attention during the video nasty campaign of the 1980s in the UK. Regardless of this background or details of this particular film, the point that cannibal films generally are exercises in orality is clear, and these, as well as films such as *The Silence of the Lambs* and *The Night of the Living Dead*, are evidence of the strong social taboos set up to maintain the clean and proper body.

In art – or more specifically in horror film, depictions of these abject states or objects are central to audience responses in terms of disgust or the 'yuk' factor (as in the vomiting in *The Exorcist*, the external womb sac in *The Brood*, the menstrual blood in *Ginger Snaps*, the eating of human flesh by Hannibal Lector), and it is worth noting that horror film narratives are also often centred around the places where the boundaries break down (graveyards in Dracula, Frankenstein and zombie or the Living Dead films, the slaughterhouse in *The Texas Chain Saw Massacre*). Drawing on Kristeva's model, Creed (1993: 61) argues that women are doubly abject. They are sexually alluring but at the same time they have disgusting bodies that not only bleed in the human sense but also menstruate and give birth in scenes of blood and gore. Many critics of horror cinema have viewed women as victims in the horror film. Stephen Neale (1980) does, for example, when he argues that horror film monsters are predominantly defined as male, with women – because their sexuality renders them desirable but also threatening to men – as their primary victims. Women are cast as victims of male monsters, he says (1980: 61), because their sexuality: 'constitutes the real problem that the horror cinema exists to explore'. Creed, on the other hand, argues that horror is centred around the monstrous-feminine because she has the power to make men fear her (because she is abject, and especially if she rejects her place in the patriarchal social order as Regan does in *The Exorcist* when she vomits on Father Merrin and forces her mother to perform cunnilingus on her). The limitation of this, however, is that it places the female character in a fixed state – as a representation of abjection and a signifier of male fear.

The female characters such as Regan, however, are also subject to character development in the narrative. At the end of the *The Exorcist*, Father Karras has taken the devil possessing Regan into himself and Regan leaves with her mother (seemingly restored to the social order). We might interpret this as representing purification. Creed (1993: 14) calls it a 'modern defilement rite':

> The horror film attempts to bring about a confrontation with the abject (the corpse, bodily wastes, the monstrous-feminine) in order finally to eject the abject and redraw the boundaries between the human and the non-human. As a form of modern defilement rite, the horror film attempts to separate out the symbolic order from all that threatens its stability, particularly the mother and all that her universe signifies.

If, as she suggests here, the horror film's confrontation with the abject serves the purpose of cleansing the 'symbolic order', the pleasures of viewing these representations of abjection falls into the category of the 'pleasure of restoration' (Hills 2004: 57). Horror films are rhythmic and repetitive. Just as they allow the repressed to return before repression is itself restored, they also allow the abject monstrous-feminine to emerge before it too is cleansed. However, Matt Hills (2004: 59) suggests that 'the abject can connote pleasurable self-transcendence and/or painful self-annihilation, depending on how this is mapped across mind/body or soul/body binaries'.

Abjection might, then, in some horror films be transcendent. Hills offers Graham Ward's analysis of *Stigmata* as an example of this, but other examples might include *Nightbreed* and *Candyman* which both end with the heroine welcoming her monstrosity. It is interesting that these films are popular with female horror fans (Cherry 1999) and Andrea Kuhn (2000) offers a feminist reading of *Candyman* which concludes that:

> [W]hile the film seems to cater to conventional genre expectations by transforming the female subject of the narrative into the object of the

> monster's abject desire, it undercuts these expectations by offering a
> fresh perspective on the old story, in which the woman establishes
> herself as subject by using the Candyman, now object of her desire, to
> rewrite the story and to make herself hero. In this case, her associa-
> tion with the world of the archaic mother, whose source she certainly
> seems to be, does not simply result in her punishment, but rather
> helps us to see through the patriarchal construct of the female martyr
> who discovers the power and lure of a femininity unleashed from
> Oedipal restraints that scares all the Trevors to death.

If applied too rigidly, perhaps, Creed's account of abjection would seem
to close down these ambiguities in favour of the purification of the
abject, so it is worth bearing in mind that this might not always be the
case in some horror films (or perhaps – as here – some readings of
horror films by some segments of the audience).

Accounts of abjection might also operate beyond Creed's focus on the
monstrous-feminine and be applied to many forms of gore film
(though they may not always contain such clear representations of the
monstrous-feminine, they frequently contain psychosexual subtexts or
encode the archaic in the mise-en-scène as *Alien* does). As many of the
examples in this discussion suggest, abjection can be linked closely to
visceral and graphic examples of horror that in aesthetic terms instil
feelings of revulsion in the audience. One of the films that Creed
explores in depth in her account of the monstrous-feminine is David
Cronenberg's *The Brood*. Indeed, many of Cronenberg's films – especially
his early works often gathered together under the label 'body horror' –
rely heavily on abjection and the associated feelings of abhorrence, disgust and revulsion. Body horror is frequently discussed in terms of
abjection being its primary intent; Mark Jancovich (2002a: 6), for
example, states that it centres around the 'collapse of distinctions and
boundaries' in which 'the monstrous threat is not simply external but
erupts from within the human body, and so challenges the distinction
between self and other, inside and outside'. This is typified in one of
Seth's early teleportation experiments in *The Fly* when a baboon is

literally turned inside out: in a classic Cronenbergian gross-out scene the door to the pod opens, the vapour clears and the mess of organs – still vaguely baboon-shaped is seen pulsing on the floor of the pod.

Cronenberg's first horror film, Shivers features a parasite that is both an organism and a sexually transmitted disease. It is seen squirming around under the skin of Nicholas's stomach (he even strokes it as though it is a baby moving inside the womb) and when he subsequently vomits the creatures up (a form of birth, perhaps) they plop viscerally to the ground below. At the end of the film when Janine infects Roger, the parasite crawls from her mouth into his as she kisses him. In what is probably the most well-known scene from the film, the parasite (which resembles a cross between a flatworm and faecal matter – both elements obviously abject) emerges from the plughole while Betts is bathing and moves up between her legs, which are spread apart, and we see her reaction as she thrashes about in the water. Jesse Stommel (2007) observes that in this scene 'it is impossible to distinguish between pleasure and pain, ecstasy and horror'. He goes on to say that:

Cronenberg's films are about upsetting these sorts of distinctions, about bodies devouring, about being devoured, about parasites that invade our bodies, about bodies mutilated and aroused by car crashes, about the intersection between biology and technology, about the limits of sexual desire (or the lack of limits). About flesh that eats and is eaten simultaneously – a sexual devouring but more often actual physical devouring as a metaphor for sex (in his films The Fly, Videodrome, Rabid, etc.). His films are about how we construct (or fail to construct) our relationship to our bodies and our sexuality.

At the end of Shivers, the now sexually liberated infected move out into the city to carry the infection far and wide. Stommel suggests that led by the two female characters, Betts and Janine, the monstrous-feminine becomes a liberatory force in this film (and in others such as Alien and Lifeforce). The monsters thus become either the protagonists in these films (Betts and Janine) or a catalyst for changes in the character (Ripley).

Similar themes of sexuality and monstrosity permeate Cronenberg's later films in the body horror subgenre. In *Rabid*, Rose becomes a sexual vampire – growing a new penetrating organ which emerges from a vaginal opening in her armpit with which she bleeds her victims during a sexual embrace. Again, this form of monstrosity is a sexually transmitted disease which rapidly spreads through Montreal. In *The Fly*, Cronenberg also explores the theme of sexual liberation through monstrosity when at first Seth is energized and becomes sexually voracious (until Ronnie complains that he cannot have any fluids left in his body). Although the carrier of the disease/monstrosity is male, the threat still resides within the abject female body, however. When she discovers that she is pregnant, Ronnie fears that the baby is a monster and she dreams of giving birth to a giant maggot. Moreover, the film can be read as suggesting that the woman – who acts as the catalyst for the sexual liberation of the repressed male scientist – is responsible for monstrosity. In a fit of jealous pique, Seth – who before his seduction by Ronnie was depicted as repressed, only ever wearing exactly the same set of clothes for example – conducts a hastily prepared experiment in which his teleporter splices his genes with that of a housefly. It can also be argued that the archaic mother is present in the mise-en-scène of the film in the form of the dark, ovoid teleport pods – when Seth transports himself he crouches naked in a foetal position within the womb-like space of the pod, and when transported the second pod gives birth to the monster Brundlefly. At the climax of the film a second birth takes place, the third pod used is an even more dark and womb-like space as it lacks the transparent panel of the other pods. Brundlefly intends to splice himself with Ronnie and the unborn baby, but when Stathis shoots out the cables connecting the pods, it this time gives birth to a fusion of Brundlefly and teleporter.

While these kinds of readings are seductive and can certainly explain the compelling attractions of such cinematic horror, it also illustrates a problem with psychoanalytic readings: namely that they do tend to close out explanations which account for differing responses in different groups of the audience. Multiple readings of these films are possible, however, since responses might well depend upon how each viewer experienced their own psychosexual development. This may well suggest different pleasures of horror film viewing for different viewers. Ashley Allinson (2002) also states that: 'The macabreness of visceral abjection […] works to categorize *Shivers* within the arena of the horror or comedy genres depending on one's reception to imagery'. Here, even the genre classification may be open to question depending upon the immediate reactions of the viewer. In another example, the horror-comedy *Slither* (which notably pastiches the bathtub scene from *Shivers*), laughter is as likely to be the primary response of viewers as is revulsion (and this variance – as Allinson points out – may be as true of a 'straight' body horror film like *Shivers* as it is of a horror-comedy like *Slither*). In his discussion of horror and comedy (he argues that they are closely matched genres, both often depending on gross-out effects), William Paul (1994) suggests that art can be playful as well as serious, and he suggests that interpretation should take into account elements other than unconscious processes. He argues that audiences respond to films in ways that are close to play, which is why laughing and screaming are both key reactions to horror films. This is not to down-play the validity of psychoanalytic readings, merely to suggest that they might not be the only explanation for those responses.

Paul states that films can contain elements that involve play and interaction similar to that experienced in a funhouse or on a roll-ercoaster ride. He argues (1994: 422) that effects films (and clearly body horror can be included here) allow the viewer to simply 'get lost in play, […] in the rush of the immediate experience'. While the play on unconscious processes may still be present in the films, the viewer may not necessarily be responding primarily to them; Paul says that 'because we do not take anything in the amusement park seriously, it is easy for us to see the emotions we indulge there as ends in themselves'. This can be seen in the very visceral responses that are observed in horror film audiences that appear to be so paradoxical. The potential problem with this alternative explanation, however, is that it may be too superficial; it is very close to the response many viewers might give – 'it's only a movie', which still does not explain why it is pleasurable.

Additionally, cultural or socio-political accounts of body horror are also possible. Ernest Mathijs (2003: 29) looks at the way in which popular and academic discussions of films that focus on 'the body as the site of violent transformation' (and he includes slasher films, rape-revenge films and zombie movies, as well as body horror in his argument), 'make clear the connections between violent invasions of the body and the role of the body in society.' Mathijs observes that comments on Cronenberg's films frequently refer to the sexually transmitted monstrous disease as a coded reference to AIDS. This, he says (p. 33), is because the monstrous transformation and AIDS are parallel examples of 'the human body in crisis'. Seth's genetic mutation (he even calls it a disease with a purpose and worries about it being contagious) simply reflects what happens to the body of a person with AIDS. In this way, The Fly can be read as a film about the global sexual crisis that emerged during the 1980s after the linking of AIDS to sexual practices. Making sociocultural references in this way anchors a film to a specific time and place, the film can thus be read not as an ahistoric, universal account of the unconscious mind, but as something that reflects the zeitgeist or cultural moment. Yet another way of looking at Cronenberg's films is as products of a specifically Canadian culture. In fact, Adam Lowenstein (2005: 147) analyzes his work as a traumatic narrative in which the comforting myths of national identity are confronted head on. Certainly, when Cronenberg refers to 'our collective unconscious' he is referring to the Canadian collective unconscious, suggesting that there could be a national/cultural element in addition to the underlying universal unconscious dimension that is worth discussing further.

These examples of alternative approaches (located in a specific culture, as thrills which are ends in themselves) to variations in audience responses to horror illustrate that a straightforward psychoanalytical account based on a model of the unconscious mind might not always give a complete picture of why certain audiences respond in particular ways. Other factors may be involved in the way the audience responds and this can be dependent upon the way the film addresses its audience. It may be, for example, that women are addressed differently by horror cinema and thus experience a different subjectivity. This may be related to the way women are represented in horror films (either as victims or as the monstrous-feminine), but it may mean also that they experience different kinds of pleasures (or displeasures), or even experience the pleasures in different ways.

THE LOOK OF HORROR CINEMA

The look is one of the most important ways the viewer is addressed in horror cinema, both in terms of the technical codes – the point-of-view shot from the slasher film, for example – and as related to the cinematic gaze of spectatorship theory. In the same way that Prawer (1990) and Abbott (2004) talk about horror being ideally suited to cinema because of film's spectral doubling, the very nature of horror can be seen as intrinsic to the processes of spectatorship. Lesley Stern (1997) draws a direct connection between horror and the look when she states that:

> Cinema, as we know it, systematically plays upon a slide between the familiar and the unfamiliar (the unheimlich). On the one hand there is a drive to depiction, to the representational familiar; and on the other there is a rendering strange through movement, through cinematic temporality. The cinema gives us the experience of time, but in temporalizing it plays all the time on a series of indeterminacies: here/there, appearance/disappearance, life/death, past/future ... The cinema taps our imagination, our unconscious, to produce a sensory affect of dissonance at the very moment of identity.

This uncanny play of images (both familiar and strange) is clearly an important element of horror cinema. This can often be seen in the viewer's reactions to images of monstrosity and horror, not wanting to look but being unable not to look as when one peers though one's fingers despite covering one's eyes with one's hands, or of responding as though the horror was 'real' even though one knows very well that it is 'only a movie'. It is interesting that Freud (1919: 123) quotes the philosopher Freidrich Schelling when he defines the uncanny as 'something that ought to have remained secret and hidden but has come to light'. Horror cinema does just that – brings out things that should have remained in the dark into the light of the projected image. It is no wonder that this can result in feelings of discomfort or dread even as one identifies with the images on screen. In other words, the experience of viewing a horror film – of looking – can give rise to the emotion of the uncanny very easily.

Stern is writing in her essay about a science fiction film rather than one of horror cinema (*Blade Runner*), but is dealing with themes related to identity and humanity. This is particularly appropriate in a film which questions whether characters who are cyborgs are truly alive and whether the hero might not be a cyborg too despite believing himself to be human. These examples are very close to the uncanny instances of metaphorical monstrosity in terms of being dyadic replicas under Schneider's typography. Furthermore, Stern describes the sequence in which Pris 'disguises' herself as one of Sebastian's dolls and then attacks Deckard as going beyond a straightforward uncanny scenario. She suggests that this enacts the uncanny via a kinaesthetic connection; it is exhilarating in terms of the momentum through time and space as Pris sommersaults towards Deckard, but at the same time it arouses dread through a sense of disembodiment. The film is littered with such references to the Freudian uncanny, but it is the emphasis on eyes in particular that is relevant here. Freud refers to the putting out of eyes in Hoffman's story (the Sandman of the title, whom the central character fears, is a bogyman who steals the eyes of children who refuse to go to bed). Certainly, eyes often convey a strong sense of the uncanny, as with uncanny feelings created by catching things out of the corner of the eye or familiar objects when seen in the dark resembling figures. More than this Freud sees the loss of eyes as symbolic castrations. In his interpretation of *The Sandman*, Freud equates the protagonist's fear of losing his eyes as castration anxiety. This can also be seen in *Blade Runner* where the replicants Batty and Roy (who as short-lived androids are already 'unmanned') visit the craftsman who made their eyes shortly before Batty kills his creator Tyrell by gouging out his eyes (a symbolic act of castrating the father figure).

In a wider sense, this emphasis on eyes being uncanny also draws attention to the look of horror cinema. Vision (the gaze) and the loss of vision (the blocking of the gaze) are frequently depicted in horror cinema, often through use of darkness and shadows that hide things from sight as much as through vision itself. Nicholas Royle (2003: 109) draws attention to the way darkness is central to Freud's account of the uncanny:

> It is darkness (rather than silence or solitude) which finally haunts his project: it is specifically 'fear of the dark', rather than fear of silence or of solitude to which we are alerted, even if the discussion indicates that the three terms under consideration ('silence, solitude and darkness') are curiously entangled bed-fellows.

Indeed, the whole notion of the uncanny is something that is brought back into the light. If 'the uncanny is what comes out of the darkness' (Royle 2003: 108), it is no coincidence that horror cinema returns again and again to images or tropes of the dark, the night, blindness, being buried alive, and losing one's way. In *The Descent*, for example, the cavers go down into the darkness where they are attacked by the blind creatures that are adapted to the total absence of light in the caves. In *The Eye*, on the other hand, Mun (who has been blind from early childhood) receives a corneal transplant – she takes her place in the sighted world (that of the light). With the return of her sight, however, she begins to see haunting glimpses of the dead all around her. Having learnt that these uncanny images are the same visions of death that the women whose corneas she has received was having, she is equally unable to communicate impending doom when she foresees it. It is only by being blinded once again, returning to the darkness, that she finds peace. This is an interesting reversal of the way in which darkness is usually coded as the place of the monstrous Other – the blind woman is at home in the darkness (emphasizing the way disability is encoded as a form of the monstrous Other); it is only in the light that she loses her bearings.

As is more usual, the characters in *The Descent* are lost in the dark, but beyond this they are lost because of a deliberate act of being led astray by Juno (who has abandoned the guidebook because she has taken them to the wrong cave anyway). Sight is obscured regardless of the fact that they are literally in the dark, since they cannot 'see' their way out of the cave, being lost is to be figuratively blind. In *The Blair Witch Project*, the filmmakers are similarly lost, but while they have light (at least during the day), again they figuratively cannot see their way out of the woods. In his essay on *The Uncanny* (1919), Freud described being lost in Venice and of returning to the same place again as he tried to find his way. A similar going around in circles occurs in *The Blair Witch Project*, and Mike discards the map – just as Juno does in *The Descent* – because it has become useless to them. Significantly, it is when night falls and they can no longer see to look for a way back to the car, that they are haunted by noises and wake to find uncanny piles of stones outside their tent. Although, like the cavers in *The Descent*, they have a night vision camera this does not help them see and they become abject, frightened figures in the darkness.

These examples draw attention to the sensation of dissonance at the moment of identity (the blurred identity of Mun as she sees what Ling, the donor of her corneas, would see; the fragmentation of identity in the characters in *The Descent* and *The Blair Witch Project* as they cannot see their way out in the caves and the woods and they literally lose themselves) that Stern says accompanies film spectatorship. In respect of the gaze, several important points regarding horror film spectatorship have been proposed in response to Laura Mulvey's (2004) model of classical narrative cinema.[7] The gaze is important in respect of understanding the processes of identification in horror cinema, particularly how this positions the spectator to align themselves with or root for a character in the world of the film, and it can therefore contribute to our understanding of the way spectators respond to cinematic horror (though bear in mind that the spectator is an idealized, theoretical version of the film viewer, and is therefore not to be confused with the real viewers in the actual audience who may not always respond in the way we might predict – as when viewers 'read against the grain' and make a negotiated or oppositional reading of the text, or when some viewers respond to *Shivers* as comedy, for example).

Subjectivity can account for the way in which the emotional and physiological responses of the spectator are oriented around a specific character (usually the hero, though of course this might be the female hero or final girl of the slasher film, and may even be the monster in some films). Take for example, the escape from the shopping mall sequence in *The Dawn of the Dead* remake (Figure 3.2). When one of the buses overturns, two of the survivors die, while Steve tries to flee and is attacked by a zombie. As they prepare to abandon the bus, Kenneth and CJ are cast in the role of active hyper-masculine heroes (they are a cop and a security guard by profession) who act without thought. However, when Kenneth tries to prevent Ana looking inside the bus, she holds back and does so anyway. The shots then focus on her and her point of view, first as she looks at the corpses inside the bus and then when she shoots Steve, now a zombie, as he rushes towards her. The shots of her show her calm determination: "I've got him!" she states as she aims her gun and fires. Her point of view shows him dropping to the ground with a bullet hole in the very centre of his forehead. This serves to build identification with Ana rather than either Kenneth (who has only shouted a warning) or CJ. The viewer is thus invested in Ana's fate rather more than the two men, which may build tension around her. As the men fire on the hoard of zombies that are rushing towards them and threatening to cut them off from the safety of the other bus, Ana holds back to retrieve the boat keys from Steve's pocket. Nicole is also urging them to hurry from the other bus, and this creates a build-up of tension around whether Ana in particular will make it since she is in a more vulnerable situation having stayed longer at the crashed bus. As the others make it onto the bus, shots of her looking up at the zombies and of Michael shouting "Ana, where's Ana?" further heighten the

Figure 3.2 Ana at the centre of the action in *Dawn of the Dead*.

tension – as the characters' concerns for Ana are emphasized, so are those of the audience. Ana then has to run and dodge the zombies who seem menacingly close, she falls (a typical ploy designed to raise anxiety levels in the viewer – it is typical for a female character to be used in this way), and then just barely makes it onto the bus, creating a final sense of relief that she is safe.

Such examples of constructed subjectivity are explained by apparatus theory. In early developments of film theory, Christian Metz argued that cinematic spectatorship could be explained by unconscious processes. In *The Imaginary Signifier* (2004: 823), he outlines the way the spectator becomes part of the process of cinema and thus identifies with himself in the cinema (the spectator here is male if we consider the look of cinema to be masculine with the female spectator forced to adopt the male gaze, though it can work in other ways depending on the film). The spectator can thus be considered part of the cinematic apparatus and the screen then becomes a mirror on which the spectator (figuratively speaking) sees their own reflection (in the sequence from *Dawn of the Dead*, this reflection is Ana). Lacan's theory of the mirror stage is one of the ways we have of understanding the desire or fascination the spectator therefore has for the characters on the cinema screen (which can be thought of as images of the Other). Lacan proposed that when the child sees the image of itself in the mirror, at first it does not see the image as separate from itself. This changes, though, such that the mirror image gradually becomes an image outside of the self. The mirror image thus becomes both self and Other. However, the desire to return to the ideal unified state when there was no Other remains. This leaves a gap between our new 'fractured ego' (post-mirror stage) and the old 'ideal ego' (before the mirror stage) that needs to be filled. In terms of the cinematic gaze, this lack can be filled by the images of the Other on the screen because they are seen as whole and unfragmented; they represent the unified self we have lost. Ana is an idealized self, she is determined – she shoots Steve without hesitation, quick thinking under pressure – she realizes Steve had the boat keys that they need to escape, and brave – she holds back and risks being caught by the zombies so that she can retrieve the keys. The question to ask here is how this might operate in horror cinema to create pleasure. Identification (as identification with Ana is constructed through the gaze) is a key point to consider in addressing this.

Mulvey's original work on the gaze has already been widely cited and applied in the analysis of a wide range of films. However, it is interesting to note that the gaze can take very specific forms in horror cinema. The slasher film in particular illustrates the way in which the gaze of cinematic horror is constructed and how this can direct responses to the film. Slasher films are famous for their use of the point-of-view shot (indeed, it has become something of a cliché). The point-of-view shot typically frames a victim as if the killer is watching them voyeuristically. Such shots are often shaky or employ a hand-held camera; they are also often framed by objects in the extreme foreground to suggest the killer is concealing themselves behind that object. According to some critics, this creates a very specific subjectivity where identification is constructed through these point-of-view shots. Roger Ebert (1981), for example, argued that slasher films (and other examples of exploitation cinema) increasingly depicted violence against women. Ebert claimed that the very absence of the killer on-screen (that comes about through the point-of-view shots and camera movements) means that the spectator identifies with the camera in objectifying the (slashed) female body. 'The more these movies make their killers into shadowy non-characters,' he says (1981: 56), 'the more the audience is directed to stand in the shoes of the killer.'

Following this line of argument, this marks out the character who is being looked at as the object of the gaze (in *Halloween*, this would be Annie, Lynda and Laurie – Bob is also killed but in Ebert's line of thinking this is more perfunctory and he is not voyeuristically stalked in the same way as the female victims are) and aligns the spectator in the cinema with the potential killer who is doing the looking (Michael). Since critics such as Ebert also presume horror to have a primarily male audience, this – taken with the fact the victims are predominantly female – is interpreted as an objectification of women that 'encourages' male violence against women. For these critics of the slasher film, the use of the point-of-view shot implies identification with the killer and therefore pleasure for the male viewer who colludes with the objectification and punishment of the female victim. It is for this reason that Ebert denounces the slasher genre as glorifying and encouraging male violence towards women. This may be too simplistic an analysis of subjectivity though (and does a disservice to the male viewers who enjoy these films as well as female ones). On the surface, it might seem to link to Mulvey's model of the male gaze, but Carol Clover (1992) argues that identification shifts from character to character in such films. It is neither static (restricted to a single character – or absence of character as argued by Ebert) nor restricted to male characters only.

It can therefore be argued that the point-of-view shot does not necessarily invite identification with the voyeur. Indeed, since the killer is rarely seen in such shots, and indeed may not exist at all in some apparent point-of-view shots (the voyeur may in some cases be an entirely innocent character and in others there may be no voyeur at all), identification may be directed elsewhere rather than with Ebert's camera-as-protagonist. Ebert's argument would suggest that in the absence of a commanding male hero, the male spectator will identify with absence rather than with a female character. Clover's model of cross-gender identification would suggest otherwise: that the male spectator can indeed identify with the female hero as part of a shifting set of identifications throughout the film. For example, at the start of the present-day (1978) sequences in *Halloween*, a voyeur is clearly suggested by point-of-view camera shots: as Laurie walks to school there is a constant sense that someone might be watching and stalking her. This is confirmed as a figure suddenly appears in the side of the frame looking out from the Myers's house as she drops off the key and then appears again as a shoulder in the corner of the screen as the camera watches her walking off down the street (the music and heavy breathing imbue these shots with added menace).

The spectator at this point might well identify with the point-of-view shot as if they too are observing Laurie. In the school scene though,

Laurie is now a character the spectator is familiar with. When she is disturbed by a car across the street that seems to suggest someone is watching or waiting, the spectator may well begin to recognize her anxiety and empathize with her. After school, the stalker is shown in extreme close-up watching the children (the camera is always slightly behind him, again suggesting his point of view) and stalking them in the car. This sets up the threat, but there is little to indicate that the spectator might be identifying with this anonymous figure. It is at this point that the narrative informs the audience via Dr Loomis that it is Michael and this serves as a warning to the spectator about the bogyman. Indeed, shortly after this, the point of view begins to be disrupted further. Laurie and her friends are alerted by the presence of the car and the viewer engages with them in their discussion of what this means. Even though this is followed by a point-of-view shot from the stalker's perspective, confirmed by the figure of Michael standing by the hedge, the spectator is more likely to experience the tension and relief as Annie goes to look and there is no one there, laughing along with Annie's teasing of Laurie. The spectator is thus thrown into the interactions between the female characters and it is the disruption of this with the point-of-view shot that builds tension.

Furthermore, at the moment the observer behind the point-of-view shot is shown as not there, the point-of-view shot immediately becomes Laurie's as she looks around to detect the voyeur. She is then startled by a figure blocking the side of the frame who appears (just as the stalker did) in an over-the-shoulder shot – but this is quickly revealed as Mr Brackett (Annie's father). Such red herring shots seem designed purely to escalate the peaks and troughs of threat followed by a jump followed by relief, which then heightens the sense of anticipation for the next cycle on the emotional rollercoaster (when the threatened danger really does appear it is all the more affecting for the red herring preceding it). In this early sequence in *Halloween*, this comes when Laurie gets home (again the spectator is very likely to be experiencing growing empathy and identification with her through this). Ron Tamborini (1996) concludes from his social-psychological research that this stimulates empathic concern leading to emotional contagion. The viewer feels the same emotion as Laurie as she looks out to see Michael standing amongst the sheets on the washing line in the neighbour's garden and is then disturbed by the 'obscene' phone call (which since this is Annie is a further red herring). This is executed via Laurie's point of view – not Michael's – and although in narrative terms it seems logical that this builds a sense of threat towards Laurie, the shots are constructed in such a way that the spectator empathizes with her.

While the opening sequence of the film is designed specifically to provoke identification with the killer, the intent is quite clearly to additionally shock the spectator out of any sense of identification via the killer's point-of-view shot later on in the film. Through this early destabilization of identification, the spectator may well question their alignment with a killer. In the first shots of the film, the spectator is clearly seeing through the eyes of a character as he (or she or it) approaches the house, moves around the side of the building, and peers in through the window at the teenagers making out on the sofa, before going upstairs. The spectator can clearly read this as an unseen character's point of view via the slightly swaying camera movements, the partial obscuring of the shot with leaves and reflections on the glass of the window, and the erratic tracking backwards and forwards around the house and up and down at the first floor window. However, there is no shot of the character to establish who it is doing the looking, and the viewer may – even at this stage – be questioning what is going on (there is certainly an edginess created in the cinematography and sound at this point).

This may well begin a disruption of subjectivity as this unseen character enters the kitchen, takes a large knife from a drawer, and then picks up and puts on a mask, after watching the boyfriend leave. The viewer may question what this character is going to do with the knife (obviously they know they have come to see a horror film from the title and publicity, and the title music and recitation of the 'trick or treat' rhyme also add to the sense of anticipation of horror). Even though the spectator sees that the hand and arm probably belong to a child wearing a clown suit for

Halloween this may well not be entirely reassuring, especially as clowns are widely regarded as disturbing. At this point in the sequence, the point-of-view shot becomes further obscured as the visual field is reduced to the eyeholes of the mask, signalling a further disruption of identification (the music also intensifies at this moment). In fact, this may well serve to distance the spectator. The shot then takes on a sexually voyeuristic tone as the teenage girl is seen naked at her dressing table. The unsettling framing is further amplified as the girl complains about 'Michael!', and the spectator hears as much as sees her being stabbed, before Michael turns to look at his hand holding the knife and his arm moving up and down to stab his sister (though the stabbing itself is not seen).

The intent here could well be to shock the spectator out of identifying with this character, to make them question their own complicity in the voyeuristic imagery and ultimately to make them question any possible identification with the killer via the point-of-view shot in subsequent scenes. After the point-of-view shot has revealed the girl lying bloodied on the floor and Michael leaving the house, the viewpoint changes to reveal the child. The disruption and shock is thus consolidated, but it also works to suggest that the point-of-view shot in general is to be distrusted. This sets up a particular pattern of subjectivity for the rest of the film. The point-of-view shot can thus be read as signalling a sense of threat to the character being looked at rather than objectifying them. This suggests a process of identification and empathy with the victim being looked at and not with the perpetrator of the violence. In focusing on the potential victim in this way, and particularly the surviving final girl (it usually becomes quite clear who she is early on in the film, as it is with Laurie), the horror is not necessarily that of voyeuristic pleasure in enacting violence on the female body, but fear of violence being done to oneself or one's friends. The spectator is thus set up for the series of escalating threats and violent attacks on the teenage characters that build throughout the rest of the film (which may be enjoyed like the rollercoaster ride).

The pleasure can thus be that of watching the potential victim fight back and survive. This is not to suggest that viewers do not take pleasure in viewing acts of violence, but it is not necessarily the dangerous and corrupting process that encourages violence against women that some critics make it out to be (though it must be accepted that there may still be some viewers who adopt this aberrant reading position). The point to consider again is that psychoanalytic-based readings of horror film spectatorship may be applied in too monolithic a way and not take into account fluctuating subject positions. As Clover notes (1992: 45–46) when discussing identification in the slasher film:

> We are linked with the killer in the early part of the film, usually before we have seen him directly and before we have come to know the Final Girl in any detail. Our closeness to him wanes as our closeness to the Final Girl waxes – a shift underwritten by story line as well as camera position. By the end, point of view is hers: we are in the closet with her, watching with her eyes the knife blade pierce the door […]. And with her, we become if not the killer of the killer then the agent of his expulsion from the narrative vision. If, during the film's course, we shifted our sympathies back and forth and dealt them out to other characters along the way, we belong in the end to the Final Girl; there is no alternative.

Identification then is not simply dependent on the point-of-view shot, but the point-of-view shot may work in conjunction with empathy for the victim within the narrative framing to create a more complex and shifting identification than might at first be thought. If spectators do not have sympathy for the early victims of the slasher (and they do not always), this may well be because they have already identified the final girl – and identify with her at the expense of the other teenage characters.

Given that identification shifts in this way, cross-gender identification (that is, male spectators identifying with the female hero) gains significance. Mulvey's original hypothesis of course was that the cinematic gaze in classical narrative cinema is predominantly male and that identification is constructed through the male character – the hero (though she did subsequently acknowledge a female gaze, this does not always apply to films in the classical narrative mould). This leaves the female spectator with no easy mechanism for identification, she either has to identify with the hero (male), or struggle to find any point of identification as the spectatorial position of the film is not constructed via the female characters (who remain the object of the male gaze). This places the female spectator in the position of having to undergo a process of cross-gender identification in order to view the film with pleasure, while male spectators can straightforwardly identify with the male. The slasher film, on the other hand, does seem to break this pattern with its female hero and disrupt identification for the male spectator. The female spectator might well easily identify with the final girl, but where does this leave the young male spectators? Clover argues that these films construct the final girl as only literally female. As the hero, she is also figuratively male. Clover argues that the male spectator too can identify with the final girl since she is coded as masculine in terms of her ambiguous name, her androgynous clothing or appearance, and her lack or avoidance of sexuality. Even though identifying with a female character might threaten the male spectator's masculinity, the coding of the character as figuratively male allows identification to take place (and this works well for the slasher film because since the male spectator is young and therefore only on the threshold of masculinity, he can recognize himself in the reflected Other of the final girl). In *Halloween*, the final girl has a name, Laurie, which could be male. She wears a plain shirt and trousers for most of the film, and cannot get a boyfriend (although she does want one) since she is too clever. Furthermore, she is played by an actress (Jamie Lee Curtis) whose star persona is based on her androgynous features and appearance.

Following Clover's model of cross-gender identification through, the audience's allegiances will shift with even the male spectators comfortably transferring their identification from the killer to the final girl. The spectator might well identify with the killer at the start of the film (as we saw with *Halloween*), but this identification is not fixed and as the narrative unfolds, this will shift to other characters before finally resting on the final girl. For example, when Annie is talking on the phone in the kitchen after having to wash her clothes, there is a brief shot of Michael standing in the doorway watching her in the background (thus the shot is an objective one framing Annie). A point-of-view shot is not needed at this stage as the threat is already firmly established, and the viewer can identify or empathize with Annie without being directed by it explicitly. After Annie is murdered, Tommy's point-of-view shot is the dominant one – but Laurie does not believe him since he has been concerned about the bogeyman all evening. Tommy sees and so does the spectator, but Laurie doesn't, and this could serve to increase the spectator's anxiety for Laurie, even if they do not identify with Tommy.

However, after she discovers the bodies of her friends and is attacked by Michael, it is Laurie's point of view that dominates (as she looks at Michael lying behind the sofa after she has stabbed him with the knitting needle, and when she is hiding in the wardrobe as Michael is breaking into it). Danger to Laurie is subsequently shown by an objective shot of Michael behind her and not through his point-of-view shot. In this way, identification crosses gender boundaries and the final girl of the slasher film (and some other examples of horror) becomes a point of identification for the male spectator on a figurative level. Since this female character is coded as masculine she offers a point of identification for young male spectators, but does not threaten their masculinity when she is depicted as being in abject terror – which a male character behaving in this way on screen could well do.

It is notable in this respect that the young male characters do seem to be portrayed as having weaknesses and they invariably die (this factor has been used to refute the arguments that it is always women who are subjected to violent attacks, though it is still true in some instances that attacks on female victims are prolonged and sexualized). It should also be noted, as Clover does, that the killer of the slasher film employs phallic weapons such as knives, chainsaws, drills. While the actual attacks on his victims are not overtly shown to be acts of sexual violence, these penetrating weapons render such attacks as sexual. When the final girl takes up these and other phallic weapons for herself (Laurie uses a knitting needle and a coat hanger in *Halloween*) she is claiming possession of the phallus for herself; again, this renders her figuratively male, facilitating the male spectator's identification with the masculinized final girl.

Horror and femininity

This account of the gaze and cross-gender identification in the slasher film, while significant in explaining the responses of the young male audience, does not, however, consider female identification in any great depth. Clover's model is of a feminized form of identification (since it is deemed to be a passive and masochistic spectatorial position). She states (1992: 53) that:

> [Horror] succeeds in incorporating its spectators as 'feminine' and then violating that body – which recoils, shudders, cries out collectively in ways otherwise imaginable for males only in nightmare.

However, since her methodology legitimately limits her focus to the male audience, it does not account for the potential of an active female gaze. Nonetheless, she does note that female identification with the final girl may provide pleasures through representation of the active female hero. This sheds little light, however, on what specific pleasures there might be for the female viewers (or indeed older male viewers), either in respect of horror cinema generally or for particular cycles or styles of horror film. As Judith Halberstam (1995: 139) points out, there needs to be consideration of 'the potential identification that horror allows between the female viewer and the male or female aggressor'.

Taking Mulvey's original hypothesis as a starting point, the cinematic gaze seems inextricably linked to gendered spectatorship where it is almost always unambiguously male. In horror film criticism, it has been pointed out that the genre frequently includes highly sexualized images of women being preyed upon by male monsters and that this is often predicated upon sexual violence (see Neale 1980, for example). This is indeed typical of classical horror films such as *The Mummy*, *King Kong*, and

The Creature from the Black Lagoon, amongst many others. With the development of feminist film theory in the 1970s and 1980s, it was inevitable that this reading would be addressed by feminist critics. Clover's account of the slasher film, for example, is a useful intervention into models of gendered spectatorship; however it is the possibility (or even maybe impossibility depending on point of view) of a female spectatorial position that demands further consideration. If the gaze is male, the female is relegated to the role of 'to be looked at-ness' (as Ann is looked at with desire by Kong, as Helen is by Imhotep in *The Mummy*, and as Kay is by the Gill Man). Although there is a possibility that the female viewer may feel sympathy for the monster (as the girl does in *The Seven Year Itch*), the female spectator is otherwise left in a position of adopting or submitting to the male gaze or rejecting the gaze entirely.

In addition to Mulvey's three looks of cinema, Barbara Creed (1993: 29) suggests there is a fourth look of horror cinema: that is, a looking away or refusal to look. On a straightforward level, scenes of horror, especially of gore or frightening monsters, may make the viewer want to look away or block their sight of the screen – as some undoubtedly do. (It is also worth noting that sound in horror cinema can have a similar effect, making viewers want to block their ears – which again serves to emphasize that sound is as important as image in creating effect.) But for the female spectator this looking away may be more complex than simply not wanting to watch a horrific scene. Linda Williams (2002) explores the refusal to look in terms of the way in which the female gaze is constructed in her account of feminine horror film spectatorship in the classic horror film. She gives an account of what happens when the heroine of the horror film is 'granted the power of the look' (2002: 61). She claims (2002: 62) that the 'woman's gaze is punished [...] by narrative processes that transform curiosity and desire into masochistic fantasy' and that this is constructed in the form of the heroine's 'terrified look at the horrible body of the monster'. Williams looks at *The Phantom of the Opera* in particular. She analyzes the scene where the heroine unmasks the Phantom and is then forced to look upon his hideously deformed face. Williams argues that the sight of his face is a punishment for daring to look, and that the female spectators are similarly punished if they too look (at the screen). Women's possession or ownership of the gaze is thus problematical and it may be that women are thus 'taught' that they should refuse to look.

An interesting account of the failure to look can be found in *The Descent*. The film opens with a clear failure to look and to see – this causes the car crash in which Sarah's husband and child are killed. One year later, she and her friends plan a trip to the Boreham Caverns in the Appalacian mountains – putting themselves in an environment where vision is obscured due to the absence of light ('Down there it's pitch black' Rebecca warns during the hike to the cave). This all-female party is thus denied access to the gaze. At first, as they descend down the hole in the ground into the first chamber there is some light, but as they drop to the lower level, they soon enter pitch darkness with only their torches for illumination. When they enter the deeper cavern and set off the flare the image is tinted with a red glow (to resemble night vision goggles or camera). From this point onwards, in many shots, the characters are reduced to partially lit figures against illuminated spots of cave wall at the centre of a largely dark screen; the spectator is thus presented with a limited field of vision that matches that of the characters' point of view. This creates a sense of claustrophobia and dread, exacerbated when Sarah gets stuck in the narrow channel and panics just before the cave-in traps them (at this point the screen becomes totally dark, signifying Sarah's point of view as she has a vision of her daughter with the birthday cake).

As they search for a way out, this partial obscurity is depicted via shots that are composed of incomplete glimpses of the creatures that inhabit the cave system: Sarah is the first to have sight of them. It is significant that Sarah – and the spectator – can see them since identification is already being organized around her, and that it is Juno who rejects Sara's account. Juno, in fact, is denying the others knowledge, having left the guidebook in the car since she is not leading them to the Boreham Caverns at all, but an unexplored cave she wants to be the first to explore – 'an ego trip' as Rebecca says. She has kept them metaphorically 'in the dark'. Then, in the cavern with several exits, Sarah uses the infra-red camera to see the animal bones as one of the creatures makes its first significant appearance (again this is in Sarah's point-of-view shot as she films with the night vision camera). None of them – including Sarah – can see clearly. There is a chaotically edited series of very short shots as they sweep their torches over the cave walls and roof searching for where the creature went, some of which do reveal a glimpse of it. This subjective sequence involves the spectator in their feelings of blind panic and the dialogue further emphasizes their vulnerability in the darkness: 'Did you see that!', 'I could barely see it!', 'I told you I saw someone!'. It is shortly after they get their first confirmed look at the creature that they are attacked.

These women do not necessarily cower, look away or block their vision as the classic heroine did (though they sometimes do – Sarah screws up her eyes when the creatures are eating Holly and then throws back her head as well when one of them comes close trying to find her in the darkness; Sam also keeps her eyes shut in similar circumstances), but they are nevertheless being punished for looking. The depiction of Juno's gaze is particularly interesting here. Immediately after she attacks the creature that takes Holly and kills the second creature that comes to its defence, and still in a murderous frenzy, she stabs Beth, who has come back to help her, through the neck. Shots of her face make it clear that Juno keeps her eyes wide open, but she fails to see that it is Beth. Failing to look is a sign that the women are putting themselves in danger. When leading Sam, Sarah is shown checking that a turn in the path is clear. However, and this is important since identification has been built around Sarah, there is no point-of-view shot. Sarah, it transpires, has failed to look enough, she did not look up and see the creature on the cave wall above them that then attacks. This inscription of looking and failing to look builds to the moment when Sarah's literal and figurative blindness is revealed – that she has been blind to her husband's affair with Juno. And the daylight she sees after she has killed Juno is ultimately revealed to be false: a dying dream or vision. Light, and with it possession of the look, has not, after all been restored to her.

Significantly, Sarah has another vision of her daughter with a birthday cake in the final moments as she awaits death, just as she did at the beginning of the film just after the car accident (which she also relives in her dreams) and when she was trapped by the cave-in. This repeated motif also suggests perhaps that her death has merely been postponed, and that the entire film is about her death. This construction of the look in the film seems quite reactionary (the women are for the most part denied the look, and when they do possess the look it is to be punished with the sight of the monstrous Other and their own deaths). The ending is nihilistic, there is no escape or rescue, although it could be said that Sarah has come to terms with dying and joins her daughter in death. There is little to suggest that the look is empowering, however, or that the woman can take on the subversive potential of the mon-strous-feminine as she does in *Candyman*, for example.

The female gaze of horror cinema can be potentially empowering in this way though. If, as Williams says (2002: 63), 'the monster's power is one of sexual difference from the normal male', then there must then be an affinity between the monster and the female (who is similarly Othered by her sexual difference). In other words, the exchange of looks between heroine and monster recognizes 'their similar status within patriarchal structures of seeing' (Williams 2002: 62). Women, like monsters, are Othered, and they are both coded as being outside of and excluded from patriarchal structures. Furthermore, she points out (2002: 63) that the monster is seen to be more appealing than the male characters in the film: 'sexual interest resides most often in the monster and not the bland ostensible heroes'. Ultimately, this means that there is a tension for the female viewer between not looking at the horrifying images – which would be the punishment for her gaze – and the potentially empowering identification with the monstrous Other that such a gaze would encompass. Williams assumes (2002: 61) that the female viewer does not dare to look: 'Whenever the movie screen holds a particularly effective image of terror, little boys and grown men make it a point to look, while little girls and grown women cover their eyes or hide behind the shoulders of their dates'. The female spectator, she concludes (2002: 61), is given 'excellent reasons for the refusal to look' since she 'is asked to bear witness to her own powerlessness in the face of rape, mutilation and murder' and on top of that is 'given little to identify with on the screen'.

Yet if, as Williams's argument suggests, the affinity between woman and monster is an identification that can give expression to female transgression, then it should be potentially possible for female viewers to appropriate that look. It is now accepted that female horror film viewers are not necessarily cowering spectators, even before the slasher film opened up a space for female identification through literal identification with the final girl. Tim Snelson and Mark Jancovich (forthcoming) reveal that in the 1930s female viewers were attracted to female monster movies such as *Dracula's Daughter* out of a purely sadistic desire to see men terrorized on screen, for example. Mary Ann Doane (1987) also states that female Gothic films such as *The Haunting* clearly address the female spectator. This evidence suggests that female viewers do look, and furthermore they take pleasure in spectacles of horror. This raises the question of whether female viewers are colluding in a 'masochistic fantasy' or are resisting viewers adopting a subversive and empowering female gaze. Williams is writing about classic horror and 'psychopathic' forms of the genre, but there are other subgenres or styles which clearly do construct a female gaze.

Candyman provides an example of a potentially empowering female gaze that is structured around an affinity with the monster. The gaze is foregrounded throughout the film. The Candyman is called into existence by looking into a mirror and saying his name five times, and Helen herself climbs through the mirror to enter the monster's lair – reuniting self and Other and taking herself back to the ideal ego perhaps. In the final moments of the film she becomes the monstrous-feminine in order to take revenge on the man who wronged her. Clearly in this respect, she cannot be contained – or repressed – by patriarchy. Furthermore, the gaze is Helen's (Figure 3.3). She is an investigator of sorts, researching (or looking into) urban legends, and she is depicted using her camera to keep a record of what she observes during her research at

Figure 3.3 Helen's gaze is highlighted in *Candyman*.

Cabrini Green. When she is attacked in the toilets the gang leader specifically says 'We hear you're *looking* for Candyman bitch' and the line is
repeated several times in the line-up at the police station. Furthermore,
she begins to experience visions after she has spoken the Candyman's
name in front of the mirror and this begins to align her with the
monster. It is interesting to note here that the look of horror cinema
can often involve the look of supernatural or inner vision (second sight,
dreaming, hallucination). There are, for example, Helen's subjective
flash forwards in *Candyman* and Sarah's visions of her daughter in *The
Descent*, as well as those films in which supernatural sight is the narrative
focus: the ability to see dead people in *The Sixth Sense*, the gift of 'the
shining' in the film of that name, or precognition in *Don't Look Now*.

In the car park scene when the Candyman appears to Helen for the
first time, she also dares to look at him: she takes off the sunglasses she is
wearing and stares directly at him. Unlike Christine in *The Phantom of the
Opera*, however, she does not flinch and block her gaze at the Candyman's
terrible form. In fact, this monster is to all intents and purposes attractive

(Figure 3.4). In line with Williams's point about bland heroes, he is far more sexually appealing than the men in the film: the insipid Trevor and his smug colleague Philip. The Candyman is closer to the vampire figure, alluring and yet monstrous (Helen even tells Jake that the Candyman isn't real, he's just a story like Dracula). His return of Helen's gaze and the timbre of his voice is seductively hypnotic. The woman's look here is also linked to her desire for the monster – as with the vampire and his victim, Helen is 'possessed' by her yearning for the Candyman, first to find out the background to the urban myth, then the history behind the myth, and finally for the man himself. As he says to her, she brought him forth: 'I came for you. […] You were not content with the stories, so I was obliged to come'.

As the object of his gaze (he invites her to 'be my victim'), however, Helen is mesmerized, her eyes glaze over and her eyelids flicker as if in orgasm (this has already been prefigured twice since she said his name in the mirror), and she loses consciousness. This in itself could be read as a variant on the victim's blocking of her own gaze, and Helen does seem to be punished for daring to look. When she wakes up, she is in the flat in Cabrini Green covered in blood and is arrested seemingly in the throws of attacking Anne-Marie; she is charged with the kidnap of Anne-Marie's baby. The film, however, goes on to make the affinity between the woman and the monster explicit. On the first occasion, this occurs in the psychiatrist's office when Helen calls on the Candyman to kill for her. 'You're mine now' he says, and then later, as she makes her way to Cabrini Green, she hears him say 'All you have left is my desire for you'. Here she also picks up a hook as she climbs into his lair so that she emulates his own hooked hand. The second time is when she is depicted as the Candyman's reincarnated lover ('It was always you, Helen'). After rejecting the Candyman's offer of 'immortality' and saving the child, she becomes the new Candyman. It is this that suggests there are possible feminist readings of the film that position Helen as a female avenger, punishing the patriarchal and misogynist male. Having died in the bonfire, the people of Cabrini Green pay her homage at her funeral – gifting her the Candyman's hook (which suggests that she is

Figure 3.4 The alluring monster of *Candyman*.

also now opposed to the white middle-class masculinity that has oppressed them, race as well as gender being inscribed in the text), and she takes her revenge on Trevor, the philanderer who wronged her, when he says her name while standing in front of the mirror.

Helen's transformation into the monster also raises interesting questions about gender. Although the Candyman desires her for his wife, she rejects him, destroys him and replaces him, becoming a monstrous 'single woman' who kills the man who cheated on her. She thus rejects heterosexual patriarchy. In addition, as a monster, she has been divested of her femininity. Her hair, which was blonde and curly signifying a socially idealized femininity, was burnt off in the bonfire. Her new, partially skinless appearance (she has only burned flesh where her hair used to be) signifies a new gender, neither masculine nor feminine. Halberstam, whose interest in horror is to historically contextualize monstrosity with respect to the body and its representations within the economic, social, and sexual hierarchies of the time, suggests (1995: 139) that 'the queer tendency of horror film ... lies in its ability to reconfigure gender not simply through inversion but by literally creating new categories'. She is suggesting here that rather than simply permitting a space for male viewers to identify with female characters (or vice versa), the whole idea of any straightforward gender identity is called into question. One of the points she makes (1995: 141) is that improper gender (as well as class and race) is allied with inhumanity (she draws on Judith Butler's work *Bodies That Matter* in this). She explains (1995: 141) that: 'improperly or inadequately gendered bodies represent the limits of the human and they present a monstrous arrangement of skin, flesh, social mores, pleasures, dangers and wounds'.

One of the films Halberstam puts forward as an example of new gender categories is *The Texas Chainsaw Massacre* 2. She says (1995: 141) that it: 'provides its viewers with a virtual skinfest and constantly focuses upon skin and the shredding, ripping or tearing of skin as a spectacle of identity performance and its breakdown'. Skin is of particular significance since it is not only the boundary of the body, but also a gendered boundary. 'Gender [...] is often a very specific "permeable membrane" – the skin. Someone's skin … precisely forms the surface through which inner identities emerge and upon which external readings of identity leave their impression' (Halberstam 1995: 141). We might therefore consider the monstrous character of Leatherface alongside Buffalo Bill in *The Silence of the Lambs* in their stitched together skin suits, or Norman Bates and Robert Elliott in *Dressed to Kill* in their women's clothing, as new gendered categories. The same is true of Brundlefly who has been literally desexed – it is frequently speculated that his penis is one of his shed body parts he keeps in his bathroom cabinet (at the end of the film his skin also literally splits apart as the final fly-like form emerges).

If the male spectator can identify across gender with the final girl and a female share a subversive affinity with the feminized monster, then identification with the Other may certainly be possible. Identification with the Other is intensely pleasurable since it is only in the mirror image that the self appears to be unified and whole – but as Lacan (1998) points out it is at the same time a misrecognition since the image is unified, whereas the self is fragmented. The image on screen is an illusion. As Davidson and Allen state (1997: 6): 'even as "I" identify with, and take pleasure in, this image of an autonomous self, "I" know that that self is not "me" precisely because it is autonomous and "I" am chaotic, disunified, fragmented'. Again there is this sense of simultaneous attraction and repulsion (just as in Kristeva's state of abjection which pre-dates the mirror stage).

This may be why mirrors frequently appear in horror films. In addition to the central use of the mirror in *Candyman*, other examples include: the possessed reflection of Ash in *The Evil Dead* which acts independently of Ash himself, the mirror attached to Mark's lethal camera tripod in *Peeping Tom* when his victims are forced to watch the distorted reflection of their own deaths, and the woman trapped in the parallel reflected world in *Into the Mirror*, as well as any vampire who casts no reflection (*Night Watch* presents an interesting variation on this where the vampire can become invisible in the real world and be seen only in a mirror). The trope of the vampire that cannot be seen in the mirror is an intriguing one. Fiona Peters (2006: 185) writes that:

> As undead, the vampire doesn't have to look in the mirror to validate his existence. […] The vampire's inability to see itself in the mirror is, rather than a lack precisely the opposite. Only us fragmented and illusory mortals need the mirror; the vampire, having no lack, has no need of a self-validating yet duplicitous and illusory reflection.

This harks back to the relationship between the self and the other, or between the Real and the Symbolic (where, according to Lacanian theory, the Real is linked to the experience of the world before language, prior to the mirror stage, and thus to the ideal ego, whereas the Symbolic is linked to language, and thus the fragmented ego after the mirror stage and the split between self and other).

The philosopher Slavoj Žižek (2001) proposes that the vampire represents a return to the Real. The vampire, he says, is like a hole in the Symbolic – it has been excluded from the Symbolic because it has been returned to the Real. Essentially, this means that we can think of the vampire as an ideal ego, not yet fragmented into self and other, or perhaps returned to the stage before the split so that self and other are 'reunited'. According to Žižek (2001: 126), it is therefore clear why vampires have no reflection: it is because they have evaded the symbolic order and do not have to rely on the process of identification Lacan proposed (or as Žižek wryly puts it, they have read Lacan). If the vampire is not fragmented into self and other, there is no other to appear reflected in the mirror, they 'cannot be mirrored' (2001: 126) because they materialize the repressed monstrous other. This also explains why vampires seem to have so much fun (as in the 'Sleep all day, party all night, never grow old, never die, it's fun to be a vampire' tagline for *The Lost Boys*): they are, as Peters says (2006: 185), open to perverse enjoyment unrepressed by the symbolic order.

It should also be understood that the mirror stage does not simply result in a sense of self, but actually constitutes the self (Lacan says that there is no self prior to the mirror stage). The result of this is that the 'self' is a precarious entity based on illusion (Lacan calls it 'fictional'). In general terms, this is why there is a need for images with which to identify (these can come from anywhere – photographs, art, magazines, advertising, television and film, even though they are not images of 'I', they are used unconsciously in the formation and structuring of the self). Horror films too offer images with which we can identify, and if we accept that they tap into the unconscious in a very specific way (via repression and abjection), they can address the need to fill the lack (the gap between ideal ego and fragmented ego). Davidson and Allen (1997: 6–7) outline the ironic nature of the image:

> [L]ike the mirror, it never can really show who 'we' are, and never does: it always gives us a picture of ourselves as somewhere else, the wrong way round, more whole and perfect than we could ever really be. We narcistically invest in finding that repetition of ourselves which will confirm who we are, but we are always both something less – less whole, less unified, less ideal – and something more – more complex, more contradictory, more unbounded – than any image we might find. Although the gaze at the mirror of representation is intended to confirm who I think I am, it will always also provoke the unnerving feeling that I am not who I thought I was after all.

If identity is so unstable, and the monster of the horror film coded as Other, this could be helpful in explaining why some members of the audience take pleasure in identifying with the monster. Whilst this might not be a universal explanation, it does account for the responses of viewers who self-identify as Other in some way (as black or homosexual, for example, or even as geeks or fans, even women fall into this group, especially if they resist conforming to the socially prescribed gender roles). They are positioned in an alienated or marginalized group of which the monster is also a member (in the same way that the monster and the female victim share an affinity in Williams's account).

Woman's relation to the look is also problematic, however, because it is narcissistic. So what the woman actually sees (Doane 1987: 142) is a 'representation of herself displaced to the level of the nonhuman'. If, as Tanya Krzywinska suggests (1995), lesbians do not see themselves represented on screen except as monsters in lesbian vampire films (as in *Daughters of Darkness*, for example), it is logical that they will identify with her since she shares their characteristics (including being Othered under the dominant heterosexual monogamous patriarchal system). This is especially true in female horror films such as *The Haunting* where the horror is organized around implied lesbian sexuality (although it is never made explicit that Nell and Theo are lesbians, this was then common in mainstream cinema). In fact, this can be observed with respect to other forms of queer sexuality. Similar identification can also occur in respect of ethnic identity too. Films where such identifications may take place – and thus explain some very particular pleasures around these specific films – include *Candyman* (black males), *The Hunger* (lesbians), *Interview with the Vampire* (gay men), and *Hellraiser* (queer and straight queer viewers). There may also be evidence of scopophilia (which is the complimentary pleasure to narcissistic identification in Mulvey's model of the gaze) involved in the pleasures of viewing such films for these people, and this would suggest that there are erotic appeals in watching alluring and attractive monsters such as the Candyman, Louis, Armand and Lestat, Miriam, and Pinhead. My own findings (Cherry 1999) reveal that female horror fans were aroused by watching the vampires in *Interview With the Vampire*, while Miriam/Catherine Deneuve is an icon to many lesbians, and Pinhead is a pinup in Japan.

Patricia White (1999) also suggests that the trope of the monster as lesbian is the logical conclusion of Linda Williams's account of the female horror film gaze. She claims (1999: 63) that the horror genre is ideologically progressive because it is concerned with the 'problem of the normal' since 'it embodies the abnormal in the figure of the monster'. She explores the potential for horror films to encourage identification across gender lines and explore perverse sexualities:

> Horror can be seen to have an affinity with homosexuality beyond its queer cast of characters or its insistent thematic elaboration of

difference in the representation of predatory or sterile desires. For horror puts in question the reliability of perception.

This means that not only can horror explore the fact that the other exists, but it can explore what forms this difference might take. White asks why it is that ghosts and hauntings (what she describes as the 'disembodied variant of horror') are so frequently associated with femininity (and hence lesbianism). Unlike Williams, who ultimately concludes that the genre discourages the (heterosexual) female gaze, she focuses on the fact that the representation of the female gaze is central to horror. She accounts for the fact that the feminine variants of horror contain disembodied monsters by drawing on Doane's point (p. 141) that 'female scopophila is a drive without an object'. *The Haunting* (a film in which a monster is never seen, but the uncanny sensations of being haunted are overwhelming) is, according to White, a dramatization not of the deficiencies in female vision, but the deficiency in terms of visibility itself. Just as women are rendered invisible, the monster of female horror is invisible (disembodied). In *The Haunting*, the ghosts are never seen, but the female figures in their white nightgowns correspond to or stand in for, are maybe even the source of, the ghosts themselves. Similarly, the lesbian is never 'seen' in the film, although the viewer – especially the lesbian viewer – knows very well that this is what the spectral disturbances are all about.

This allows for potential – and pleasurable – identification between the female spectator and the monster. Furthermore, this is not necessarily masochistic and certainly does not accord with socially prescribed gender roles. Clover's proposition that the radical potential of the horror film lies in the way it forces identification between the male viewer and the female victim can be extended. What these examples also illustrate is that there are variations in responses to horror that are not always resolved by monolithic or universal and ahistorical theories of the unconscious. Cognitive processes – how we think, not just about ourselves and our identity, but about the world in general – can provide alternative accounts of our various responses to cinematic horror and the pleasures (or otherwise) that the viewing of horror entails.

BEYOND PSYCHOANALYSIS

Clearly, it is not altogether certain whether any single, universal and ahistoric explanation for the pleasures of horror exists. As the example of lesbian women's responses to the female vampire illustrates, there can be variation in the way different groups interpret or respond to different kinds of cinematic horror (and this can be explored further with empirical audience research). This, of course, lays reductive accounts of horror cinema based solely on the blanket application of a single psychoanalytical concept open to doubt. One of the main reasons psychoanalysis has been questioned is in respect of it being unscientific (it cannot be proven by experiment), though even this is open to dispute – as Michael Levine (2004: 37) points out Freud himself viewed psychoanalysis in scientific terms and developed his theories by observing everyday life and analyzing cultural texts in addition to drawing on clinical case notes. In adopting a cognitivist approach (that is, developing an account of horror based on the way people think and respond to the world around them), Cynthia Freeland (2000: 34) rejects psychoanalytic approaches to film outright, claiming that psychoanalysis is 'an outmoded theory of the mind'. However, others such as Steven Schneider (2004b) argue that while psychoanalysis is not genuinely scientific in the way that cognitivism is (Schneider describes it as metaphysical because it cannot be experimentally tested), it may still be a useful analytical tool for exploring the allegorical or mythological meanings of particular films. What may be worth bearing in mind is Joan Hawkins's point (2002) that Freudian or other psychoanalytical methods may only provide an incomplete reading of a film, making it advisable to consider how other approaches might complement or counter a psychoanalytic reading (Wood's approach which incorporates ideological meaning is useful in this respect).

Overall, these different approaches are evidence of the major debates within horror film theory that have taken place in recent years, not only between those who take a stance in opposition to psychoanalysis, but also between theorists working in the same area. Some of the most productive arenas of debate have been amongst theorists taking philosophical and psychological approaches to horror cinema, and in particular cognitivism. Like psychoanalysis, this is an account of the mind, but it sees people as rational beings whose actions are a result of thought processes (rather than the 'victims' of their unconscious) and thus explores how those cognitive processes operate in respect of horror film viewing. One of the major interventions in the cognitivism versus psychoanalysis debate has been *The Philosophy of Horror* by Noel Carroll (1990). Carroll states that horror is a paradox, and he poses questions that he calls 'paradoxes of the heart', that is, how the viewer can be actually frightened by something that they know full well does not exist, and more importantly why the viewer is attracted by something that is inherently unpleasant. His approach to these questions is based on cognitive responses to 'art-horror' (the term that he uses for fictional horror texts which the viewer knows to be unreal but which nevertheless horrify them). In his definition of 'art-horror' and the emotions that it engenders, Carroll argues for cognitivism and indirectly against psychoanalysis. He rejects the psychoanalytic explanation for the intensity of the viewer's responses because he doubts they are actually identifying in a psychoanalytic sense with the unpleasant image on the screen. He advances an alternative account of responses that is instead based on cognitive psychology and analytic philosophy.

Carroll (1990) defines horror cinema in terms of the two emotions that he considers central – fear and disgust. There are points of connection here with abjection as discussed by Barbara Creed. However, Carroll (1990: 47) argues that disgust arises not from abjection but because of the monster's 'interstitiality' (it falls between the conceptual categories in which we cognitively place objects we come across): zombies and vampires disgust because they cannot be categorized as either alive or dead, werewolves because they fall between the classes of human and animal, the alien entity in *The Thing* because it cannot be classified as a whole but as a conglomeration of various body parts and organs. Carroll therefore bases his argument on a cognitive theory of the emotions, one that seeks to identify emotions in terms of the object that determines or creates that emotion, rather than an unconscious process. He argues that the horror film must contain something that elicits the emotion of horror, that is that makes the viewer afraid (creates fear) and revolted (creates disgust). That something, he concludes, must be a monstrous entity that is harmful (in order to make the viewer afraid) and impure (in order to disgust them), and further that monsters are defined as things not explained by science.

Although the viewer knows the monster does not exist, they can still be art-horrified by it because they can imagine themselves into the required emotional state by entertaining the notion that this thing does exist. Carroll equates this (quoted in Privett and Kreul 2001) with the kinds of thoughts we might have when standing on the edge of a cliff and imagining stepping off the edge – we know that we won't, but it can still make us shudder. This is not a result of the workings of the unconscious, but a cognitive process. Viewers can think themselves into an emotional state that is like fear or like disgust (this is why it is art-horror, to differentiate it from feelings of actual, real world fear and disgust). Carroll (1990) goes on to explore the ways he thinks this is constructed and played out in the horror film, and argues that it is principally (though not always – a close-up of a monstrous entity that can do that in its own right) through characters who respond in the same way as the viewer is expected to respond. These characters thus serve to cue the emotional responses of fear and disgust in the viewer (the cowering heroine of the classic horror film or the Final Girl of the slashers are good examples of this). Of course, the concept of identification also explains this, but Carroll (1990: 95–96) argues that the viewer does not share the psychological state of the character as they would if they identified, but rather recognizes on a cognitive level how the character is feeling in a particular situation. He terms this 'assimilation' – accessing the characters' perspective without sharing their psychological state.

This explanation for emotional responses to horror is all well and good. It is an alternative explanation for an observable process that takes place when people watch a horror film. There is much to commend this argument, just as there is the psychoanalytic explanation, and the version one prefers might well depend on the theoretical angle one is coming from. Where Carroll's work has proven more contentious is, first, in his definition for the source of the horror in the film text, and second, in the limitations of his assumptions about sources of pleasure for horror film viewers. He argues (1990: 186) that:

> The emotion of art-horror is not our absolutely primary aim in the consuming of horror fictions. […] Rather, art-horror is the price we are willing to pay for the revelation of that which is impossible and unknown, of that which violates our conceptual schema.

What he is saying, then, is that we don't actually enjoy horror. What we enjoy is satisfying our curiosity about monsters that are beyond our knowledge. He is proposing (p. 192) that: 'the art-horror we feel is finally outweighed by the fascination of the monster, as well as […] by the fascination engendered by the plot in the process of staging the manifestation and disclosure of the monster'. This fascination is therefore a property of the narrative. Carroll draws on the writings of the eight-eenth-century philosopher David Hume when he argues that the plea-sure of watching a tragic play is the result of a satisfying conclusion to narrative expectations generated by a good plot (and not the result of taking sadistic pleasure in the tragedy). In the same way, in the horror film pleasure derives from the way in which the monster is presented within the narrative structure. The narrative contains a mystery or enigma surrounding where the monster comes from, what it is, what it wants, how it can be destroyed, and so on. Carroll says (1990: 181–82) that this plays on the viewer's curiosity. The pleasure comes from experiencing the narrative reasoning that results in the monster being identified, confronted and overcome. Pleasure does not, in Carroll's model, come from the monster itself.

For example, in his co-existentialist account – the one where for the average viewer pleasure is strong enough to outweigh disgust; in the opposing integrationist account the disgust contributes to the pleasure for the specialist viewer (1990: 191) – there are no pleasures to be gained from the sight of Regan's head spinning 180 degrees, of her lacerated, oozing body writhing on the bed, or of her vomiting on Father Merrin in *The Exorcist*, only disgust. The viewer would not watch unless there were some other pleasures available that outweighed the disgust and this pleasure comes from curiosity about the monster and its eventual disclosure. *The Exorcist* is a good example in this respect as it presents a series of possible explanations for Regan's behaviour – medical tests, psychiatric evaluations and then finally investigation by the priests, resulting in the revelation that a devil is possessing Regan and the exorcism that casts it out. In addition, there is a police investigation into the desecration of the church and later Burke's death. Pleasure comes from the disclosure of the monster (Carroll 1990: 106 calls this 'the play of ratiocination' and 'the drama of proof'), having curiosity about the nature of evil satisfied and seeing good overcome that evil. The fascination here compensates for the disgust, 'our curiosity is stimulated and rewarded' (Carroll 1990: 193).

Carroll (1990: 193) accounts for the seemingly contrary pleasures experienced by the specialist viewers by assuming that they watch horror films 'simply for the gross-out'. For these viewers (he calls them 'connoisseurs of gore'), films that are not extremely disgusting are likely to be regarded as inferior. Here the disgust is essential to pleasure, rather than contingent to it. He explains this as a metaresponse (a response to a response). What he means by this is that the pleasure these viewers are seeking is in proving that they are a person who can withstand being disgusted. They want to watch excessively graphic horrors to demonstrate just how much disgust they can handle: they are metaresponding to their own revulsion. These viewers would watch a film like *Saw III*, with its reputation for raising the level of gore in the film outweighing negative reviews, simply because it promises extremely graphic and disturbing imagery. Their pleasure would come from demonstrating that they can stomach the disgust when Troy has to rip the chains from his body, when Allison's ribcage is torn off to reveal her internal organs, when Lynn's head is blown apart, or when Timothy's limbs are contorted until the shattered bones burst through the skin.

Carroll assumes here that these viewers are adolescent males who are using horror films as endurance tests or macho rites of passage. It is also interesting that the endurance test Carroll supposes specialist viewers are putting themselves through is mirrored in the film by Jeff being forced to walk through the meat-packaging plant witnessing the gruesome deaths of the people involved in his son's death. The final montage of the film containing all the traps in the three *Saw* films up to that point supports this argument in that it reminds the fan of all the gruesome moments that they have watched before.

The difficulty with Carroll's work in this respect – and this applies to his accounts of both average and specialist viewers – is that it significantly underestimates both the fact that people might actually enjoy the horror and what pleasures different audience members might gain from different types of horror films, including identification with the monster. Daniel Shaw (1997) recognizes this problem when he observes just that his young son loves monster movies and gains unique pleasure out of being horrified:

> In Carroll's view, we are **not** ambivalent about the monsters in horror fiction. […] This seems to make the relationship between audience and monster too unproblematic, unpleasant and uncomplicated. My son Patrick loves the monster, and not just when the monster is lovable (like Frankenstein is at certain moments), even as he loves to be chased by just about anyone that he can get to chase him. He loves to be scared, and is constantly (and ineffectually) sneaking up behind someone and acting like a monster.

Obviously, one anecdotal observation is not sufficient proof of a phenomenon, but as a typical female fan of vampire films in my own study (1999) similarly states, she does not just love the vampires when they are in repose but when they are in their most bestial of forms too. Shaw goes on to propose that: 'any satisfying account of the reasons why so many of us love horror fictions has got to recognize that our primary source of pleasure is the monster, or horrific human, which we relate to in a profoundly ambivalent fashion'. Certainly findings from empirical studies of horror film audiences and fan cultures can shed light on how we might interpret such theoretical accounts of pleasure and would indeed suggest that further elaboration of theory is sometimes required.

As Shaw also suggests here with his reference to the 'horrific human' (which would include Jigsaw and other human killers) in addition to a monster, the importance Carroll places on a supernatural monster in his definition of horror seems overly limiting. In defining the monster as having to be an entity that is both dangerous and impure and 'not believed to exist now by contemporary science' (1990: 27), he precludes a large number of films that contain monsters which can and might well exist in the real world. This means that any horror (or horror-related) film with a human killer (which means most serial killer films, many exploitation, rape-revenge films and examples of torture porn, and several slasher movies) does not meet his requirements. When he also argues that the emotional responses of fear and disgust must be expressed by characters towards the monster within the diegesis of the film (in order for the viewers' responses to follow these cues), he also excludes those horror films with a sympathetic monster or a monstrous entity that does not horrify the characters (this might well include vampire movies in which vampirism represents a welcome throwing-off of repression and films like *Nightbreed* where the human characters are monstrous and the monsters are oppressed outsiders).

As discussed before, Carroll has problems for example with *The Fly*. Since Ronnie continues to express feelings for and concern about Seth as he mutates into the human-fly creature, the film cannot therefore art-horrify. However, what he seems to overlook are the different responses that different audience segments might exhibit or the fact that fear and disgust can be located other than with the monster. There is no clear connection between the characters and the viewer's responses to the images of gore in *The Fly*, though moments of disgust are abundant as Seth mutates into Brundlefly (he peels his fingernails off, his teeth fall out and his ear drops off, his skin becomes a mass of tumourous flesh – he comes to resemble the Elephant Man, and he vomits digestive juices which dissolve flesh). However, Seth himself seems morbidly fascinated by his transformation, keeping a 'museum' of discarded body parts in his bathroom cabinet, while girlfriend Ronnie exhibits the sympathy towards Seth which one would have towards a loved one with a terrible, disfiguring disease. The viewer's disgust is concentrated around the physical decay of disease, ageing and death that Cronenberg presents as the ultimate fate of all humans rather than simply as a frightening and impure monster. Carroll uses this as a basis for his rejection of *The Fly* as horror, but this does rather seem to overlook the point that monsters can provide points of identification.

Certainly, Carroll does not acknowledge the possibility of identification with a monstrous entity when it is the protagonist who is turning into a monster (where the transformation may represent a coming to terms with normal processes of change such as puberty, disease and ageing as is central in Cronenberg's body horrors). This is in fact quite common in werewolf and vampire cinema, 1950s horror-sci fi such as *The Incredible Shrinking Man*, films based on the work of Clive Barker such as *Candyman*, *Nightbreed* and *Hellraiser*, as well as body horror including *The Fly*. In all these films the viewer is invited to identify with the character undergoing the transformation, and this might deal with fears about the processes of change but it can also be about embracing difference (as with lesbian vampires). In *The Fly* there is also the narrative development as Ronnie's disgust and revulsion is directed towards her pregnancy. She does not know if this conception took place before or after Seth had been gene-spliced with the housefly and therefore does not know whether her child is also monstrous or not. This is signalled through her desperation for an abortion, but is also primarily expressed in a dream in which she gives birth to a giant maggot. Fear and disgust on her part, and potentially then for female viewers (since this undoubtedly taps into fears every pregnant woman has that the child might not be healthy and whole), is directed towards the monstrous thing inside her.

This limitation of Carroll's account, that the viewer's disgust mirrors a character's response to a threatening and impure monster, raises problems with a number of other films widely categorized as horror. The

Saw films, of course, do not contain a disgusting monster: Jigsaw is a man dying of cancer, the puppet he uses as a surrogate – while devilish in appearance and uncanny – cannot be described as disgusting in any way, nor can his apprentice Amanda. The disgust in the film is focused primarily around Jigsaw's (and Amanda's) traps and what they do to the human body (we may empathize with the plight of the victims, but the characters are also the loci of the disgust and the empathy is thus designed to make the experience of viewing more painful), the responses are displaced onto the unspeakable acts of the killer. While Jigsaw and Amanda are cruel, disturbed killers, they are still human, and while they may incite abhorrence towards them in the viewer, Jigsaw's plight at least can be understood and maybe even sympathized with to a small degree (he is convinced that he is teaching his victims a valuable – if cruel and excessive – lesson). Even though *The Exorcist* does depict a supernatural entity, it is not seen. Disgust again centres around the body of the victim and the effects that demonic possession has on it.

There have been several responses to Carroll that address these and other problems with his account, but Matt Hills's engagement (2003) with the limitation of Carroll's account caused by the requirement of a supernatural, threatening and impure monster is particularly valuable here. The problem with Carroll's definition is that it is entity-based and thus excludes horror films that do not contain such an entity. Hills (2003: 142) proposes that an event-based model is required instead. His event-based account of art-horror explains responses to films such as *The Haunting* and *The Blair Witch Project* that depend upon more suggestive forms of horror that bypass cognitive processing. Hills argues (2003: 146) that these films are designed to disorientate the viewer – they might do this stylistically (as *The Blair Witch Project* does via hand-held camera work which was reported as giving some viewers motion-sickness) or through shifts of perspective (such as when Eleanor is lying in bed in *The Haunting* and the pattern on the wallpaper seems to change to suggest an otherworldly presence). The crucial point that Hills makes is that the responses generated by these devices (others could be the use of off-screen sound, images that mainly consist of darkness, or a series of extreme close-ups) are not narrative entities and cannot be accounted for by narrative analysis (there is no narrative disclosure of the monster in *The Haunting*, for example). Rather, these devices disrupt the narrative in a way that is 'cognitively unsettling for the audience' and creates an 'objectless affect or anxiety' (p. 149) that permeates the films.

This is similar to Cynthia Freeland's account (2004: 197) of 'art-dread' in 'films depicting threats of imminent deep but inexplicable evil'. Art-dread is associated with horror movies based on mood and atmosphere that create feelings of unease, foreboding and awe. It is the label Carroll gave to the emotion generated by those films that fell outside his definition of horror because they lacked a monster, though Freeland points out (2004: 191) that there is not a clear demarcation between films which create art-horror and those which create art-dread. In cognitive terms, art-dread is (2004: 195) 'an imaginative exercise of conceptualisation, seeing that the world is not as it should be or as we wish it were'. Good examples of this are *The Sixth Sense*, *The Others*, *The Birds*, *Cat People* and *The Blair Witch Project*. The sense of dread created by these films is enjoyable because (p. 193) they offer: 'imaginative and plausible encounters with evil and cosmic amorality, they help us ponder and respond emotionally to natural and deep worries about the nature of the world'.

In *The Naked and the Undead* (2000), Freeland argues that audiences have a direct interest in the horrific, and the appeals of horror are produced via horror films' unique presentations of evil. People enjoy watching horror films, she says, because they depict human encounters with evil that either understand and defeat it or succumb to its power and temptation. Films may thus be affirmative or negative in their depictions of evil, both are pleasurable for the viewer – either in seeing evil overcome, or in seeing evil-doers punished for their sins. Films that create dread also often have an ending that confronts the viewer's perceptions of the world (2004: 192); in *The Sixth Sense* it is revealed that Malcolm has been dead all along, and in *The Others* that Grace and her children are the ghosts haunting the house where they died. In both these examples, the viewer comes to the realization that they too 'see dead people'. This often creates a sense of cosmic justice. Freeland points out that Heather's tearful confession at the end of *The Blair Witch Project* suggests she must die because (2004: 194) she has 'violated certain cosmic limits'. Similarly, in *The Others*, Grace is condemned to this spectral existence because she killed her children and committed suicide. As Hills does, Freeland points out that an effective sense of dread is created by narrative events in conjunction with mise-en-scène, cinematography, editing and sound. She also makes the important point that acting is crucial. In *The Others* (2004: 196): 'The pinched, pale face of Nicole Kidman ... shows that this woman knows something is very wrong in her house and her children'. In the art-dread that these films thus create they fall into the uncanny form of horror that Freeland discusses in *The Naked and the Undead* (2000: 215–71) and which she opposes to the graphic form that uses gore to demonstrate that evil exists. The appeals of such uncanny horror films (2004: 239) lie in the fact that they are repulsive and dreadful, and also intriguing.

These approaches also address the problem that cognitive accounts do not allow for an active audience (now well established within media and cultural studies). As Tim Groves (2006) states: 'Cognitive film theory effectively argues for a uniform emotional response among viewers', suggesting that ultimately cognitive approaches can be as reductive as psychoanalysis. Cognitivism, he says, 'cannot adequately account for why people can and do have different affective reactions and experiences to the same film'. It cannot, for example, explain the variety of tastes and responses amongst viewers. Certainly, some viewers will love a film and others hate it for reasons that might relate to gender, class, ethnic or sexual identity, or to cultural or historical context. Matt Hills, for example (2004: 144–45), compares the way audiences of the Universal horror films in the 1930s responded differently to audiences of today, and Freeland (2004) points out that what causes dread will change for different people at different times. In the case of *Frankenstein*, the film is unchanged and the characters in it still express fear and disgust at the monster, but today's audiences are much less likely to react in this way than 1930s audiences were. Obviously, as Hills says (2004: 145), when compared to the film technology used to create monsters and horrific scenes today, the 1930s horror films are much less convincing to contemporary audiences and thus unlikely to create the intended emotional responses. In the case of *Cat People*, it is still universally admired for its eerie atmosphere, but as Freeland says (2004: 197), the tunnel scene is not as powerful now as it was in 1942.

This suggests that any account of horror must also take into account time and place. Andrew Tudor (2002) for example questions Carroll on the grounds that his question – why horror? – is too narrow. Tudor (2002: 54) proposes instead that we should ask 'why do *these* people like *this* horror in *this* place at *this* particular time?' and therefore base an account of pleasure on the specific films of a particular historical period, in one national horror cinema, for a specific audience. This takes account of the fact that horror films can vary widely, as can the kinds of viewers they are aimed at. More importantly, it also engages with the sociocultural and political ideologies encoded in the film as Wood's account of the return of the repressed does.

4

HORROR AND THE CULTURAL MOMENT

In claiming that Noel Carroll's question 'why horror?' is too narrow, Andrew Tudor (2002) argues that different audiences make sense of different kinds of horror in different ways (in fact, different kinds of horror film work in different ways). Although theoretical accounts of the pleasures of horror do acknowledge variations in responses, these are not always explored in depth. Tudor suggests that what are required in order to fill these gaps are 'particularistic accounts' (2002: 50) that can illustrate how particular types of horror films are consumed by particular audiences under particular circumstances or social situations. What works as horror and the pleasures that horror cinema engenders can undoubtedly be explained theoretically in a number of ways but any explanation must also consider what works for particular social groups in particular cultures at particular times. It is important therefore to consider horror cinema historically and culturally in order to determine how the horror film reflects and addresses the anxieties of the age.

As Robin Wood (2004) has said in response to his earlier essay on the return of the repressed, he fully intended his account to link the psychoanalytical with the political. Pointing out that the changing forms of horror cinema have been 'strongly influenced by cultural-political evolution' (2004: xiii), he stresses that psychoanalysis has 'great resonance […] but only insofar as it is melded with a political awareness' (2004: xv). Such an approach can be used to explain sudden shifts in the genre – such as the emergence of the slasher film in a period of social and cultural change after the Vietnam war (Dika 1990) – at one end of the scale, and ideological representations in key films – the way in which *Edward Scissorhands* deals with the fear and prejudice surrounding disability, for example (Church 2006) – at the other. Wood is particularly interested in the way George Romero's zombie films encode radically different political meanings (moving them away from a straightforward account of the return of the repressed). Thus, *Night of the Living Dead* concerns race and the civil rights movement in the 1960s, *Dawn of the Dead* is a response to the emergence of the consumer society in the 1970s and *Day of the Dead* is about the crisis of masculinity in the wake of feminism in the 1980s. Certainly, this can mean that the socio-political context of the film must be taken into account alongside theoretical explanations when exploring responses to specific films or cycles. An interesting exercise in this respect would be to compare how the remakes (Night in 1990, Dawn and Day in the 2000s) rework these themes or introduce new ones.

Horror can of course be seen as a set of universal anxieties (and certainly horror can sometimes translate well from one culture to another and across time). Wells (2000: 6–7) lists the 'grand narratives' of horror as:

- social alienation
- the collapse of moral and spiritual order
- a deep crisis of evolutionary identity
- the overt articulation of humankind's innermost imperatives
- a need to express the implications of human existence in an appropriate aesthetic

It is easy to see that these conditions underpin much of contemporary horror cinema, just as they did classical horror films, and also that these narratives can be identified in, amongst other national cinemas, Italian,

Spanish, British, Asian, Indian, Nigerian, Mexican, New Zealand and Canadian horror film, just as they can in American. These themes are accessible to audiences across different periods and cultures (although, of course, the horror moments may not work as effectively for all audiences). But over and above this, horror films do tap into very specific elements of the zeitgeist or cultural moment as the Living Dead films demonstrate. Films may well have meanings which later audiences or those outside the country of origin may not recognize and they may also have additional and possibly unintended meanings for those audiences. It may be, for instance, that Japanese horror films such as *Ringu* which have become popular outside Japan have cultural meanings which Western viewers are not picking up. It may be worth considering the differences in the plots of the Japanese original and the Hollywood remake (of *Ringu* and *The Ring*, as well as other 'pairs' such as the originals and remakes of *Ju-on: The Grudge* or *Dark Water*) in order to identify how different factors – either universal or cultural – might be presented in different ways, left out or added.

According to Barry Keith Grant (1986), the ability of film to reflect contemporaneous political, social and cultural trends (predominantly attitudes or values held by a society or a group in a particular time and place) is particularly true of genre cinema. The collaborative nature of production (being the work of many individuals within an industrial system) means that cinema acts as a 'barometer' reflecting the cultural climate. It is not that any one film will necessarily reflect the cultural moment, but that the evolving conventions within a genre or the rising popularity and decline of particular genres can be seen as a reflection of changing cultural mores. The ideological subtexts of films are always about the time and place in which they were made, whatever their historical or geographical setting (a Gothic film such as *Bram Stoker's Dracula* set in the 1890s is just as much about sexuality in the 1990s as is *The Silence of the Lambs*). The fact that horror cinema deals with anxieties that are of great concern to the culture can thus explain some of the pleasures for the audience. Addressing contemporary social anxieties (which may be the subject of frenzied media coverage) in this way can allow the viewer to also work through these fears, and further it can also explain why horror is so enduring and always popular.

As Paul Wells (2000: 3) states, 'the history of the horror film is essentially a history of anxiety in the twentieth century'. It is key here to identify the ways in which different horror narratives reflect the cultural moment – in other words, how horror changes and adapts to the social, cultural and historical anxieties of the time and place in which the films were made. Many horror films directly articulate these anxieties, whether it be of the atomic bomb in post-World War 2 Japan in *Godzilla*, of the 1970s rise in divorce rates and the breakdown of the nuclear family in *The Brood* or domestic violence in *The Shining*, of the 1970s 'Me Generation' of selfish parents in *A Nightmare on Elm Street*, of the difference of cultural Other be they the unemployed 1970s rural working classes in *The Texas Chain Saw Massacre*, or the African-American male in *Candyman* and the gay male family in *Interview with the Vampire*, or of 'mad cow' and foot and mouth disease in twenty-first century Britain in *28 Days Later*. Examples are numerous and it is possible to analyze just about any horror film in these terms. The following sections explore a number of key issues which horror cinema deals with directly; many others may come to mind and these could easily be explored in a similar way using relevant films.

POLITICS AND CONTROL

Mark Jancovich's work is a good example of the way accounts of horror can take political ideology into consideration. In *Rational Fears* (1996), he contests the way genre criticism has a tendency to view genres as coherent and hermetically sealed objects. One of his points, relevant here, is in respect of the 'tendency to conflate very different forms in a manner which can ignore or minimise both historical change across periods, and differences or struggles within any particular period' (1996: 10). We might usefully add to this the differences between horror films produced under different cultural circumstances (this could primarily take into account national differences, but the differences between mainstream and independent production might be another factor which could be explored). Jancovich suggests (1996: 15) that discussions of genre should focus on 'the relationship between [the] texts and the period in which they were made'. For example, he links the 1950s invasion narratives of films such as *The Thing (from Another World)* and *Invasion of the Body Snatchers* to Cold War ideology, fear of Soviet aggression, xenophobia and the unquestionability of authority. In this respect, he questions whether the invasion narratives did indeed legitimate Fordism (the mass culture theory which stated that the rationalization of industrial and cultural production from the 1930s to the 1960s would give rise to a complacent population conditioned to accept the authority of scientific rationality) and concludes that they do not. In fact, he states (1996: 26) that they 'often criticize the system by directly associating the alien with it'.

In his analysis of *Invasion of the Body Snatchers* he notes that it has been seen as both anti-communist and anti-McCarthyite. Such opposing viewpoints are possible because both political systems seek to impose conformity on their populations. What is telling is that the alien duplicates in the film are whole in every way except that they lack emotions. It is this lack of emotion that renders the duplicates monstrous. On the one hand, this can be read as the threat of Communism – a political ideology that suppresses difference. On the other, it can be interpreted as a reflection of the way people are conditioned into standardized behaviour patterns by American society itself (Capitalism). The pods are speeding up a process that is happening anyway. Only Miles realizes what is happening and resists, and he is brushed aside by the authorities because he is irrational – he does not conform to behavioural norms. It is useful here to think of the way in which this stripping away of identity and individuality has been reworked in later versions of the film. The 1978 version is obviously not invested with the same McCarthyite politics since these were associated with the particular historical cultural moment in which the 1956 version was made. The same plot – the replacement of humans by emotionless pod-people – is now a commentary on mindless consumerism, the alienation of urban living (the setting has moved from small town America to the city) and the diagnosis of those who do not fit into society or adopt its behavioural norms as mentally ill (David is a celebrity psychologist who advocates shock therapy and blames the effects of the pods on emotional isolation).

In the 1993 version, now just called *Body Snatchers*, the setting is transposed to a military base – a choice that stresses the links between militarism and the alien pod people since both are subject to high levels of conformity. Against this backdrop, the depersonalization can be read in the context of the end of the Cold War (which led to America losing a key role as a world superpower keeping Communism at bay), the first Gulf War (which saw American military imperialism in the service of multinational corporations in order to protect the supply of oil), and Bush Sr's clashes with environmentalism (the plot also concerns the monitoring of toxic waste which can be read as the threat of encroaching ecological catastrophe which the American military-industrial complex does nothing to avert). In addition to this, the lead role is given to the teenage Marti, a character already alienated within her family. In *The Invasion*, the 2007 version, it is worth noting that the pessimism of the ending of all three previous versions is invalidated in a post-9/11 sense of triumphalism as the US military save the world from the alien menace (even though the pod people have brought peace to the Middle East, solved the crisis in Darfur, ended the Iraq war and brought in free healthcare for every American). This sends a message that wars, humanitarian disasters and social injustice only have a solution in a depersonalized world 'where human beings cease to be human' (as Yorish says in the film), and it certainly seems that this could be read as a particularly neo-conservative line which validates the war on terror.

In *Horror* (1992), Jancovich relates the proliferation of American horror films since the late 1960s, as well as its acceptance into the mainstream, to the failure of Fordism. In an argument based – like Wood's – on Marcuse, he demonstrates that rather than becoming complacent, the population became increasingly anxious and paranoid and was critical not just of science and technology, but authority in general. By the 1960s, the modern world was a nightmare of regulation and the population was powerless to resist it. In particular, bombardment by media and advertising images led to insecurity and loss of identity. This led on the one hand to the rejection of the authoritarian systems of modernism (Fascism, Stalinism, the 'technocratic society') and on the other to the rise of the 'individualist' and even 'survivalist' positions of postmodernity as people sought to hold on to what little was left to them. The post-Fordist system that emerged in the 1960s and 1970s saw challenges to the trade union movements (organized labour), the re-privatization of nationalized industries and new flexible working conditions (short-term contracts, job insecurity). This led to increased levels of helplessness and anxiety which were reflected not only in the rise of horror within contemporary culture, but also changes in its form.

Jancovich states (1992: 85) that in horror cinema of this time:

> These feelings of helplessness and anxiety are frequently dealt with in relation to two key institutions: the family and the military. The military is presented as the ultimate system of scientific technical rationality. It not only seeks to dominate and control the population, but also threatens it with ultimate annihilation. The family, on the other hand, is presented with much more ambivalence. As a primary site of socialisation and male authority, it is frequently presented as a source of horror, an institution which threatens forms of violence and domination which are both physical and psychological. On the other hand, it can also provide an image of community and interaction that challenges the system of rational domination. At its best though, it remains a precarious institution, and the role of the father presents a distinct problem. Paternal authority is rarely a solution to forms of domination within contemporary horror, but more usually the problem itself. The families which are defined as a challenge to forms of domination are usually clearly distinguished from the patriarchal family.

These transformations can be observed taking place in the various remakes of *Invasion of the Body Snatchers*, as the representations of community and family evolve-seen firstly in *Body Snatchers* as Marti struggles to emerge as an adult individual from her father's authority, and secondly in *The Invasion* where, as a divorced mother, Carol struggles to save her son from his father. The family – and the fragmentation of the family – is depicted in many American horror films of the 1970s on, not least *The Exorcist, The Brood, The Shining* and *The Stepfather*. The way in which the role of the military changes is also significant, from an institution indistinguishable from the aliens in the 1990s to the mechanism for the survival of the human race (or the individual in American society) in the 2000s.

These changes have also led to the disappearance of the traditional hero from the horror genre, with the monster and the victims now being the main characters (as they are in the slasher film and we can see how this develops through *Psycho, The Texas Chain Saw Massacre, Halloween* and *A Nightmare on Elm Street* as the heroine becomes increasingly self-sufficient and the male characters more ineffectual). Throughout the horror genre the victim's survival is no longer dependent on the intervention of an authority figure, but on her own capabilities. This reflects the changing roles of women in Western cultures. The horror genre has invariably presented confrontations with the forces that threaten women within society and give them more space than other genres in which to act (for example in the post-war films such as *Cat People*). However, in contemporary American horror women have acquired an even greater importance. Female heroes now take on the monster themselves, as Marti does in *Body Snatchers* and Carol does in *The Invasion*. As Jancovich observes (1992: 86), this development is not inherently feminist, but is linked to the same processes that led to feminism and has allowed self-consciously feminist horror texts to emerge.

Loss of control has also led to representations of chaos or social breakdown in the contemporary American horror film. Traditional horror presented the problem as an opposition between order and disorder, normality and abnormality, the conscious and the unconscious self. In contemporary horror it has become increasingly difficult to distinguish between these oppositions. As a result narrative closure is much less likely, contemporary horror narratives frequently have open or provisional endings. Thus from the 1970s on we see apocalyptic narratives (*Night of the Living Dead*), the birth of the Antichrist (*Rosemary's Baby, The Omen*), a preoccupation with consumerism (*Dawn of the Dead, Christine*), the dysfunctional family (*Texas Chain Saw Massacre, The Shining*), an obsession with serial killers (*Halloween, Friday the 13th*), and the crisis of identity and the transformation of the body (*The Howling, The Thing, Shivers*). We see this ambivalence emerging in the closing scenes of the 1978 version of *Invasion of the Body Snatchers* (which ends on Matthew's scream as he points Nancy out as still human) and *Body Snatchers* (where, even though she and Tim escape, the films ends with Marti stating in a voiceover that 'you can only stay awake so long'). In this way these horror films are a document of anxieties in the post-war, post-Fordist, postmodern America, but the ending of *The Invasion* (with its clear resolution in favour of the survival of humanity) may suggest a reactionary post-9/11 sensibility in some examples of the American horror film.

These discourses are of course particularly about American anxieties about 'technocratic regulation of American social life' (Tudor 2002: 51). As Tudor states (2002), such an approach makes the assumption that 'texts appeal to their audiences in part because they express in accessible and entertaining popular cultural terms the characteristic fears of their time'. Here they are very much about the changing focus of those fears as the American nation moves from the Cold War to the war on terror, but other national horror cinemas might well reflect their own sets of political anxieties. A similar tracing of shifting attitudes to the military could be undertaken across British horror films from *Witchfinder General* in the 1960s to *Deathwatch*, *28 Days Later* and *Dog Soldiers* in the 2000s, for example.

IDENTITY AND DIFFERENCE

Regardless of the ideology encoded in these films, they all centre on a monster or form of monstrosity that is represented within the text in opposition to the dominant ideological stance. This can be linked, as Wood suggests, to social and cultural anxieties surrounding the outsider or those who are socially marginalized (the Other). The history of horror is thus the history of the way other people and groups exhibiting markers of difference have been regarded and depicted by their society. This can encompass many factors, including disability, age and religion, but the examples discussed here – race, sexuality and class – have been chosen because they are central to the genre (or at least the forms it takes in British, American and European horror cinemas).

The concept of identity is one that is widely discussed and theorized in the areas of philosophy, sociology and media theory, particularly with respect to how identity is conceptualized within postmodern thought. David Gauntlett (2002) has argued that identity has moved from the more fixed traditional identities of the past to more fluid and knowingly constructed identities of today (the postmodern period). He argues that categories such as gender, for example, have changed along with social change (as a result of feminism, for instance). However, it is important to remember that aspects of identity cannot easily be separated out from each other or from background and upbringing. Gauntlett's warning (2007) that it can be difficult to establish what identity means should be heeded. As he states (2007: 209), '[t]he idea of "identity" can seem vague and abstract'. Reducing identity to a set of categories such as gender, ethnicity, and physical ability (which Gauntlett says become even more fuzzy when inspected closely) is an almost impossible task. Nevertheless, changes in horror cinema and its representations of monstrosity can be usefully analyzed in respect of social and cultural attitudes towards aspects of identity. The main consideration to bear in mind is that any one factor of identity cannot easily be analyzed without considering others: gendered identities can be strongly linked to class or racial identity, for example, and the one cannot be discussed without considering the other.

It may also be necessary to tease out the encoding of identity. It may not always be as straightforward as, for instance, identifying *Candyman* as an example of race horror. *Nosferatu*, for example, encodes the vampire as a Jew – at the time a hate figure in Germany blamed by some for the nation's humiliation under the Treaty of Versailles after World War 1. Count Orlok possesses many of the characteristics of the negative stereotype found in anti-semitic propaganda cartoons of the period. He has sharp rat-like features, a hunched spine, hooked nose and pointed ears, and clawed grasping hands like the caricature of a Jewish money-lender. Cartoons of this period depicted Jews sucking the life out of the German nation or being responsible for Germany's decline – the links to vampirism being implicit in these representations. In the film, Orlok is also accompanied to Bremen by a plague of rats and the rats themselves are plague carriers, again echoing the propaganda that implied Jews spread the plague (he too has rat-like fangs close together at the front of his mouth). In the fact that Orlok also attempts to seduce a beautiful, virtuous, young Aryan woman, it could also be said that he is a threat to racial purity.

This reading does not necessarily mean that the film itself is anti-semitic. Orlok's characteristics can also be read as evidence of his sexual status as a vampire – he is, as Roger Dadoun (1989: 58–59) suggests, the Pointed One, a conglomeration of points that are 'the paraphernalia of fetishism'. He is 'walking phallus or "phallambulist"'. What is clear though is that the demonization of a racial and religious group can be encoded in unconscious ways within the culture (this had been prevalent with respect to Jews in Europe since the middle ages and was thus deeply ingrained – at an unconscious level – in the German psyche). It is certainly not unknown for minority and marginalized groups in other times and places to be the subjects of explicit racism or other form of prejudice that is then encoded in this way in popular cultural texts (radical texts can similarly present an oppositional ideological viewpoint). For example, one of the early formulaic elements of the American horror film (and one so iconic that it is still reproduced today in contemporary films such as Edward Scissorhands as well as other popular culture texts such as The Simpsons) is the torch-wielding mob that hounds the monster to its (seeming) death.

Typical sequences can be seen in Frankenstein and Bride of Frankenstein. When the townsfolk in these films take up arms and torches to hunt for the monster they closely resemble in dress, poses and actions the lynch mobs that had been active in America in the first half of the twentieth century. Lynchings of freed slaves had been common in the aftermath of the American Civil War, but had recurred in the 1920s and 1930s – after the release of Birth of a Nation in 1915 when the Ku Klux Klan had reformed, and in the 1950s and 1960s – during the period of civil rights activism. The resemblance of the mobs in the Universal Frankenstein films to the lynch mobs that were so recently a blot on American history is clear: the creature can be read as a representation of racial difference. He is a large hulking brute, is dressed in worn workman's clothing, and represents a threat to the virtuous woman. He is accused of crimes that may not have been intentional (if they occurred at all) and is subjected to extrajudicial punishment. (A similar argument can be applied to King Kong.) As Nosferatu did with the Jewish stereotype, these characteristics reflect the dominant negative stereotyping of the African-American male of the time. It is notable also that with the resurgence in lynchings during the civil rights campaign, images very similar to those of actual lynching parties occur at the end of Night of the Living Dead.

As Stephen Harper (2005) attests, Night of the Living Dead 'clearly and insistently engages with its contemporary social and political milieu' and so we must, as Harper does, understand the film in its historical context. Indeed, Harper sees the film as 'one of the most important cultural records of its era' (the late 1960s). Harper provides a detailed discussion of the film as social document (and he also provides a clear example of the way a film can be re-interpreted by audiences at different moments in time). One of the most important contemporary issues dealt with by the film is race. Although it is never mentioned by any of the other characters, the hero is African-American. That there are no other non-white characters in the film (the rest of the people trapped in the house and the various authorities on the television bulletins together with the hunting parties) means that a sense of difference surrounds Ben as the only non-white character. The zombies themselves are an amorphous mass that never really takes on any identifying characteristics of its own, although since Ben is mistaken for one of them at the end they could be also seen as representatives of a racial other that threatens white America.

Previous film zombies are indeed significantly inflected with race: the zombie being a feature of Haitian culture and associated with the African roots of communities transposed to the new world as slaves in films such as I Walked with a Zombie. Harper also draws the links with slavery in The Plague of the Zombies, a Hammer film made a year before Romero's, in which villagers are turned into zombies in order to provide slave labour in a Cornish tin mine. But beyond these general links, at the time Romero was making his film race was a serious issue in America. The civil rights movement peaked in the 1960s, and achieved significant changes in America against segregation (which still existed in some states) and discrimination, although several civil rights workers were murdered and churches bombed, while Malcolm X was assassinated in 1965 and Martin Luther King in 1968. In this climate, lines of dialogue such as 'we don't know how many of them there are', 'well, if you have a gun, shoot 'em in the head, if you don't, get a torch and burn 'em, they go up pretty easy – beat 'em or burn 'em' and 'another one for the fire' could easily be seen as racist remarks that might be spoken by a member of the Ku Klux Klan.

Reinforcing this, the hunting parties are dressed in very similar fashion to the members of lynch mobs shown in photographs from the 1920s and 1930s. The final credits of the film draw irrefutable attention to the resemblance. The grainy still images (giving a documentary feel) of Ben's body being thrown on the pyre (Figure 4.1) recall well-known images of actual lynchings (Figure 4.2) with similar style of dress, stance and physical appearance. Ben's evasion of the contaminating bite of the zombies and his survival (not to mention that he predominates in the battle between himself and the middle-aged, traditional family man Harry to protect the lone, single female) is thus significant. His unexpected death at the hands of the posse at the moment of escape is thus all the more shocking and – in the posse's resemblance to a lynch party – reconfigures the racist past of the USA. The freeze frames under the end credits of Ben being dragged on meat hooks and

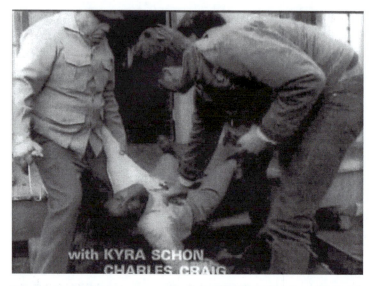

Figure 4.1 Ben's body is thrown on the fire under the end credits of *Night of the Living Dead*.

Figure 4.2 The burning corpse of William Brown (28 September 1919, Omaha, Nebraska).

thrown on a bonfire almost exactly reproduce the actual archive images. There are undoubtedly other sociopolitical readings that can be made of *Night of the Living Dead* – of gender, family, and youth, for example, but the inscription of race is significant. The fact that the film retains a significant appeal more than 40 years after its release is also important. Like many low-budget films conceived of and executed by young visionaries (and Romero can certainly be counted amongst this group of horror film auteurs), its aesthetics are clearly a result of the conditions of production, but its power remains, not only in the iconic images of the unrelenting zombie hoard but in its shockingly brutal ending.

Candyman also deals with gender identity (as already explored), and this is closely tied to racial and sexual categories. Helen transgresses not just her gender but social anxieties about interracial marriage; Candyman's crime (for which he too was lynched) was to be both a free man and in love with a white woman (miscegenation laws were not fully repealed in the USA until 1967). In *Candyman*, the monster is clearly depicted as a threatening racial other (ambiguously, since he threatens the poor black community too – though this may ostensibly be because their homes are on the site of his murder), but his role in urban myth can also be read as taking revenge on the children of the white community. Furthermore, he also elicits sympathy as a victim of racism. As Pinedo says (1997: 128): 'the monster of *Candyman* is a product of white racism'.

The evidence of racism also dominates the film in the location of Cabrini Green. This location creates a strong link between race and class or wealth. The African-American community is living in poverty, cut off (literally by the freeway) from the rich white Americans; Helen's apartment is identical to Anne-Marie's, but the white woman's block has been refurbished into luxurious condominiums while the black woman's has been left to decline. *The People Under the Stairs* also foregrounds the link between race and wealth. The hero of the film is a young African-American boy Fool with dreams of being a doctor inspired by the fact his dying mother cannot afford healthcare. The family is threatened with eviction from their cramped ghetto apartment by the wealthy white landlords, and it is this aberrant couple (a brother and sister who kidnap children who they then mutilate and discard in the basement of their huge house when they fail to live up to their standards) who are coded as monsters (they are incestuous child abusers, and 'Father' is a fetishist who hunts the discarded children while wearing a gimp suit). Where The People Under the Stairs is significant is in its reversal of the racial other as monster; here it is the wealthy white racists who are the locus of monstrosity, and in the fact that Fool defeats these monsters, frees their victims, and redistributes their wealth to his neighbours from the ghetto. It is not insignificant that this film was made at a time of increasing levels of poverty and unemployment at the end of the Bush Sr. presidency.

Just as race, class and gender can be strongly linked in representations of monstrosity, so can class, gender and sexuality. Count Orlok in Nosferatu, despite being a walking phallus in Dadoun's account, is very different from later versions of Dracula and other vampires in that he is far more monstrous in appearance. The more attractive appearance of most vampires can be linked to the encoding of sexuality (rather than race) in the look of the monster with the vampire as an embodiment of non-normative (that is non-monogamous, non-straight) sexuality. This 'haemosexuality' as Christopher Freyling labels it in his book Vampyres (1991) suggests that vampires reflect the cultural moment's attitudes towards queer sexualities (and here queer can mean any non-normative sexuality including the 'straight queer'). Of all horror subgenres or styles, the vampire has proven the most adaptable at reflecting social attitudes revolving around gender, sex and sexuality, as well as the way these aspects of identity are often inscribed into class. As already seen, the fact that vampire films deal explicitly with sexuality means that they speak directly to members of the audience who self-identify as anything other than the bourgeois, heterosexual norm. In attempting to explain their popularity, we might also think about the way in which the figure of the vampire is often brought to the centre and coded as charismatic or alluring – in Martin, Near Dark, Interview with the Vampire, Cronos, Underworld, and Blade (an interesting example of the heroic vampire figure), for example. The vampire in these films is an appealing and sympathetic monster, not only as an extremely attractive (and often sexually arousing) figure as he or she is in most cases, but as someone who stands outside of 'normal' society and embraces their difference, meaning that viewers will frequently desire them or want to become them.

Dadoun (1989) has also described the vampire as an 'eidolon' (from the Greek for idol). The vampire is thus both a spectral double and an idealized image. The vampire in this sense is a reflection of whatever aspects of society and culture it needs to be for the time. As Nina Auerbach says in *Our Vampires, Ourselves* (1995: 145), every age 'embraces the vampire it needs, and gets the one it deserves'. On one level, vampire films encode fears of sexually transmitted diseases (from syphilis at the time Bram Stoker wrote *Dracula*, through the AIDS at the time of *Interview with the Vampire*). There is clearly a fear of the contaminating blood of the vampire, but on another level other aspects of sexuality are evident. Hammer's Dracula and Karnstein[1] films, as Peter Hutchings (1993a) points out, are a document of changing attitudes towards gender, from middle-class conceptions of female sexuality in the late-1950s to a patriarchal anti-feminist backlash in the 1970s. Equally, *Interview with the Vampire* (Figure 4.3) encompasses anxieties about the homosexual family and gay male reproduction or adoption. As Harry Benshoff (1997: 272) has pointed out the film presents its queer monster tropes in an ambivalent way:

> Although Lestat's penchant for little boys and Louis's homoerotic longing for his dead brother are downplayed or missing from the film (Louis now has a dead wife), the film *is* very sympathetic to its queer vampires, and the bulk of its running time is devoted to the vampires' exploring their own queer identities. […] Yet the idea of a male couple (and a male couple raising a child) is once again represented as unnatural and steeped in violence, much of it directed against women.

Benshoff observes that when he has viewed the film at a public screening the most horrifying moment in the film for the teenage audience is when Armand, having confessed his desire, seems about to kiss Louis. This

Figure 4.3 The gay male family in *Interview with the Vampire*.

reassertion of heterosexuality by drawing away from the frightening queer sexuality, Benshoff argues (1997: 272), means that the narrative expresses 'fears of sexual difference in general and homosexuality specifically'. It is also important to note that Lestat, Louis and Armand are dressed in the manner of upper class fops or dandys. On one level, this feminizes them, but it is also a signifier of queer.

Benshoff (1997: 49–50) makes a similar observation in the opening framing sequence of *The Bride of Frankenstein* where Lord Byron and Percy Shelley are inviting Mary to continue her horror story; 'their status as sexual transgressors is made clear', he says. Benshoff argues (1997: 50) that at the time (and he considers director James Whales's own homosexuality as extremely significant), a tale of queer sexuality can only be produced using the conventions of the horror film. *The Bride of Frankenstein* certainly encodes queer sexuality, just as much as class and race, into the text. Just after the creature has been chased by the torch-wielding villagers, he takes refuge in a crypt where he encounters (and is entertained by) Dr Pretorius (played by the outwardly queer actor Ernest

Thesiger). The contrasts between these two figures is clear: the creature is lumpen and awkward in his movements, his clothes are shabby and ill-fitting, he grunts and speaks in half-sentences; Pretorius is effete and mannered, he commands others and wears the garb of a medical man, and he lays out a well-prepared meal despite being in a place of the dead. There is a strong contrast between the working class codings of the creature and the aristocratic bearing of Pretorious, however Pretorius is also excessively camp in his mannerisms and voice. Gay male reproduction is again brought to the fore in both Pretorius's and Frankenstein's creation of living monsters.

As social attitudes towards sexuality, as well as race, class, disability and other factors of identity, change, so too might the representations of monstrosity, though it may only be that these become more ambiguous (as with homosexuality in *Interview with the Vampire* or race and gender in *Candyman*). However, as Benshoff notes (1997), production histories too are worth exploring in such accounts. A more outwardly queer horror cinema has emerged in the 2000s as gay, lesbian and other queer filmmakers make films such as *Hellbent*. Equally, the independent short horror film *Killer Cure* made by the Shoot Your Mouth Off collective (which produces films by disabled filmmakers) presents disability in very different ways (as *The People Under the Stairs* does with race) to the classic encoding of disability as an outward sign of inner monstrosity.[2]

MEDIA AND TECHNOLOGY

In addition to anxiety surrounding identity, horror cinema may also deal with external social or cultural issues that affect the self on the level of everyday life. If horror films reflect the anxieties of the age, then these may be related to the minutiae of everyday life, just as much as to major events or concerns such as the AIDS epidemic, the war on terror or climate change. Horror films deal with everyday experiences or the sociocultural contexts of many people's (and especially younger people's) lives, in the way the slasher films deals with teen sexuality for example or the werewolf films examine male puberty, for example. Other topics could easily be discussed, but one aspect of everyday life that has been key in contemporary horror cinema is technology and the new media culture that has been engendered by the Internet, games consoles, mobile phone communication and multi-channel television. Technology has advanced at a far faster pace in the last decades of the twentieth century than ever before and technological (along with associated media and communication) change has become a constant. It is unsurprising then that in the 1990s and 2000s, horror cinema has reflected the way technology and the media have become increasingly dominant in people's lives. It is no surprise either that some of these films approach film narrative and aesthetics in novel ways that are quite different to classical narrative forms.

One of the first films to gain widespread attention for so doing was *The Blair Witch Project*, first, through the marketing of the film and, second, in the way the film was directed, shot and edited (in both cases as though it was genuine found footage). The marketing effectively exploited the Internet with a website and other material which resembled a missing persons campaign. This website contained an elaborate archive of historical information about the legend and material found during the search for the filmmakers.[3] This was reinforced in the 'real world' by realistic-looking missing posters (many put up around locations where young people were most likely to be found) directing readers to the website. In addition, a mockumentary *The Curse of the Blair Witch* about the background to the Blair Witch and the missing students was screened on The Sci-Fi Channel in the run-up to the film's release. The campaign – based around the tag that 'In October of 1994 three student filmmakers disappeared in the woods near Burkitsville, Maryland while shooting a documentary … A year later their footage was found.' – was designed to be convincing enough to support rumours that this was an actual case (Figure 4.4).

This was then convincingly backed up in the shooting style of the film. As the statement from directors Dan Myrick and Ed Sanchez (quoted in Jones and Jolliffe 2006: 637) explains: 'We sent the actors

Figure 4.4 Marketing and fictional world collide in the search for the missing students of *The Blair Witch Project*.

out into the woods and […] directed them by remote control. […] It took an immense amount of trust to allow them to shoot and improvise their lines'. This 'remote control direction' involved giving the actors backstory documents and directing notes for each day's shooting. The shoot took place largely as it is seen in the finished film, with the actors themselves doing the filming, flags being left by the crew to mark the routes the actors were to take, and directions for the actors left each day in tubes at various pre-arranged places around the locations being used for the film. The narrative of the film thus sets the actors up not just as characters, but as filmmakers themselves. The constant filming is the raison d'etre of the film (in narrative terms the film itself would not exist without it), and the unremitting point-of-view camerawork predates and anticipates the documentation of everyday life now in evidence on blogs, YouTube, webcams, and other Internet sites.

Moving image technology thus becomes the central focus and often the source of the horror. Josh, Mike and Heather are not simply curious about the legend of the Blair Witch, it is to be the subject of their film project. But are they really so different from other groups of young people who feature in the rural-urban horror film? 'You damn fool kids'll never learn' says the older fisherman as they embark on a trek that seems to be going in the direction of death and foreshadows their destruction: Black Hills Forest, Coffin Rock, the Cemetery Trail. This is not just a film about urban youth getting lost in the wilderness though; it is also about the way in which technology gets in the way of seeing. (In this way, it also perhaps interestingly links back to theories of the gaze in horror cinema.) On route to the Cemetery Trail, Heather says: 'I know exactly where we're going. Josh is looking at the map now, even though I know where we're going' before having an argument with Mike about whether or not they are lost. Mike cannot fathom such low technology, saying of the map, 'This is Greek to me, it's useless', but more significantly he then complains about Heather's constant surveillance, displacing his discomfort onto the video camera: 'I don't know why you have to have every conversation on video'. The hike is largely shot through this video camera and thus is literally (and diegetically) Heather's point of view.

It is shortly after this that they find the first piles of rocks, which they assume to be the cemetery. Josh knocks over one of the piles in the dark, Heather puts it back, kisses her hand and touches it to the stones ('You can't be too careful,' she says, but she has already been careless in overconfidently and arrogantly denying that they are already lost). On what they then think is the return journey to the car, Josh and Mike are confused that they are going a different way. Again, there is disagreement about whether they are lost, and when Heather suggests camping before nightfall (even though she has been insisting they are on route to the car) the argument again comes back to the camera. 'Turn the camera off and get us home' says Mike, suggesting that it is Heather's insistence on filming that is getting in the way of them seeing the way out of the woods – it is literally blocking her sight as she holds it to her eye. Heather refuses though: 'No, I'm not turning the camera off. I wanna mark this occasion'. She also refuses to hand over the map to Josh (which uselessly is in her pocket – again, out of sight – she cannot get at it because she is filming).

After this night, three piles of rocks appear (perhaps their own gravemarkers). Again, this becomes a point of contention. Josh wants to leave, 'All I want to do is get to the goddamn car […] we're obviously not wanted here' but Heather seems to want to stay: 'I can't believe we have to leave just when shit's happening'. For her, this is an interesting development for their film, which she is still thinking about in terms of the end product, and seems more important than personal safety or even practical considerations such as returning the film equipment. Again, Josh recognizes this impediment to clear and sensible vision and tells her to 'put the fucking camera down'. This is emphasized when Heather discovers that she has lost the map ('the least responsible thing she could have possibly done'). Later Mike confesses: 'I kicked that fuckin' map into the creek yesterday. It was useless. I kicked that fucker into the creek'. Again this prefigures a significant escalation in tension as they come across the voodoo grove with stick figures hanging from the branches of the trees. Heather lingers – she seems still to be taking a director's rational approach but is also obsessed, whereas Mike, already clearly unstable with his erroneous belief that the map was useless, becomes unhinged and starts screaming. Heather finally admits that they are lost, but she still films.

As the horrors escalate after another disturbed night and finding Josh's pack has been opened and the contents strewn about and covered with slime, Heather is still trying to resolve the mystery. 'Why you?' she asks – still filming. Mike screams at her: 'Are you not scared enough?' The camera seems to be insulating her. Mike and Josh again protest about Heather's constant filming and obsession with 'going around doing your documentary thing'. Further evidence is supplied by the way she becomes exceedingly possessive and violent when Josh tries to wrest the camera from her. She bites him – in a parody of the witch who devours children (and *Blair Witch* is clearly a version of Hansel and Gretel). But as he films Heather after she has calmed down, Josh empathizes with her motivations: 'I see why you like this video camera so much. […] It's not quite reality. […] It's totally like a filtered reality, man. It's like you can pretend that everything's not quite the way it is'. Thematically, this is a key moment in the film, suggesting that this filtered vision is itself a trigger for the horror.

They are all beginning to break down under the stress, but Heather will still not turn off the camera despite Mike's pleas. It is only when they discover they are walking around in circles that Heather begins to lose it. Josh takes up the camera again and taunts Heather, directing her in a manic fashion as if she were an actress in need of motivation. The camera has now become a weapon or a torture device; it is the object that has trapped them in a media hell. Josh is then literally lost: he disappears. Heather is confronted with that loss as symbolic of death when she opens the strange bundle made from a torn strip of Josh's shirt, it is bloody and contains human teeth and hair. Her point-of-view in the video camera sees her looking, then looking away, only to look back and dwell on the objects. This occurs shortly before Heather's on-camera confession and acceptance of the blame – a key image in the publicity for the film and a picture of abject despair (Figure 4.5). The film is clearly a descent into madness as well as death, and the final discovery of the house symbolizes both as the final destination of the journey. The fact that it is left unclear as to what really happened, whether this is simply madness or something supernatural is never resolved. The picture becomes jumpy and disjointed as Heather and Mike both film as they frantically run around the house trying to locate Josh – the final frames show only the juddering of the film after Heather has fallen giving no narrative resolution (the viewer has known from the very start that they had never been seen again, but the film does not provide an answer to what happened to them beyond getting lost). Technology (the video and film footage) shows this, but it leaves only loose ends, as if it, rather than the witch, is the tool of their destruction.

Similar themes of technology and the media being alienating have been dealt with in non-horror films, Slacker for example, but it is in horror cinema where media technology as a source of anxiety is truly felt.[4] Cloverfield, being even more recent, is more focused on the anxieties of twenty-first-century life as lived through a lens as much as it is

Figure 4.5 The on-camera confessional of *The Blair Witch Project*.

about a monster, which in any case is an unknown and unknowable entity within the film. In fact, *Cloverfield* has been described as the first film for the MySpace Generation: Bruce Newman writes[5] that 'If this isn't exactly the first YouTube movie, it may be the first to fully discard what snooty scholars call "film grammar" in favor of a new video-based visual language employed by that website, as well as Facebook and My Space'. Newman also suggests that *Cloverfield* is:

> The ultimate movie for people who don't feel a cataclysm has really happened until they can videotape it, upload it and stream it live to the rest of the world. It's a movie that deserves to be seen on the big screen, but whose natural home – and ultimate destination, no doubt – is a Web server, from which it can be downloaded to an iPod.

Clearly, this is a flashback to The Video Backpacker of *Slacker*, though the technology that kept this character rooted in his home can now be carried around in one's pocket.

Cloverfield, like *The Blair Witch Project*, used internet viral marketing – this time involving the J.J. Abrams fan community, and presented the narrative as found footage, in this case in a camera found on the site of Central Park after the destruction of Manhattan. This footage – screened just as it was found on the tape – is an eyewitness account of an attack and rampage by some kind of extraterrestrial monster that begins during a farewell party for Rob, who is leaving for a job in Japan. Hud is filming farewell messages from Rob's friends at the party and keeps on filming during the attack. Occasional flashbacks to a trip Rob and Beth made to Coney Island a month before are provided by brief segments of the footage previously recorded by Rob on the same tape. The first sequence on the morning of Beth and Rob's trip contains significant comments on the nature of new media: Rob films Beth unawares as she is waking up and protests by saying 'I could just see this ending up on the Internet' – a comment perhaps not on the lack of privacy in everyday life, but on a culture where everything about the self is exposed to perusal and everyday life is opened up for public viewing. Nothing it seems is 'real' until it has been recorded and replayed. When the attack begins and people rush out into the street confused, the Statue of Liberty's head crashing into the road results not in a great deal of running and screaming, as we might expect in a classical narrative, but in a standing still, turning round and taking of pictures on mobile phones. The first instinct, it seems, is to record the event – commenting perhaps on the way so many people now experience the world as mediated through a lens (just as Heather did in *The Blair Witch Project*) or on a personal screen.

It is true of course that the film taps into another significant anxiety: 9/11. The sequences straight after the initial attack resemble the footage of the Twin Towers endlessly cycled on news and other programmes, with the buildings collapsing and thick pall of smoke and debris billowing down the street, with the dust and fires choking the survivors. And as with 9/11, there is initial confusion about the source of the attack. The hand-held point-of-view footage, mainly that of Hud as he films his friends attempts to rescue Kate and escape from the monster, also resembles video eye witness footage now commonly used in news reports. The story is fast-paced and action-packed with scary edge-of-the-seat monster movie tropes (the death of Rob's brother when the monster attacks the Brooklyn Bridge, the friend in jeopardy that they have to rescue, the attack by the creature's offspring in the underground tunnel, the infection of Marlene after she is bitten, the climb up the toppled building to find Beth, the helicopter crash, Hud being eaten by the creature[6]) but as a narrative is what in a classical film would be an entirely peripheral story to the main action.

It is a very different narrative mode than that of the classic monster movie told from the narrative point of view of scientists, military and government characters who are seeking to resolve the enigma as seen in *The Thing* or *The Invasion*. In this sense the film might be deemed post-classical – the sole focus is on bystanders, a small group of people that would in any other film be background non-speaking roles. The horror thus becomes claustrophobically their horror – which is all the more terrifying because of their complete lack of access to any information. In their final confessionals to the camera Rob says ' … some thing attacked the city. I don't know what it is. If you found this tape, if you're watching this right now, then you probably know more about it than I do' and Beth 'I don't know why this is happening' – there has been no resolution for these characters (and shortly before he disappears in *The Blair Witch Project*, Josh is similarly bewildered about why his belongings have been slimed). The ending, as in *The Blair Witch Project*, is bleak, not only do they die but a backwards message at the end of the credits states that 'it's still alive'. And although there is a hidden suggestion of where the monster came from (a streak in the sky of something falling into the sea can be seen in the background of the final sequence from Coney Island – and it is notable for the MySpace Generation claims that this, along with the backwards message have garnered a great deal of Internet discussion and can only be spotted by freezing and replaying the scene) the enigma is never really resolved. Although, this narrative approach is clearly meant to reflect the democratization of news with mobile phone footage and bystander witness reports that have become prevalent across the Internet as well as incorporated into traditional news programming (where there is now 24 hours to fill, rather than an hourly bulletin once or twice a day), it also seems to be saying that even though we all now have the ability to record all that we witness, this does not provide us with any answers.

Technology has of course been the means by which horror is identified or the threat communicated in many other horror films. Indeed, *Bram Stoker's Dracula* is a prime example of the foregrounding of technology (as it was in the novel) to record the horror, and *The Last Broadcast* or *Man Bites Dog* (in which documentary crews follow the serial killers around) are interesting examples which comment on the media itself. Even in plots not directly related to such technology, similar thematic material can emerge. In *Saw*, when Adam and Lawrence discover they are being watched through a two way mirror, the killer is shown watching on a monitor: 'I can see you', he says, and then: 'Don't look at me, I can't help you' – a metaphor for the surveillance society and reality television. As Adam says: 'So, that's what this is. Reality TV'. He has rationalized his plight by equating it with the predominant media culture of television shows such as *Survivor* and *Big Brother*. Other contributions to the cycle include [•REC] which presents the plot of an outbreak of a rage-inducing virus as footage recorded by a television reporter and her cameraman,[7] and *Diary of the Dead* which presents a zombie attack from the point of view of a group of film students. More interesting perhaps are those films where the technology itself is the threat, as in *Ringu* and *One Missed Call* with their vengeful ghosts who haunt via videotape and mobile phone. It is perhaps no surprise that the key films in this area are Japanese, being the product of a culture that has been the focus of the late-twentieth-century technological revolution and the commodification of technology.

In *Ringu* (Figure 4.6), the Japanese horror film that kick-started the popularity of Japanese and Asian horror cinema (such as *The Host*) in the West, the telephone and the video recorder are directly implicated in the horror. The victim only has to watch a tape to be cursed ('You will die in one week') and the curse is announced by phone ('You saw it'). This suggests that technology is not just an alienating barrier to recognizing

Figure 4.6 Technology is the conduit for horror in *Ringu*.

the horror as it is in *The Blair Witch Project* or a worthless substitute for sight and knowledge as it is in *Cloverfield*, but is an actual conduit for a supernatural entity. Televisions switch on of their own accord and give access into the real world for the evil spirit. A ringing phone becomes something to be feared, technology is a harbinger of death rather than something that can make life easier, aid communication, or entertain. The victims have a look of extreme fear on their faces when they die, and of Masami, the friend who witnessed Tamoko's death, it is said she 'went crazy, she's in hospital, she won't go anywhere there's a TV … '. Significantly again, the protagonist Reiko is an active producer of moving image material: she is a reporter working for a television news company, and parts of the action take place in the television studio and editing suite.

The filmic image itself uses photographic, video and camera footage to relay a series of uncanny images. When Reiko conducts an interview about the urban myth, the subject is shown in the washed out video image. In the photo of Tamoko and her friends after they have watched the cursed video their faces are blurred and distorted. When Reiko looks at the shelves of videos in the reception at Izu the image becomes a grainy video shot that draws attention to the unboxed tape cassette (the music also becomes strange and Reiko's voice develops an echo – this leads directly into her watching the cursed tape), and of course the images on the tape itself – the combination of static, grainy partial images that are 'edited' in a discontinuous fashion. These comprise the impossible angles of some of the shots, the mysterious words and phrases – Sada, eruption, brine and goblins, not to mention Sadaku emerging from the screen in the money shot at the end of the film when Ryuji (Reiko's ex-husband) dies. These images create further uncanny moments when they 'cross over' into real life, such as when Reiko wakes to 'see' The Towel Man (the veiled pointing figure) superimposed over Yoichi's mattress and opens the sliding doors to discover her son watching the tape.

Uncanny disturbing moments in the film are frequent and unsettling: the general use of sound effects and shadows, as when Yoichi (Reiko's son) goes upstairs during Tomoko's funeral, when Reiko finds the cabin in Izu or when the flashbacks are in a grainy video image, are typical horror film stylistics. Other elements are specifically Japanese, and might require some cultural knowledge to fully appreciate the horror.[8] The appearance of Japanese ghosts (who are traditionally female) derives from funeral rites in the Edo period of the sixteenth and seventeenth centuries. The dead would be dressed in a white burial kimono and if they were female their hair would be loose (at this time women wore their hair long but always wore it up in elaborate buns). The female ghost of Japanese folklore is thus depicted dressed in white with long dishevelled hair, just as Sadako is (Figure 4.7). She is also associated with summer and humidity or water and haunts the living in a desire for revenge (as in Ju-On: The Grudge, Honogurai mizu no soko kara, and others). One of the most famous traditional Japanese ghost stories is Yotsuya Kaidan which tells of Oiwa who becomes a vengeful spirit (again she is usually depicted in white with long tangled hair) after being poisoned by her husband. One effect of the poison was to cause her eye to droop, and a similar effect is shown in Ringu where one of Sadako's eyes is shown almost entirely white and with distorted eyelids. Oiwa also manifests from a lantern

Figure 4.7 Sadako: an incarnation of the vengeful female ghost in *Ringu*.

and this could be interpreted as a link in the way Sadako manifests as the flickering light on the television screen. Furthermore, in Japanese popular cultural, urban legends are very popular, as are television programmes about Shinrei Shashin or spirits appearing in photographs (both of which are elements in *Ringu*). These may not be directly readable by a Western audience, but they are nonetheless disturbing images. Other cultural elements have Western equivalents – Sadako's ability to will someone to death through fury (an idea already known to Western audiences as well in *The Fury*) and the idea of being entombed alive in the well (a common trope of the American gothic of Edgar Allen Poe where people are buried alive or bricked up behind walls), for example. It is perhaps no coincidence that these films are primarily suggestive horrors, unsettling the viewer with their suggestion that technology has an uncanny life of its own.

As many other films attest, anxieties about technology can also be represented in much more graphic ways. Amongst David Cronenberg's films for example, *Videodrome* depicts in very visceral imagery what happens when technology 'invades' the mind and the body – in Max's hallucinatory world his body literally becomes a video player when a slot opens up in his stomach, and when Seth steps out of the pod after having teleported himself he asks 'Is this life or is it Memorex?' – he has become a hyperrealistic copy of himself. Anxieties surrounding the dominance of technology in Japan are again evident in *Tetsuo* – like Cronenberg's work, another body horror version of the impact of technology on human flesh. *Tetsuo* deals with the way in which technological hardware, mechanical devices and the motorcar, impact upon human flesh. (It is interesting that there are allusions to J.G. Ballard's *Crash* in the scenario of *Tetsuo* since Cronenberg later adapted the novel for his own film version.) In the opening sequence the Metal Fetishist slices open his thigh and inserts a large threaded screw (almost as if he were using it to replace his femur). As he does so drawings of runners on crumpled paper burst into flame, suggesting perhaps that he is trying to make improvements to his body to make it stronger and faster, though the burning images could also suggest that this is futile for him. The Fetishist's wound fails to heal and the man discovers maggots infesting his flesh. When he does run, it is into the path of an oncoming car and this collision between metal and flesh triggers a similar obsession (hinting at infection or disease transmission) in the salaryman who is driving the car. At first the salaryman finds a small metal spike growing from his cheek, but he gradually transforms until he is all scrap metal. It is the salaryman who grows pistons and valves in his ankles that allow him to move with amazing speed.

Tetsuo is shot in grainy black and white, often in extreme close-up and punctuated with almost abstract shots of industrial equipment and tangled metal objects, pipes, cables, wires, tools, bolts and screws. These shots sometimes suggest technology growing inside the salaryman – after one such sequence, the skin of his arm is bursting with pipes and wires. Lighting strobes and the music replicate the sounds of industry. The conjunction of metal and flesh is not clean and efficient, but is grotesque, engorged and encrusted. Blood spurts as wires, screws and pipes burst from split, fragile skin – and in the black and white footage the blood appears like viscous black oil intended to lubricate the machinery of the mechanized body (another example of Halberstam's reconfigured genders perhaps). These images of body horror are enhanced by the sound effects, as for example when scratching, screeching metal, ricocheting bullets and a cacophony of other metallic sounds contrapuntally accompany shots of the salaryman's girlfriend eating. There are bizarre point-of-view shots (which appear as flickering cathode ray tube images) from a bio-mechanoid cluster of scrap metal (in which the Metal Fetishist seems hidden) on a tube platform as a woman reaches out to touch it and then poke it with a pencil.

It appears that the Fetishist is surviving fused with scrap metal (there are similarities to the artwork of H R Giger) and needs contact to infect and possess a victim; this operates in a very different way to the point-of-view aesthetic of The Blair Witch Project and Cloverfield, and also from the point-of-view shot of the slasher film. Here it seems totally distancing and alienating; the Metal Fetishist seems to be looking out from another world (like the woman in the radiator or the man in the planet in Eraserhead). What point-of-view shots there are tend to be of the salaryman examining his own mechanized flesh, as when he examines his cheek in the shaving mirror or pulls up his sleeve to see the metal growing in his arm – as if like Seth in The Fly he does not recognize himself but is fascinated with what he is becoming. Technology is thus depicted as dangerous and dehumanizing. The film ends with a fight between these two men mutated into giant bio-mecha creatures. The urban landscape of the film resembles nothing so much as the same industrial gothic aesthetic Lynch created in Eraserhead. This landscape is run down and largely deserted. The sense of alienation in this post-human technological landscape is indicated via the fact that characters are nameless and the main character is known by his job – a salaryman, itself symbolic of the nameless, faceless workplace drone of Japanese culture. In the final sequences these men become nothing more than machines. This sense of nihilism is prevalent throughout violent postmodern horror cinema.

VIOLENCE AND TORTURE

The history of horror is also a history of social anxieties about violence, and this can be explored not only through examples of violence in horror films, but through society's responses to those films. As a genre, horror has often been denigrated as dangerous, linked to what is perceived as the decline of moral values and subjected to media or political campaigns calling for it to be controlled or banned. Certainly, horror cinema has frequently dealt with 'difficult' topics, but this is inherently a part of its nature and one of its main purposes. Jonathan Lake Crane (1994) argues that violent horror films do not create or contribute to the creation of a more violent society but are a response to it. He states that the horror film now embraces far more violent imagery in an attempt to keep up with escalating violence in society. Crane's argument that violence dominates post-1960s horror cinema is perhaps a little premature. Although he says (1994: 2) that 'spooky films [...] with just a hint of spurious violence are gone' (an argument undermined by the resurgence in the uncanny that has come with the popularity of Asian and Mexican-Spanish horror cinema, together with its remakes and copies), it is still true that a large number of violent horror films are produced, and the violence depicted in them is increasingly extreme. He proposes that this is because we are now living in increasingly violent times and that living in a violent society or world does not (1994: 1) 'diminish our taste for blood'. This is not simply a straightforward case of 'bloodlust', however, and he argues (1994: vi) that audience responses to cinematic violence are more complex than this and therefore that horror films are more than the 'moronic efforts designed to sate sadistic and illegitimate appetites' that many critics portray them as. Rather such 'extraordinarily negative productions' (1994: 5) offer 'a vivid visual approximation of what it feels like to live in an inordinately dangerous world – a world, which, like the purposeless scenes of graphic mayhem randomly scattered through the slasher film, has also stopped making sense'.

The series of *Saw* films are a good case study in this respect. *Saw* is structured around the victims Adam and Lawrence as they attempt to work out how to escape from the factory bathroom (Figure 4.8). The enigma at the start of the film is that, as Lawrence ponders, 'they must want something from us, the question is what?' There is a sense of meaninglessness (a metaphor for the emptiness of postmodern life, perhaps) set up from the very start. Furthermore, the answer to what 'they' want would seem to be only pain and suffering. As Crane (1994: 4) points out with regard to slasher films, these films could be said to have a 'nihilistic context': 'violence in the contemporary shocker is never redemptive, revelatory, logical or climactic (it does not resolve conflicts)'. Despite the fact that Jigsaw intends his traps to be 'tests' or 'games' that will teach the victim a valuable lesson, this never seems to work. The one victim for whom it does seem to work is Amanda, but then in later films she becomes Jigsaw's apprentice and rejects his underlying principle by ensuring the victims can never escape death even if they escape the trap. The only thing the victims are expected to do is enter into the game that is being played without fully knowing the rules or the motivation of the game-master. Adam and Lawrence, like the previous

Figure 4.8 Torture is the game in *Saw*.

victims who must win the game to live, are expected to find solutions to problems or solve clues they are given by a process mainly of guesswork or trial and error, more than by logic and deduction. If they make the wrong move they are tortured – when Lawrence attempts to fool Jigsaw about giving Adam the poisoned cigarette, he is electrocuted, but to win the game they must carry out violent acts that are against their own moral and ethical codes (it is apt in this respect that Lawrence is a medical doctor charged with keeping the Hippocratic oath) or thrust them into a no-win situation – Lawrence is given until 6 o'clock to kill Adam or his wife and daughter will die.

Adam is set up in the film as a passive observer in life (a variation on the postmodern zombie, perhaps), and asked whether he is 'going to watch [him]self die today, or do something about it'. Adam's message also contains the question 'what do voyeurs see when they look into the mirror?' He is a photographer who works as a private investigator taking undercover photographs of rich men – a sleezy, amoral profession. In this, he is linked to Gordon who he has photographed going to a seedy hotel for a liaison with a medical student and also to the disgraced detective Tapp who has commissioned him. Saw thus depicts a society that is stagnant and corrupt. Tapp, when he suspects Lawrence, tells him: 'We arrested a dentist last week. He liked to play with kids a bit too much. He lived two blocks from you. The sewer lines run under this neighbourhood too, Doctor'. Society is not just crime-ridden, it is corrupt to the core. Perhaps also it is doomed. Tapp discovers that the killer's lair is on Stygian Street – a name that links it to the river Styx, the boundary between Earth and Hades in Greek myth. It is when he goes to Stygian Street (crosses the boundary) that his own world becomes a hell – Tapp has his throat cut when accosting the killer and his partner Sing is killed by a booby trap. Tapp is subsequently taken off the case and the force, his obsession with the meaningless crimes destroying his life.

In this nihilistic view of the world, Jigsaw's victims are demeaned by the degrading acts and violent self-harm which – though apt punishments in Jigsaw's terms – they are forced to endure. Adam is made to feel about in the encrusted toilet (reflecting his seedy profession), Lawrence saws through his own ankle (like a surgeon mutilating a cancer patient to save them). Of the previous victims, Paul (an unsuccessful wrist slasher) is forced to crawl naked through a cage of razor wire and bleeds to death in an attempt to survive, Mark (a malingerer) is poisoned and smeared with a flammable substance in a room lit only by a candle – he burns to death trying to open the safe which contains the antidote, Amanda – an addict – has to retrieve a key from the stomach of a paralysed cellmate in order to get out of the reverse bear trap that will rip open her head, and Zep (though the reasons for his test are unclear) is forced to become Jigsaw's proxy when he is given slow-acting poison. The postmodern condition is such that, as Crane says (1994: 8), 'it is impossible to end a horror film with any plausible orientation to the future'. We are 'inhabiting a world in which the future has vanished before everyday signs of the last things' (1994: 5) – we could consider gun crime, knife crime, AIDS, bird flu, the war on terror, and climate change, amongst others, as some of these signs, 'watching a horror film is a reality check' (1994: 8). Indeed, there is no redemption even for Adam and Lawrence at the end of *Saw*; Lawrence shoots Adam and crawls away, mutilated (and even in the sequels we never learn what happened to him, though it might be supposed he bled to death), while Adam, surviving the gunshot, is entombed in the bathroom by Jigsaw (and as we learn in the sequel, starves to death).

We might also consider that subsequent *Saw* films have significantly increased the levels of pain and torture inflicted on the victims. Again, it is useful to think about the way in which Crane links this to contemporary nihilism. In horror cinema, the monster has returned to human dimensions (1994: 9). The horror is no longer the sight of the monster's terrible body and it does not therefore have to be created with special effects. Instead (1994: 9–10), the visceral sights of horror cinema are the terrible effects the monster has on us:

> Special effects are now mobilized around human evisceration not only to terrify the audience but also to give credence to the fact that to be

human is to suffer spectacular abominations. The only *object* of terror is the body; consequently, special effects are now concentrated on flaying the flesh off the body.

Saw II does just this with its 'venus flytrap' spiked head trap and the hand trap that kills Addison, while *Saw* 3 has the classroom trap where Troy has to rip the chains from his skin, the angel trap which eviscerates Allison, and the rack trap that twists Tim to pieces, and *Saw* 4 depicts the hair trap that scalps Brenda and the bedroom trap in which Ivan's limbs are torn off. These devices for the torture and dismemberment of the body are increasingly the sole raison d'etre of the films. As J. G. Ballard (who wrote the novel *Crash*) is quoted by Crane (1994: 5) as saying, these films allow audiences to 'confront the terrifying void of a patently meaningless universe by challenging it at its own game, to remake zero by provoking it in every conceivable way'. Or, as social-psychological and audience research identifies, viewing these films can be related to sensation seeking (Zuckerman 1996) or testing one's own threshold for fictional violence (Hill 1997).

Such examples of violent horror cinema do mean that horror films generally tend to get caught up in more general criticisms of violent entertainment. There is, of course, a lot of overlap between horror cinema (not least because it is such a varied genre with shifting boundaries) and other genres that have violence as a key narrative element. These include mainstream genres such as thrillers, psychological thrillers, crime films, gangster films and melodramas, as well as other culturally denigrated forms such as the cult film, exploitation cinema (including rape-revenge films and 'snuff' movies[9]) and video nasties. In recent years, such cycles have been given various labels including 'new brutalist cinema' and 'torture porn', though essentially they retain many of the same features: namely, the foregrounding of acts of extreme violence, these violent acts perpetrated by amoral or psychologically damaged characters, and which are shown in graphic and highly gory special effects sequences. Or as film critic David Edelstein (2006) summarizes: 'blood, guts and sadism'.[10] He includes in his list such disparate titles as

Hostel, *Wolf Creek*, *Saw*, *The Devil's Rejects*, *Irréversible* and *The Passion of the Christ*. As is only to be expected, it is the more extreme versions of horror, the films that push hardest against the boundaries of 'good taste' or up the ante in terms of their effects or examples of violence, that draw the most attention. However, these films also offer similar commentaries on the postmodern condition as outlined by Crane in respect of slasher films. The so-called 'torture porn' films are a case in point.

It is films like *Ichi the Killer* and *Hostel* – for which Edelstein devised the label torture porn – which have attracted a great deal of attention in terms of their cultural legitimacy (or otherwise). Horror cinema, alongside a number of other popular cultural forms of entertainment perceived as low culture (this includes comics, alternative music genres such as rap and metal, and violent computer games), is frequently discussed in pejorative terms in the media and made the scapegoat for social decline and criminal acts of violence. As Crane states (1994: vii), 'Low culture – the entertainment of the young, minorities, the working class or the disenfranchised – is under serious fire'. Mainstream critics, he goes on to say, 'have decided we should be protected from "illicit" cultural objects.' In fact, even though he describes himself as a 'horror maven', Edelstein seems to do just that. He declares himself baffled by 'how far this new stuff goes' and seems to be bemoaning the fact that such films are now given 'a place of honour' in the multiplex, when before 'explicit scenes of torture and mutilation were … confined to the old 42nd Street, the Deuce, in gutbucket Italian cannibal pictures like *Make Them Die Slowly* [aka *Cannibal Ferox*]'. Perhaps the main point he is wishing to make here is the loss of the cult fan's favoured texts to the mainstream (reverse snobbery), but it nevertheless reinforces the cultural status (or lack of it) of these films.

It is not simply the cultural illegitimacy that makes these films the object of media outcries, however, but the linking of them with real-life violence. It is not always the most graphic films depicting extremes of violence that are blamed for real-life criminal acts either. Well-received popular hits that garner a lot of media coverage do seem to be more likely to be played up in the blame discourses of such cases. Films as disparate as *The Matrix* (implicated in the Columbine shooting and at least four other cases where it was argued that the killers believed they were living within 'the Matrix'), *The Basketball Diaries* (blamed in at least three school shootings in the USA, including Columbine again), *The Fisher King* (which is said to have inspired a copycat mass murder in a restaurant, the killer having had a ticket to the film in his pocket), *Taxi Driver* (which inspired John Hinckley Jr's attempt to assassinate Ronald Regan) and *Natural Born Killers* (the husband of a woman injured in a copycat crime spree sued Oliver Stone and Time Warner for inciting violence, though the case was eventually dismissed) have been cited as inspirations for murder. In one sense, these films are cited because they are widely available, mainstream titles that contain scenes of violence close to real life (political assassinations, college massacres, sniper incidents and other acts of mass murder, and crime sprees involving shootings).

Regardless of whether the films concerned may have influenced the perpetrators or not, this illustrates that it is not always the most extreme or exploitative films that are blamed for inciting real-life acts of violence. However, many of the instigators of moral panics, be they politicians, newspapers, clergy or activists manning the moral barricades, may focus their protests around the more extreme films for sensationalist effect. This apparent contradiction may give support to the argument that these films are being used as scapegoats to mask more deep-seated problems (which may be that the perpetrators are suffering from psychological disturbances, but may also be related to sociopolitical aspects such as unemployment, domestic violence, family breakdown, poverty, poor access to education or other social resources, and social alienation) than actually being dangerous in their own right (Buckingham 1997: 37).

The horror genre is not the only aspect of popular culture to be so scapegoated. Rap, goth and heavy metal, comic books, violent video games, Internet social networking sites, pornography, Victorian penny dreadfuls, and so forth have all been blamed at various times. Horror films – or at least certain kinds of horror films – do make easy targets for some of the campaigners, be they politicians, members of special interest or religious groups, or other sections of the media (groups that Cohen 1980 refers to as the 'moral barricade'). They attract attention through their often lurid publicity materials and the way they seek to depict more and more extreme images of horror, death and attacks upon the body. The focus of the argument in such cases is on whether or not a film can 'deprave and corrupt' or trigger viewers into acts of violence. Despite there being a wealth of research in the area of mass media effects,[11] no single definitive answer to the question of whether the media are capable of directly influencing people or not has been accepted by those on opposing sides of the argument (especially in general as opposed to academic circles).

This lack of a clear conclusion leaves horror open to concerted campaigns or moral panics by those with a vested interest. While horror films reflect and respond to the anxieties of the cultural moment in terms of their narrative themes or representations of violence (as Crane argues), they are also seen as a source of anxiety for some sections of society at large. In particular, they are an easy target for groups who wish to find a concrete example of what they see as the decline of moral values or good taste. One of the most famous instances of this in the UK was Mary Whitehouse's and *The Daily Mail*'s video nasties campaign in the early 1980s. Although this campaign (which saw then unregulated videos being seized from video hire shops and prosecutions under the Obscene Publications Act) was couched in terms of taste, it also served a political purpose for the then Tory government facing re-election. With riots taking place around the country (caused by discrimination, poverty and unemployment), the idea that video nasties were causing violence could be used to support the Tories law and order agenda. The result was the Video Recordings Act of 1984 and the BBFC being charged with certificating videos in line with film certification.

The majority of the videos banned under the act are now available on DVD. The debate, however, will not go away. In January 2008, MPs were campaigning for new powers to ban videos after the BBFC passed *SS Experiment Camp* (one of the few remaining original nasties still banned) for release on DVD.[12] The history of horror cinema in the UK is full of examples of such censorship dating back to the 1930s. At this time, these included the censorship of *Frankenstein* so that the creature is no longer shown throwing the girl into the water as if she was another flower (which had the effect of making the creature look more calculating and evil than naïve and innocent) and the banning of *Freaks* for exploiting the disabled (although this was far from true). The prosecution under obscenity laws and subsequent banning on video of over 70 titles – including *The Evil Dead*, *I Spit on Your Grave* and *Last House on the Left* – during the campaign by Mary Whitehouse to outlaw such video nasties was one of the most concerted attacks. Legitimate horror films were also caught up in the subsequent passing of the Video Recordings Act, including the decision by the BBFC to deny video certification to *The Exorcist* (even though it continued to be screened in cinemas up until its eventual release on video in 1999). Other cases include concern over voyeurism in *Henry: Portrait of a Serial Killer*, the outcry over *Child's Play 3* after the murder of James Bulger[13] during which video store owners were urged to burn their copies of the film by *The Sun*; and the banning of *Crash* from cinemas in Westminster by order of the council under the powers given to local authorities (although this meant the film could not be screened in the West End or Leicester Square, it could be seen in neighbouring boroughs such as Camden). Such campaigns have even ended up being commented on in horror films themselves. Wes Craven deliberately confronts the view that horror film viewing is dangerous in *New Nightmare*, for example, when he suggests that they in fact keep evil at bay.

Certainly, the aim of these campaigns and acts of censorship sometimes seem to have very little to do with actual responses to violent material (Barker and Petley 2001). Any account of the pleasures cinematic horror engenders in the viewer should also address the question of why some people equally strongly dislike such films and seek to avoid their 'negative' effects without necessarily denigrating the genre and blaming it for various social ills. This example from a comment piece on Eli Roth, *Hostel* and torture porn[14] illustrates that the reasons for a negative response may be just as personal as a positive one:

Make it Stop: I don't know what makes someone enjoy watching prolonged torture scenes, but it is becoming increasingly obvious that many people do. As a film critic, my own reaction is certainly extreme, but it lies in the opposite camp from enjoyment. I cannot find macabre fun in such scenes – as some critics claim to – or relax and tick off the film-maker's knowingly ironic references to a back catalogue of other horror films. Instead, I feel nauseated and intensely depressed. The sight of bloodied people begging for their lives, at length, doesn't feel like entertainment: it feels like a very grim reality. (McCartney, 1 July 2007)

An important question in this respect is why some people do take such pleasure in vicariously and safely experiencing disturbing or upsetting sequences (sometimes quite extreme and graphic ones), while others experience such displeasure that they avoid or shy away from the genre generally or certain kinds of horror films in particular.

Here, the writer seems genuinely disgusted – rather than art-horrified – by scenes of violence and torture. As Zillman and Weaver (1996) note in their account of horror film viewing as gender socialization, the ability to cope with depictions of horror in fictional films and entertainment is something that can be acquired with repeated viewing. This is not to suggest, however, that such viewers are desensitized in any general sense, but that mastery of fictional scenes of horror can be 'learnt'. Individual viewers are also likely to have personal boundaries as to what they can or will watch, or self-censoring for their own comfort (Hill 1997: 51). It is not perhaps as easy as saying people divide straight-forwardly into those who embrace and those who reject horror. More-over, in discussing torture porn, McCartney reveals her own very personal negative responses to a form of cinematic horror involving extremes of violence. Her rejection of such material relates to her background and experiences in her own life that mean that it has very uncomfortable associations for her (in this case living and growing up in Northern Ireland during the Troubles).

Press coverage such as this often serves to make horror appear negative, disreputable or even dangerous, and is thus part of a wider debate on the mass media effects of horror and related genres. On another level, however, there are several important considerations to be made that can again contribute to a broader understanding of the forms and functions of the genre. As illustrated by McCartney's comments, readings of horror can vary widely and we can consider many examples of horror cinema to be polysemic texts open to different interpretations and responses by different demographic or psychographic groups at different times. Clearly, the identity and background of the viewer is a major consideration here, but beyond this there are also the coded reflections of social anxieties which contribute to the themes and narrative subtexts of horror films made in particular national and historical moments. These socio-cultural and ideological sets of meanings can be used as a means of explaining why certain kinds of horror are produced at specific times and places and thus explain developments in national horror cinemas and the evolutionary changes that take place within the genre.

A FINAL WORD

Horror as we have seen can elicit a range of responses in the viewer, these responses being created through cinematic and aesthetic cues that trigger or tap into psychological states or cognitive processes. Beyond these desired responses or emotional effects, however, horror films speak to their audiences in many ways. It is often the ideological imperative of the narrative of a film that gives it meaning in a historical or cultural context: the point of analysis here is to ask what the film has to say about the world it reflects. This is important because over and above meeting the basic desire in the viewer to be scared, the horror genre seems to be a form that is easily adaptable at addressing a range of ideological issues. Horror films invariably reflect the social and political anxieties of the cultural moment.

Overall, this account has looked at the way horror cinema 'works'. At the way horror films create images of gore and the uncanny, the way these cinematic and stylistic devices create responses of terror and disgust in the viewer, the way they speak to audiences on an intimate personal level, addressing their innermost fears and desires. It has also looked at the role of horror cinema in society and culture. At how horror films engage with social anxieties and are in turn regarded by society, at how it represents various identity groups. It has explored how we might better understand the audience and their psychological and cognitive responses. Along the way, this account has considered a range of theories and a wide selection of films. By necessity these could only summarize the theoretical accounts and touch on the vast number of horror films in the current and back catalogues. Any interested reader should regard this as a steppingstone to deeper exploration of the 'black lagoon' of horror cinema. The bibliography suggests further reading and one can do no better than to begin with Paul Wells's *The Horror Genre* (2002) for an overview of the genre's history and themes, and the collection of extracts from the key theoretical approaches in *Horror: The Film Reader* edited by Mark Jancovich (2002). The filmography, meanwhile, can be used to suggest further viewing, perhaps by sub-genre, director, or national cinema as a starting point. Just keep repeating – it isn't only a movie …

FILMOGRAPHY

13 Ghosts (William Castle, 1960, USA)

28 Days Later (Danny Boyle, 2002, UK)

Alien (Ridley Scott, 1979, UK/USA)

American Psycho (Mary Harron, 2000, USA/Canada)

An American Werewolf in London (John Landis, 1981, UK)

The Amityville Horror (Stuart Rosenberg, 1979, USA)

Anthropophagus (Joe D'Amato, 1980, Italy)

Audition (aka Ôdishon, Takashi Miike, 1999, South Korea/Japan)

The Birds (Alfred Hitchcock, 1963, USA)

Black Christmas (Bob Clarke, 1974, Canada)

Black Sabbath (aka I Tre Volti Della Paura, Mario Bava, 1963, Italy/
    France/USA)

Blackmail (Alfred Hitchcock, 1929, UK)

Blade (Stephen Norrington, 1998, USA)

Blade Runner (Ridley Scott, 1982, USA/Singapore)

The Blair Witch Project (Daniel Myrick and Eduardo S{aacute]nchez,
    1999, USA)

Blood Feast (Herschell Gordon Lewis, 1963, USA)

Bloody Smile (aka Mangryongui Kok, Yoon Kyo Park, 1980, South Korea)

Body Snatchers (Abel Ferrara, 1993, USA)

Bram Stoker's Dracula (Francis Ford Coppola, 1992, USA)

The Bride of Frankenstein (James Whale, 1935, USA)

The Brood (David Cronenberg, 1979, Canada)

A Bucket of Blood (Roger Corman, 1959, USA)

Cabin Fever (Eli Roth, 2002, USA)

The Cabinet of Dr Caligari (aka Das Cabinet des Dr Caligari, Robert Wiene, 1919, Germany)

Candyman (Bernard Rose, 1992, USA)

Cannibal Ferox (Umberto Lenzi, 1981, Italy)

Cannibal Holocaust (Ruggero Deodata, 1980, Italy)

Carrie (Brian de Palma, 1976, USA)

Cat People (Jacques Tourneur, 1942, USA)

Cherry Falls (Geoffrey Wright, 2000, USA)

Child's Play 3 (Jack Bender, 1991, UK/USA)

City of the Living Dead (aka Paura nella Cittá dei Morti Viventi, Lucio Fulci, 1980, Italy)

Cloverfield (Matt Reeves, 2008, USA)

The Creature from the Black Lagoon (Jack Arnold, 1954, USA)

Cronos (Guillermo del Toro, 1993, Mexico)

The Crow (Alex Proyas, 1994, USA)

The Curse of Frankenstein (Terence Fisher,1957, UK)

Dark Water (aka Honogurai Mizu no Soko Kara, Hideo Nakata, 2002, Japan)

Daughters of Darkness (aka Les Lèvres Rouge, Harry Kumel, 1971, Belgium/France/Germany)

Dawn of the Dead (George A. Romero, 1978, Italy/USA)

Dawn of the Dead (Zack Snyder, 2004, USA)

Day of the Dead (George A. Romero, 1985, USA)

Dead Ringers (David Cronenberg, 1988, Canada/USA)

Dead Silence (James Wan, 2007, USA)

Deliverance (John Boorman, 1972, USA)

Demon Pond (aka Yashagaike, Masahiro Shinoda, 1979, Japan)

The Descent (Neil Marshall, 2005, UK)

Destiny (aka Der Müde Tod, Fritz Lang, 1921, Germany)

A Deusa de Mármore (Rosângela Maldonado, 1978, Brazil)

The Devil's Mansion (aka Le Manoir du Diable, Georges Méliès, 1896, France)

The Devil's Rejects (Rob Zombie, 2005, USA/Germany)

Diary of the Dead (George A. Romero, 2007, USA)

Doctor X (Michael Curtiz, 1932, USA)

Don't Look Now (Nicolas Roeg, 1973, Italy/UK)

Dr Jekyll and Mr Hyde (Rouben Mamoulian, 1931, USA)

Dracula (Tod Browning, 1931, USA)

Dracula (Terence Fisher, 1958, UK)

Dracula (John Badham, 1979, USA/UK)

Dracula's Daughter (Lambert Hillyer, 1936, USA)

Edward Scissorhands (Tim Burton, 1990, USA)

Eraserhead (David Lynch, 1977, USA)

The Evil Dead (Sam Raimi, 1981, USA)

The Exorcist (William Friedkin, 1973, USA)

The Eye (aka Gin Gwai, Oxide Pang Chun and Danny Pang, 2002, Hong Kong/UK/Singapore)

Eyes Without a Face (aka Les Yeux Sans Visage, Georges Franju, France/Italy)

The Faculty (Robert Rodriguez, 1998, USA)

As Filhas do Fogo (Walter Hugo Khouri, 1978, Brazil)

Final Destination (James Wong, 2000, USA)

The Fly (David Cronenberg, 1986, Canada/UK/USA)

Forbidden Planet (Fred M. Wilcox, 1956, USA)

Freaks (Tod Browning, 1932, USA)

Frankenstein (James Whale, 1931, USA)

Friday the 13th (Sean S. Cunningham, 1980, USA)

From Dusk Till Dawn (Robert Rodriguez, 1996, USA)

The Fury (Brian de Palma, 1978, USA)

Ginger Snaps (John Fawcett, 2000, Canada/USA)

Godzilla (aka Gojira, Ishirô Honda, 1954, Japan)

The Golem (aka Der Golem, Carl Boese and Paul Wegener, 1920, Germany)

Gorilla at Large (Harmon Jones, 1954, USA)

Ju-on: The Grudge (Takashi Shimizu, 2003, Japan)

Halloween (John Carpenter, 1978, USA)

Happy Birthday to Me (J. Lee Thompson, 1981, Canada)

The Haunting (Robert Wise, 1963, UK)

Hellbent (Paul Etheredge-Ouzts, 2004, USA)

Hellraiser (Clive Barker, 1987, UK)

Henry: Portrait of a Serial Killer (John McNaughton, 1986, USA)

The Host (aka Gwoemul, Joo-ho Bong, 2006, South Korea)

Hostel (Eli Roth, 2005, USA)

House of the Lute (Yuhuo Fen Qin, Shin Hon Lau, 1979, Hong Kong)

House of Wax (André de Toth, 1953, USA)

The House on Haunted Hill (William Castle, 1959, USA)

The Howling (Joe Dante, 1981, USA)

The Hunger (Tony Scott, 1983, UK)

I Know What You Did Last Summer (Jim Gillespie, 1997, USA)

I Spit on Your Grave (aka Day of the Woman, Meir Zarchi, 1978, USA)

I Walked with a Zombie (Jacques Tourneur, 1943, USA)

I Was a Teenage Werewolf (Gene Fowler Jr, 1957, USA)

Ichi the Killer (aka Koroshiya 1, Takashi Miike, Japan/Hong Kong/South
Korea)

The Incredible Shrinking Man (Jack Arnold, 1957, USA)

The Innocents (Jack Clayton, 1961, UK)

Interview with the Vampire (Neil Jordan, 1994, USA)

Into the Mirror (aka Geoul Sokeuro, Sung-ho Kim, 2003, South Korea)

The Invasion (Oliver Hirschbiegel, 2007, USA/Australia)

Invasion of the Body Snatchers (Don Siegel, 1956, USA)

Invasion of the Body Snatchers (Philip Kaufman, 1978, USA)

Irréversible (Gasper Noé, 2002, France)

Jaws (Steven Spielberg, 1975, USA)

Killer Cure (Stephen Carolan, 2005, UK)

King Kong (Merion C. Cooper and Ernest B. Schoedsack, 1933, USA)

Kwaidan (Masaki Kobayashi, 1964, Japan)

The Last House on the Left (Wes Craven, 1972, USA)

Lifeforce (Tobe Hooper, 1985, UK)

Macabro (Lamberto Bava, 1980, Italy)

The Mad Magician (John Brahm, 1954, USA)

Maléfique (Eric Valette, 2002, France)

Man Bites Dog (aka C'est Arrivé Près de Chez Vous, Rémy Belvaux and André Bonzel, 1992, Belgium)

Martin (George A. Romero, 1977, USA)

Mary Shelley's Frankenstein (Kenneth Branagh, 1994, UK/Japan/USA)

The Masque of the Red Death (Roger Corman, 1964, UK)

The Mummy (Karl Freund, 1932, USA)

The Mummy (Terence Fisher, 1959, UK)

The Mummy (Stephen Sommers, 1999, USA)

My Bloody Valentine (George Mihalka, 1981, Canada)

Mystery of the Wax Museum (Michael Curtiz, 1933, USA)

Nadja (Michael Almereyda, 1994, USA)

Near Dark (Kathryn Bigelow, 1987, USA)

New Nightmare (Wes Craven, 1994, USA)

Night of the Demon (Jacques Tourneur, 1957, UK)

Night of the Living Dead (George A. Romero, 1968, USA)

Nightbreed (Clive Barker, 1990, USA)

The Nightmare Before Christmas (Henry Selick, 1993, USA)

A Nightmare on Elm Street (Wes Craven, 1984, USA)

Night Watch (aka Nochnoy Dozor, Timur Bekmambetov, 2004, Russia)

Nosferatu (aka Nosferatu, eine Symphonie des Grauens, 1921)

The Omen (Richard Donner, 1976, USA)

One Missed Call (aka Chakushin Ari, Takashi Miike, 2004, Japan)

The Terrible Secret of Dr Hichcock (aka L'Orribile Segreto del Dr. Hichcock, Riccardo Freda, 1962, Italy)

The Others (Alejandro Amenábar, 2001, USA/Spain/France/Italy)

Onibaba (Kaneto Shindô, 1964, Japan)

Peeping Tom (Michael Powell, 1960, UK)

The People Under the Stairs (Wes Craven, 1991, USA)

Pi (Darren Aronofsky, 1998, USA)

The Picture of Dorian Gray (Albert Lewin, 1945, USA)

The Phantom of the Opera (Robert Julian, 1925, USA)

Phantom of the Rue Morgue (Roy Del Ruth, 1954, USA)

Poltergeist (Tobe Hooper, 1982, USA)

Prom Night (Paul Lynch, 1980, Canada)

Psycho (Alfred Hitchcock, 1960, USA)

Rabid (David Cronenberg, 1977, Canada)

[•REC] (Jaume Balagueró and Paca Plaza, 2007, Spain)

Repulsion (Roman Polanski, 1965, UK)

Resident Evil (Paul W. S. Anderson, 2002, UK/Germany/France)

Ringu (Hideo Nakata, 1998, Japan)

The Rocky Horror Picture Show (Jim Sharman, 1975, UK/USA)

Rosemary's Baby (Roman Polanski, 1968, USA)

Saw (James Wan, 2004, USA)

Saw II (Darren Lynn Bousman, 2005, USA)

Saw III (Darren Lynn Bousman, 2006, USA)

Saw IV (Darren Lynn Bousman, 2007, USA)

Scanners (David Cronenberg, 1981, Canada)

Scream (Wes Craven, 1996, USA)

Scream 2 (Wes Craven, 1997, USA)

Se7en (David Fincher, 1995, USA)

Shaun of the Dead (Edgar Wright, 2004, UK)

The Shining (Stanley Kubrick, 1980, UK/USA)

Shivers (David Cronenberg, 1975, Canada)

The Silence of the Lambs (Jonathan Demme, 1991, USA)

Silent Night, Deadly Night (Charles E. Sellier Jr, 1984, USA)

The Sixth Sense (M. Night Shyamalan, 1999, USA)

Sleepaway Camp (Robert Hiltzik, 1983, USA)

Slumber Party Massacre (Amy Jones, 1982, USA)

SS Experiment Camp (Sergio Garrone, 1976, Italy)

The Stepfather (Joseph Ruben, 1987, USA)

Suspiria (Dario Argento, 1977, Italy)

Tetsuo (Shinya Tsukamoto, 1988, Japan)

The Texas Chain Saw Massacre (Tobe Hooper, 1974, USA)

The Texas Chainsaw Massacre 2 (Tobe Hooper, 1986, USA)

The Thing (John Carpenter, 1982, USA)

The Thing (from Another World) (Christian Nyby, 1951, USA)

The Tingler (William Castle, 1959, USA)

Two Thousand Maniacs! (Herschell Gordon Lewis, 1964, USA)

Ugetsu Mongatari (Kenji Mizoguchi, 1953, Japan)

Underworld (Len Wiseman, 2003, USA/Germany/Hungary/UK)

Vampire Hunter D (Yoshiaki Kawajiri and Jack Fletcher, 2000, Japan/ Hong Kong/USA)

Videodrome (David Cronenberg, 1983, Canada)

A Virgem da Colina (Celso Falcão, 1977, Brazil)

Whatever Happened to Baby Jane? (Robert Aldrich, 1962, USA)

When a Stranger Calls (Fred Walton, 1979, USA)

The Wicker Man (Robin Hardy, 1973, UK)

Witchfinder General (Micheal Reeves, 1968, UK)

Wolf (Mike Nichols, 1994, USA)

Wolf Creek (Greg McLean, 2005, Australia)

NOTES

1 The horror genre: form and function

1 In case these need identifying, they are *Dawn of the Dead*, *The Blair Witch Project*, *Halloween*, *Alien*, *Dracula*, *The Fly*, *Ringu*, *Saw*, *Interview with the Vampire*, *Cloverfield* and *I Spit on Your Grave* (though since some of these are relatively 'generic' there might well be other films which contain the same or similar scenes).

2 Including novels, folklore, real life atrocities, Grand Guignol theatre, pre-cinema phantasmagoria shows, and so on.

3 The name given to this group of films means 'yellow' and derives from the cover colour of the pulp novels on which the film genre is based.

4 As Cronenberg notes in an interview with Scott Thill in *Wired* (December 2007: 15) he did not invent the term and does not consider his films in this way himself.

5 All figures supplied by www.boxofficemojo.com, www.boxofficeguru.com, www.the-numbers.com, and www.imdb.com.

6 Joyce Woolridge, *Bram Stoker's Dracula* review, *Fortean Times*, no. 85, 1992, p. 47.

7 See online at: < http://www.channel4.com/film/newsfeatures/microsites/S/scary/index.html > (accessed 12 January 2007).

8 Gene Siskel, 'Looker turns ugly after half-hour', *Chicago Tribune*, October 30 1981, p. C2.

9 The term 'video nasty' was applied pejoratively to the flood of cheap, exploitation films released on video when the market was still unregulated. In the 1980s, the National Viewers and Listeners Association under the leadership of the campaigner Mary Whitehouse, and *The Daily Mail* instigated a moral panic over these videos (discussed in more depth in the final chapter), but the term has subsequently been applied to exploitation or graphic horror films in general.

10 Michael Saunier (2007) *Slumber Party Massacre* Does Not Waste Valuable Time, best-horror-movies.com. Available online at: < http://www.best-horror-movies.com/slumber-party-massacre.html > (accessed 16 January 2008).

11 Justin Kerswell (undated) *Slumber Party Massacre* review, Hysteria Lives. Available online at: < http://www.hysteria-lives.co.uk/hysterialives/Hysteria/slumber_party_massacre.html > (accessed 16 January 2008).

12 This should not necessarily be confused with desensitization (which is often used in arguments about the effects of viewing horror). Learning to deal with one's negative emotions is not the same as a lowering of one's tolerance for real-life violence or inhibitions to commit acts of violence.

13 These observations are non-empirical descriptions of the original slasher film audience. Zillman and Weaver's study (1996) may suggest that there are more women in the audience than this implies (as does my own research). This illustrates that the assumption of a male audience for horror during the slasher cycle was widespread, and although this may have changed somewhat in recent years it still persists.

14 Anon (2007) 'Freddie Kruger' attacker jailed, BBC News, 4/4/2007. Available online at: < http://news.bbc.co.uk/1/hi/england/leicestershire/6526129.stm > (accessed 22 October 2007).

15 Andrew Hindes (1997) 'Scream 2 Showcases Demographic Power', *Variety* 16 December 1997.

16 David Skal (1990) describes the sacks of fan letters that Lugosi received from his adoring female fans.

2 Horror aesthetics and affect

1 Claudia Puig (2003) *28 Days Later* review, USA TODAY, 26 June 2003. Available online at: < http://www.usatoday.com/life/movies/reviews/2003-06-26-later_x.htm > (accessed 3 March 2008).

2 Wesley Morris (1999) *The Blair Witch Project* review, *The San Francisco Chronicle*, 16 July 1999. Available online at: < http://www.sfgate.com/cgi-bin/article.cgi?f = /e/a/1999/07/16/WEEKEND2729.dtl > (accessed 6 March 2008).

3 Simon Crook (2006) *Hostel* review, Empire, March 2006. Available online at: < http://www.empireonline.com/reviews/reviewcomplete.asp?FID = 132329 > (accessed 16 December 2007).

4 Anon (2006) BBC News report, 31 October 2006. Available online at: < http://news.bbc.co.uk/1/hi/entertainment/6101704.stm > (accessed 3 March 2008).

5 This recalls the publicity stunts used in the 1930s to 1950s that Berenstein (1996) describes.

6 The Overlook Film Encyclopaedia volume on Horror (1995) lists *The Devil's Manor* as the first ever horror film. Although the film is not currently available, unrestored footage can be seen in a documentary extra available on StudioCanal's 2008 boxset of Méliès films.

7 Reproduced on The Missing Link website. Available online at: < http://www.mshepley.btinternet.co.uk/melies.htm > (accessed 10 March 2008).

8 This camera angle was used in Expressionist films like *The Cabinet of Dr Caligari* and given the name Deutsch angle in recognition of its use in German cinema, but the name became corrupted to Dutch in the English-speaking world.

9 *The Birds* itself is an interesting use of sound to create horror with its electronic 'musical' score of screeching bird sounds.

10 These may not be novel or innovative necessarily, but digital technologies have opened up and made easier certain techniques (just as they have with filming and editing).

11 Quoted on the *Dead Silence* official website. Available online at: < http://deadsilencemovie.net/ > (accessed 12 June 2008).

12 The film is also sexually provocative, showing Frankenstein's liaison with his housemaid while planning to enter into an arranged marriage with his cousin. When he learns she is pregnant, he engineers it so that the creature will kill her. In Hammer and Beyond, Hutchings (1993a) discusses the gender and class representations in the film.

13 Available online at: < http://www.fangoria.com/ > (accessed 22 July 2008).

14 Available online at: < http://www.visimag.com/shivers/index.htm > (accessed 22 July 2008).

15 Quote taken from an interview conducted with Clive Barker by Brian J. Robb, Brigid Cherry and Paul Cockburn, and reproduced in Cherry (2005).

16 Roger Ebert (1974) *The Texas Chain Saw Massacre* review, Chicago Sun Times, 1 January 1974. Available online at: < http://rogerebert.suntimes.com/apps/pbcs.dll/article?AID = /19740101/REVIEWS/401010319/1023 > (accessed 12 November 2007).

17 Which they do in *Hellraiser*, as I argue elsewhere (Cherry 2005).

3 Horror cinema and its pleasures

1 The id is the part of the personality that exists within the unconscious and is that part which according to Freud's pleasure principle demands that all needs and desires are met without thought of others or of the reality of the situation. It exists in counterbalance with the ego, that part of the personality that exists within the conscious and is based on the reality principle so that it allows us to meet the needs of the id while considering how this will impact upon reality, and the superego that is our moral and ethical conscience.

2 In an interview for *Val Lewton: The Man in the Shadows*, released 2008, Chapter 3.

3 This story, familiar to many as the ballet *Coppelia* or from the opera *The Tales of Hoffman*, centres around a young man who falls in love from afar with an inventor's 'daughter' who is in fact a life-size dancing doll.

4 Capitalism is included here since there is an economic dimension in that Western society is based on labour, and labour must be distanced from child-rearing, which has resulted in the patriarchal ideal of the two-parent

family where the man works and the woman takes care of the home and family.

5 heckler-2 1999 'Holy poop', IMDb message boards. Online posting. Available online at: < http://us.imdb.com/title/tt0078935/usercomments?start = 250 > (accessed 16 April 1999).

6 Will Laughlin (date unknown) A Brief Nasty Overview. Available online at: < http://www.braineater.com/nasties.html > (accessed 13 January 2007).

7 The cinematic gaze is made up of the look of the camera during the production of the film, the look of the spectator in the cinema when it is screened, and the looks by and between characters within the diegetic world of the film itself.

4 Horror and the cultural moment

1 Based on Sheridan LeFanu's novel *Carmilla* (1872).

2 *Killer Cure* can be viewed on YouTube.

3 This can be found at www.blairwitch.com

4 Given that *The Blair Witch Project* is so centred on technology, it seems ironic that Heather, Josh and Mike are not allowed GPS or mobile phones (since this would presumably invalidate the plot).

5 Bruce Newman (2008) '*Cloverfield* mantra: If it's scary, get it on video' in *Oakland Tribune*. Available online at: < http://findarticles.com/p/articles/mi_qn4176/is_20080118/ai_n21209268 > (accessed 18 January 2008).

6 The film gives a nod to the traditional monster movie with footage from *Them!*, *The Beast from 20,000 Fathoms*, and *King Kong*.

7 In an interesting piece of self-reflexivity that demonstrates just how effective the horror is in attracting an audience one of the trailers for [●REC] uses night-vision footage of the audience responding to the film (this can be viewed on YouTube).

8 Japanese ghost films date back to the 1960s with *Onibaba*, *Ugetsu Mongatari* and *Kwaidan*.

9 Although it has never been established that an actual snuff movie in which actors were actually killed during the making of a film exists, the term has

come to be more generally applied to actuality films such as the *Faces of Death* series.

10 David Edelstein (2006) 'Now playing at your local multiplex: torture porn', in *New York Magazine*. Available online at: < http://nymag.com/movies/features/15622/ > (accessed 28 January 2006).

11 See *Ill Effects* (Barker and Petley 1997/2001) for example.

12 Marie Woolf (2008) 'MPs press for ban on SS camp video nasty', in *The Sunday Times*. Available online at: < http://entertainment.timesonline.co.uk/tol/arts_and_entertainment/film/article3257530.ece > (accessed 27 January 2008).

13 The judge in the case suggested that the killers had been influenced by the film even though there was no evidence to suggest they had ever watched it.

14 Jenny McCartney (2007) 'Make it stop', in *The Daily Telegraph*. Available online at: < http://www.telegraph.co.uk/arts/main.jhtml?xml = /arts/2007/07/01/svtorture101.xml > (accessed 1 July 2007).

BIBLIOGRAPHY

Abbott, S. (2004) 'Spectral Vampires: *Nosferatu* in the Light of New Technology', in S. Hantke (ed.) *Horror Film: Creating and Marketing Fear*, Jackson, MI: University Press of Mississippi.

Allinson, A. (2002) 'Keeping his Body of Work in Mind: A Chronology of David Cronenberg's Success as Canadian Auteur and Industry Pillar', *Senses of Cinema*. Available online at: http://www.sensesofcinema.com/contents/directors/02/cronenberg.html (accessed 22 October 2007).

Altman, R. (1999) Film/Genre, London: BFI.

Auerbach, N. (1995) *Our Vampires, Ourselves*, Chicago, IL: University of Chicago Press.

Baird, R. (1997) 'Startle and the film threat scene', *Images: A Journal of Film and Popular Culture*, 3. Available online at: http://www.imagesjournal.com/issue03/features/startle1.htm (accessed 14 September 2002).

Barker, M. and Petley, J. (eds) (2001) *Ill Effects: The Media/Violence Debate*, London: Routledge.

Barthes, R. (1966) *Image-Music-Text*, Waukegan, IL: Fontana.

Benshoff H. (1997) *Monsters in the Closet: Homosexuality and the Horror Film*, Manchester: Manchester University Press.

Berenstein, R. (1996) *Attack of the Leading Ladies: Gender, Sexuality, and Spectatorship in Classic Horror Cinema*, New York, NY: Columbia University Press.

Bordwell, D. (1989) *Making Meaning: Inference and Rhetoric in the Interpretation of Cinema*, Cambridge, MA: Harvard University Press.

——(2001) 'Aesthetics in Action: Kungfu, Gunplay and Cinematic Expressivity', in E. C-M. Yau (ed.) *At Full Speed: Hong Kong Cinema in a Borderless World*, Minneapolis, MN: University of Minnesota Press.

Bordwell, D. and Thompson, K. (2008) *Film Art: An Introduction*, Maidenhead: McGraw-Hill.

Brownlow, K. (1992) *The Parade's Gone By ...* , Berkeley, CA: University of California Press.

Buckingham, D. (1997) 'Electronic Child Abuse? Rethinking the Media's Effects on Children' in M. Barker and J. Petley (eds) *Ill Effects: The Media/Violence Debate*, London: Routledge.

Buscombe, E. (1970) 'The Idea of Genre in the American Cinema', *Screen*, 11.2: 33–45.

Cantor, J. and Oliver, M. B. (1996) 'Developmental Differences in Responses to Horror', in J. B. Weaver and R. Tambourini (eds) *Horror Films: Current Research on Audience Preferences and Reactions*, Philadelphia, PA: Lawrence Erlbaum.

Carroll, N. (1990) *The Philosophy of Horror, or Paradoxes of the Heart*. London: Routledge.

Charney, M. J. (1997) 'Beauty in the Beast: Technological Reanimation in the Contemporary Horror Film', in M. A. Morrison (ed.) *Trajectories of the Fantastic*, Westport CT: Greenwood.

Cherry, B. (1999) 'Refusing to Refuse to Look: Female Viewers of the Horror Film', in R. Maltby and M. Stokes (eds) *Identifying Hollywood Audiences*, London: BFI.

——(2005) 'Broken Homes, Tortured Flesh: *Hellraiser* and the Feminine Aesthetic of Horror Cinema', *Film International*, 17: 10–21.

——(2008) 'Subcultural Taste, Genre Boundaries and Fan Canons', in L. Geraghty and M. Jancovich (eds) *The Shifting Boundaries of Genre: Essays on Labeling Films, Television Shows and Media*, Jefferson NC: McFarland.

Church, D. (2006) 'Fantastic Films, Fantastic Bodies: Speculations on the Fantastic and Disability Representation', *Offscreen*, 10.10. Available online at: http://www.offscreen.com/biblio/phile/essays/fantastic_films_fantastic_bodies/ (accessed 14 March 2007).

Clover, C. (1992) *Men Women and Chainsaws*, London: BFI.

Cohen, S. (1980) *Folk Devils and Moral Panics: The Creation of the Mods and Rockers*, Oxford: Martin Robertson.

Cook, D. A. (2004) *A History of Narrative Film*, New York, NY: W. W. Norton.

Cook, P. (2007) *The Cinema Book*, London: BFI.

Crane, J. L. (1994) *Terror and Everyday Life: Singular Moments in the History of the Horror Film*, Thousand Oaks, CA: Sage.

Creed, B. (1993) *The Monstrous-Feminine: Film, Feminism, Psychoanalysis*, London: Routledge.

——(2000) 'The Naked Crunch: Cronenberg's Homoerotic Bodies', in M. Grant (ed.) *The Modern Fantastic: The Films of David Cronenberg*, Westport, CT: Praeger.

Cronenberg, D. (1984) 'Appendix: Festival of Festivals', 1983 Science Fiction Retrospective', in W. Drew (ed.) *David Cronenberg: Dossier 21*, London: BFI.

Dadoun, R. (1989) 'Fetishism in the Horror Film', in J. Donald (ed.) *Fantasy and the Cinema*, London: BFI.

Davidson, P. and Allen, L. (1997) *The Bisexual Imaginary: Representation, Identity and Desire*, London: Continuum.

Derry, C. (1987) 'More Dark Dreams: Some Notes on the Recent Horror Film', in G. A. Waller (ed.) *American Horrors: Essays on the Modern Horror Film*, Chicago, IL: University of Illinois Press.

Dickstein, M. (1980) 'The Aesthetics of Fright' in B. K. Grant (ed.) *Planks of Reason*, Metuchen, NJ: Scarecrow Press.

Diffrient, D. S. (2004) 'A Film is Being Beaten: Notes on the Shock Cut and the Material Violence of Horror', in S. Hantke (ed.) *Horror Film: Creating and Marketing Fear*, Jackson, MI: University Press of Mississippi.

Dika, V. (1990) *Games of Terror: Halloween, Friday the 13th and the films of the Stalker Cycle*, Toronto: Fairleigh Dickinson University Press.

Doane, M. A. (1987) *The Desire to Desire: The Woman's Film of the 1940s*, Bloomington, IN: Indiana University Press.

Ebert, R. (1981) 'Why Movie Audiences Aren't Safe Any More', *American Film*, March: 54–56.

Eisner, L. (2008) *The Haunted Screen: Expressionism in the German Cinema and the Influence of Max Reinhardt*, Berkeley, CA: University of California Press.

Evans, W. (1984) 'Monster Movies: A Sexual Theory', in B. K. Grant (ed.) *Planks of Reason*, Metuchen, NJ: Scarecrow Press.

Eyman, S. (1997) *The Speed of Sound: Hollywood and the Talkie Revolution, 1926–1930*, Baltimore, MD: John Hopkins University Press.

Ezra, E. (2000) *Georges Méliès: The Birth of the Auteur*, Manchester: Manchester University Press.

Feuer, J. (1992) 'Genre Study and Television', in R. Allen (ed.) *Channels of Discourse, Reassembled: Television and Contemporary Criticism*, Chapel Hill, NC: University of North Carolina Press.

Frayling, C. (1991) *Vampyres*, London: Faber and Faber.

Freeland, C. A. (2000) *The Naked and the Undead: Evil and the Appeal of Horror*, Oxford: Westview Press.

——(2004) 'Horror and art-dread', in S. Prince (ed.) *The Horror Film*, Piscataway, NJ: Rutgers University Press.

Freud, S. (2003) [1919] *The Uncanny*, London: Penguin (trans David McLintock).

Fowler, A. (1989) 'Genre', in E. Barnouw (ed.) *International Encyclopedia of Communications, Vol. 2*, Oxford: Oxford University Press.

Gauntlett, D. (2002) *Media, Gender and Identity*, London: Routledge.

——(2007) *Creative Explorations: New Approaches to Identities and Audiences*, London: Routledge.

Gledhill, C. (2007) 'Genre', in P. Cook (ed.) *The Cinema Book*, London: BFI.

Grant, B. K. (1986) 'Experience and Meaning in Genre Films', in B. K. Grant (ed.) *Film Genre Reader*, Austin, TX: University of Texas Press.

Groves, T. (2006) 'Entranced: Affective Mimesis and Cinematic Identification', *Screening the Past: An International Electronic Journal of Visual Media and History*, 20. Available online at: http://www.latrobe.edu.au/screeningthepast/20/entranced.html (accessed 30 August 2007).

Halberstam, J. (1995) *Skin Shows: Gothic Horror and the Technology of Monsters*, Durham, NC: Duke University Press.

Hardy, P. (1995) *The Overlook Film Encyclopedia: Horror*, New York, NY: Overlook.

Harper, S. (2005) 'Reappraising an Undead Classic', *Bright Lights Film Journal*, 50. Available online at: http://www.brightlightsfilm.com/50/night.htm (accessed 14 December 2007).

Hawkins, J. (2002) 'Revisiting the Philosophy of Horror', *Film-Philosophy*, 6.6. Available online at: http://www.film-philosophy.com/vol6–2002/n6hawkins.html (accessed 23 April 2008).

Heffernan, K. (2004) *Ghouls, Gimmicks and Gold: Horror Films and the American Movie Business, 1953–1968*, Durham, NC: Duke University Press.

Highley, S. L. and Weinstock, J. A. (eds) (2004) *Nothing That is: Millennial Cinema and the Blair Witch Controversies*, Detroit, MI: Wayne State University Press.

Hill, A. (1997) *Shocking Entertainment: Viewer Response to Violent Movies*, Luton: University of Luton Press.

Hill, J. (1998) 'Film and Postmodernism', in J. Hill and P. Church-Gibson (eds) *The Oxford Guide to Film Studies*, Oxford: Oxford University Press.

Hills, M. (2003) 'An Event-Based Theory of Art-Horror', in S. J. Schneider and D. Shaw (eds) *Dark Thoughts: Philosophical Reflections in Cinematic Horror*, Metcheun, NJ: Scarecrow Press.

——(2004) *The Pleasures of Horror*, London: Continuum.

Hutchings, P. (1993a) *Hammer and Beyond: The British Horror Film*, Manchester: Manchester University Press.

——(1993b) 'Masculinity and the Horror Film', in P. Kirkham and J. Thumim (eds) *You Tarzan: Masculinity, Movies and Men*, New York, NY: St Martin's Press.

——(2000) '*The Masque of the Red Death*', in *The International Dictionary of Films and Filmmakers*, Farmington Hills, MI: St James Press. Available online at: http://findarticles.com/p/articles/migx5212/is2000/ain19127374 (accessed 12 November 2003).

——(2003) *Dracula*, London: I. B. Tauris.

——(2004) *The Horror Film*, Harlow: Pearson.

Jancovich, M. (1992) *Horror*, London: Batsford.

——(1996) *Rational Fears: American Horror in the 1950s*, Manchester: Manchester University Press.

——(2002a) 'Introduction', in *Horror The Film Reader*, London: Routledge.

——(2002b) 'Genre and the Audience: Genre Classifications and Cultural Distinctions in the Mediation of *The Silence of the Lambs*', in M. Jancovich (ed.) *Horror The Film Reader*, London: Routledge.

——(2002c) 'A Real Shocker: Authenticity, Genre and the Struggle for Distinction', in G. Turner (ed.) *The Film Cultures Reader*, London: Routledge.

Jenkins, H. (2007) *The Wow Climax: Tracing the Emotional Impact of Popular Culture*, New York, NY: New York University Press.

Johnson, T. (1997) *Censored Screams*, Jefferson, NC: McFarland.

Jones, C. and Jolliffe, G. (2006) *The Guerilla Filmmaker's Handbook*, London: Continuum.

Kermode, M. (1998) *BFI Modern Classics: The Exorcist*, London: BFI.

Kitses, J. (2004) *Horizons West*, London: BFI.

Kramer, P. (1998) 'A Powerful Cinema-going Force: Hollywood and Female Audiences since the 1960s', in M. Stokes and R. Maltby (eds) *Identifying Hollywood's Audiences: Cultural Identity and the Movies*, London: BFI.

Kristeva, J. (1982) *Powers of Horror*, New York, NY: Columbia University Press.

Krzywinska, T. (1995) 'La Belle Dame Sans Merci?', in P. Burston and C. Richardson (eds) *A Queer Romance: Lesbians, Gay Men and Popular Culture*, London: Routledge.

Kuhn, A. (2000) '"What's the Matter, Trevor? Scared of Something?" Representing the Monstrous-Feminine in *Candyman*', Erfurt Electronic Studies in English, 2000. Available online at: http://webdoc.gwdg.de/edoc/ia/eese/artic20/kuhn/12000.html (accessed 4 September 2004).

Lacan, J. (1998) *Four Fundamental Concepts of Psychoanalysis*, New York, NY: W. W. Norton.

Langford, B. (2005) *Film Genre: Hollywood and Beyond*, Edinburgh: Edinburgh University Press.

Levine, M. (2004) 'A Fun Night Out: Horror and Other Pleasures of the Cinema', in S. J. Schneider (ed.) *Horror Film and Psychoanalysis: Freud's Worst Nightmare*, New York, NY: Cambridge University Press.

Lindsey, S. S. (1996) 'Horror, Femininity, and Carrie's Monstrous Puberty', in B. K. Grant (ed.) *The Dread of Difference: Gender and the Horror Film*. Austin, TX: University of Texas Press.

Lowenstein, A. (2005) *Shocking Representation: Historical Trauma, National Cinema, and the Modern Horror Film*, New York, NY: Columbia University Press.

Mathijs, E. (2003) 'AIDS References in the Critical Reception of David Cronenberg', *Cinema Journal*, 42.4: 29–45.

Metz, C. (2004) 'From The Imaginary Signifier: Identification, Mirror', in L. Braudy and M. Cohen (eds) *Film Theory and Criticism*, Oxford: Oxford University Press.

Mulvey, L. (2004) 'Visual Pleasure and Narrative Cinema', in L. Braudy and M. Cohen (eds) *Film Theory and Criticism*, Oxford: Oxford University Press.

Naremore, J. (1995) 'American Film Noir: The History of an Idea', *Film Quarterly*, 49.2: 14–17.

Neale, S. (1980) *Genre*, London: BFI.

——(2000) *Genre and Hollywood*, London: Routledge.

Needham, G. (2002) 'Playing with Genre: An Introduction to the Italian Giallo', *Kinoeye*, 2.11. Available online at: http://www.kinoeye.org/02/11/needham11.php (accessed 22 November 2007).

Newman, K. (1992) 'The Pleasures of Horror', *Sight and Sound London Film Festival Supplement*, October, 16–18.

Nielsen, B. (2004) '"Something's Wrong, Like More Than You Being Female": Transgressive Sexuality and Discourses of Reproduction in *Ginger Snaps*', *thirdspace* 3.2: 55–69.

Paul, W. (1994) *Laughing Screaming: Modern Hollywood Horror and Comedy*, New York, NY: Columbia University Press.

Peirse, A. (forthcoming) 'Destroying the Male Body in British Horror Cinema', in S. Fouz-Hernández (ed.) *Mysterious Skin: Male Bodies in Contemporary Cinema*, London: I.B. Tauris.

Perry, T. (2006) *Masterpieces of Modernist Cinema*, Bloomington, IN: Indiana University Press.

Peters, F. (2006) 'Looking in the Mirror: Vampires, The Symbolic and the Thing', in P. Day (ed.) *Vampires: Myths and Metaphors of Enduring Evil*, Amsterdam: Rodopi.

Phillips, K. R. (2005) *Projected Fears: Horror Films and American Culture*, Westport, CT: Greenwood.

Pinedo, I. C. (1997) *Recreational Terror: Women and the Pleasures of Horror Film Viewing*, New York, NY: State University of New York Press.

Powell, A. (2005) *Deleuze and Horror Film*, Edinburgh: University of Edinburgh Press.

Prawer, S. S. (1980) *Caligari's Children: The Film as Tale of Terror*, New York, NY: Da Capo Press.

Privett, R. and Kreul, J. (2001) 'The Strange Case of Noel Carroll: A Conversation with the Controversial Film Philosopher', *Senses of Cinema*, 13. Available online at: http://www.sensesofcinema.com/contents/01/13/carroll.html (accessed 13 March 2003).

Rebello, S. (1999) *Alfred Hitchcock and the Making of Psycho*, New York, NY: St Martin's Press.

Robb, B. (1998) *Screams and Nightmares: The Films of Wes Craven*, London: Titan Books.

Royle, N. (2003) *The Uncanny: An Introduction*, Manchester: Manchester University Press.

Ryall, T. (2000) 'Genre and Hollywood', in J. Hill and P. Church-Gibson (eds) *The Oxford Guide to Film Studies*, Oxford: Oxford University Press.

Said, E. (2003) *Orientalism: Western Conceptions of the Orient*, London: Penguin.

Schatz, T. (1981) *Hollywood Genres: Formulas, Filmmaking and the Studio System*, New York, NY: Random House.

——(2004) 'Film Genre and the Genre Film', in L. Braudy and M. Cohen (eds.) *Film Theory and Criticism*, Oxford: Oxford University Press.

Schneider, S. J. (1999) 'Monsters as (Uncanny) Metaphors: Freud, Lakoff, and the Representation of Monstrosity', *Cinematic Horror, Other Voices: The (e)journal of Cultural Criticism*, 1.3. Available online at: http://www.othervoices.org/1.3/sschneider/monsters.html (accessed 14 September 2001).

——(2004a) 'Toward an Aesthetics of Cinematic Horror', in S. Prince (ed.) *The Horror Film*, Piscataway, NJ: Rutgers University Press.

——(2004b) *Horror Film and Psychoanalysis: Freud's Worst Nightmare 2004*, Cambridge: Cambridge University Press.

Shaw, D. (1997) 'A Humean Definition of Horror', *Film-Philosophy*, 1.4. Available online at: http://www.film-philosophy.com/vol1_1997/n4shaw (accessed 9 May 2003).

Skal, D. (1990) *Hollywood Gothic: The Tangled Web of Dracula from Novel to Stage to Screen*, London: Andre Deutsch.

Sonnenschein, D. (2001) *Sound Design: The Expressive Power of Music, Voice and Sound Effects in Cinema*, Studio City, CA: Michael Wiese.

Snelson, T. and Jancovich, M. (forthcoming) '"No Hits, No Runs, Just Terrors": Exhibition, Cultural Distinctions and Cult Audiences at the Rialto Cinema in the 1930s' in R. Maltby, P. Meers and D. Biltereyst (eds) *The Glow in Their Eyes: Global Perspectives on Film Cultures, Film Exhibition, and Cinema-going*, Edinburgh: Blackwell.

Stam, R. (2000) *Film Theory: An Introduction*, Edinburgh: Blackwell.

Stern, L. (1997) 'I Think, Sebastian, Therefore … I Somersault: Freud and the Uncanny', *Australian Humanities Review*, November. Available online at: http://www.lib.latrobe.edu.au/AHR/archive/Issue-November-1997/stern2.html (accessed 12 February 2002).

Stommel, J. (2007) '"Pity Poor Flesh": Terrible Bodies in the Films of Carpenter, Cronenberg, and Romero', *Bright Lights Film Journal*, 56. Available online at: http://www.brightlightsfilm.com/56/bodies.htm (accessed 12 July 2007).

Tamborini, R. (1996) 'A Model of Empathy and Emotional Reactions to Horror', in J. B. Weaver and R. Tambourini (eds) *Horror Films: Current Research on Audience Preferences and Reactions*, Philadelphia, PA: Lawrence Erlbaum.

Tarratt, M. (1986) 'Monsters from the Id', in B. K. Grant (ed.) *Film Genre Reader*, Austin, TX: University of Texas Press.

Tudor, A. (1974) *Theories of Film*, London: Secker Warburg.

——(1986) 'Genre', in B. K. Grant (ed.) *The Film Genre Reader*, Austin, TX: University of Texas Press.

——(1989) *Monsters and Mad Scientists: A Cultural History of the Horror Movie*, Oxford: Basil Blackwell.

——(1997) 'Why Horror? The Peculiar Pleasures of a Popular Genre', *Cultural Studies*, 11.3: 443–63.

——(2002) 'Why Horror? The Peculiar Pleasures of a Popular Genre', in M. Jancovich (ed.) *Horror The Film Reader*, London: Routledge.

Twitchell, J. B. (1985) *Dreadful Pleasures: An Anatomy of Modern Horror*, Oxford: Oxford University Press.

Waller, G. A. (ed.) (1987) *American Horrors: Essays on the Modern Horror Film*, Chicago, IL: University of Illinois Press.

Weiss, E. (1982) *The Silent Scream: Alfred Hitchcock's Soundtrack*, London: Associated University Presses.

Wells, P. (2000) *The Horror Genre: From Beelzebub to Blair Witch*, London: Wallflower.

White, P. (1999) *Uninvited: Classical Hollywood Cinema and Lesbian Representability*, Bloomington, IN: Indiana University Press.

Williams, L. (2002) 'When the Woman Looks', in M. Jancovich (ed.) *Horror the Film Reader*, London: Routledge.

——(2003) 'Film Bodies: Gender, Genre, and Excess', in B. K. Grant (ed) *Film Genre Reader III*, Austin, TX: University of Texas Press.

Williams, L. R. (1999) 'The Inside-Out of Masculinity: David Cronenberg's Visceral Pleasures', in M. Aaron (ed.) *The Body's Perilous Pleasures: Dangerous Desires and Contemporary Culture*, Edinburgh: Edinburgh University Press.

Wood, R. (1986) *Hollywood From Vietnam to Reagan*, New York, NY: Columbia University Press.

——(2002) 'The American Nightmare: Horror in the 70s', in M. Jancovich (ed.) *Horror The Film Reader*, London: Routledge.

——(2004) 'Foreword', in S. J. Schneider (ed.) *Horror Film and Psychoanalysis: Freud's Worst Nightmare*, New York, NY: Cambridge University Press.

Worland, R. (2007) *The Horror Film: An Introduction*, Oxford: Blackwell.

Wright, W. (1975) *Six Guns and Society: a Structural Study of the Western*, Berkeley, CA: University of California Press.

Zillman, D. and Weaver, J. B. (1996) 'Gender Socialization Theory of Reactions to Horror', in J. B. Weaver and R. Tamborini (eds) *Horror Films: Current Research on Audience Preferences and Reactions*, Philadelphia, PA: Lawrence Erlbaum.

Žižek, S. (2001) *Enjoy Your Symptom! Jacques Lacan in Hollywood and Out*, London: Routledge.

Zuckerman, M. (1996) 'Sensation Seeking and the Taste for Vicarious Horror', in J. B. Weaver and R. Tamborini (eds) *Horror Films: Current Research on Audience Preferences and Reactions*, Philadelphia, PA: Lawrence Erlbaum.

INDEX

3D cinema 74
9/11 anxiety in horror 172, 175, 192
13 *Ghosts* 75, 78
28 *Days Later* 55, 56–57, 58

abjection: audience, reactions to 122–24; corpses 112; mother figure 115–16, 117; monstrous-feminine 119–20; sexuality 121–22, 124; taboo subjects 116–18; trans- formation, human to monster 113–15, 120–21; women 118–19, 122
advertising, 19, 20f, 48–50, 75, 186–87f
aesthetics of horror 88–89, 93
Alien 18, 27, 87, 105, 116
Altman, Rick 24, 26, 27, 31
American Psycho, 70
American Werewolf in London, An 70–71, 113
anti-American anxiety in horror 171–73

anxieties, horror as reflective of: 9/11, 172, 175, 192; AIDS 124; anti-American 171–73, 174–75, 178–79; family breakdown 109–10, 173–74; Fordism 172; Jews 176–77; military 172, 174, 175; racism 176– 82; technology 186–89; violence 200–211
apparatus theory 131
Aronofsky, Darren: *Pi* 66, 79
art-dread 89, 98, 164, 165
art horror 156–58, 163–64
audience: age and gender of 39–40, 41–42, 220n13; co-existentialist viewers 24; definition of horror film 24; demonizing of 40–41; effect of horror films on 5, 16, 45–47, 52–59, 93, 201; emotions, effect of horror on 36–39, 43–47; female viewers 42, 119, 140–54; identification with characters 128–40; integrationist viewers 24; marketing to 48, 186; sensory

affects on 81; specialist viewers 159–60; *see also* abjection; identity; uncanny; unconscious

banning of films 90, 207–8
Barker, Clive: 81, 83–84; *Hellraiser* 82, 87; *Nightbreed* 161
Benshoff, Harry 183–84
Berenstein, R. 48–50
birth 111–12, 116, 122
Blackmail 69
Blade Runner 126–27
Blair Witch Project, The: 9, 128; camera angles 65–66, 163; dread 165; review of 55–56, 57, 58; use of technology/media in 186–90, 191f
blindness 127–28
Blood Feast 79
body genres 22–23, 46–47
body horror: 4, 22, 48, 199; in Cronenberg's films 82, 120–24, 162, 198
Body Snatchers 172, 174, 175
Bram Stoker's Dracula 15–16, 50, 194
Bride of Frankenstein, The 177–78, 184–85
Brood, The 109, 111–12, 116, 120
Brown, Rita Mae *Slumber Party Massacre* 25, 35
Buscombe, Edward 17

Cabinet of Dr Caligari, The 61, 63, 68
camera shots: in *Blair Witch Project* 186–90; in *Cloverfield* 190–94; dolly zoom 66, 68; Dutch angles 65, 221n8; point of view shot 132–36; shock cut 85–88; in *The Texas Chain Saw Massacre* 88–89, 91
Candyman: 81; advertising poster 50; and female gaze 145–49; female viewers 119–20; gender/race/sex 181; mirrors in 150
Cannibal Holocaust 117–18
cannibalism 117–18

Carrie 112, 115, 117
Carroll, Noel 23, 24, 46, 98, 156–64
Cat People 87, 166
Cherry Falls 22, 27
children as monsters 108
cleanliness, rituals of 115, 116–17
Clover, Carol 27, 40, 98, 133, 137, 138, 140, 141
Cloverfield 65, 190–94
cognitive theory of emotions 155–66
colour, use of in horror 73–80
Coppola, Francis Ford: 15; *Bram Stoker's Dracula* 15–16, 50, 194
Corman, Roger 101
Crane, Jonathan Lake 200, 201, 203, 205
Craven, Wes: 34; *A Nightmare on Elm Street* 21, 25, 34, 41, 107; *The People Under the Stairs* 181–82; *Scream* series 8–9, 42, 70
Creed, Barbara 97, 112, 113, 116, 118, 119, 120, 141, 156
Cronenberg, David: 4, 81, 82, 98–99; *The Brood* 109, 111–12, 116, 120; *Dead Ringers* 80; *The Fly*, *see* main entry; *Rabid* 122; *Shivers* 120, 123; *Videodrome* 82, 198, 120–22, 198
Crow, The 50
Curse of Frankenstein, The 75, 76–78t

Daily Mail and video nasties campaign 207–8
darkness, use of in horror 30, 127–28, 142
Dawn of the Dead 129–32, 168
Day of the Dead 168
Dead Ringers 80
Dead Silence 71–73
Descent, The 127, 128, 142–44
Devil's Mansion, The 61
Diffrient, David Scott 85–87, 88
disgust while watching horror 156, 158–60, 161–63; *see also* abjection

Doctor X 74
Dracula 49, 77

Eraserhead 79, 92, 199
ethnicity 153
Evil Dead, The 9, 65–67f, 83, 150
Exorcist, The: box office takings 8;
    colour, use of 80; disgust at
    content 111, 118, 159, 163; and
    family breakdown 109; "modern
    defilement rite" 119; monstrous-
    feminine 112, 115; and
    repression 110; screenings of 58
Eye, The 127–28
eyes, loss of 126–27

family breakdown 109–10, 173–74
fear, as feminine 49–50
female viewers: 38, 48–50, 51;
    cross- gender identification
    137–38; identi- fication, general
    140–54
femininity: 108–9; failure to look
    141–44; feminine gaze 140;
    heroine and monster, affinity
    between 144–50, 153–54;
    monstrous-feminine 112, 145
film making: and genre 31, 34–35
    see also technological advances
film types 5t–6t, 7
Final Destination 86
Fly, The: 23; AIDS connection 124;
    body horror 82, 120–21, 122;
    disgust 161–62
Fordism 171, 172
foreign horror: German Expressionism
    62–65; Italian 79; Japanese 7, 22,
    48, 194–97, 198–99
Frankenstein 165, 177–78
Freeland, Cynthia 83, 89, 92, 94,
    155, 164–65, 166
Freud, Sigmund: eyes 126; the
    uncanny 102–5, 128; the
    unconscious 99–100
Friday the 13th 21, 25, 27, 107

Gauntlett, David 176
gaze, cinematic: 128–37; cross
    -gender, 133, 137–40; exchange
    of looks, heroine/monster
    144–50, 153–54; failure to look
    142–44; looking away (female)
    141–42
gender: audience 39–40, 41–42;
    cross- gender identification 133,
    137–38; gender identification
    128–54; horror films as practice
    for gender roles 38–39; marketing
    to 48–51; new gendered identities
    149–50
genre: audience, defined by 42–44;
    body 46–47; categories of 29–30;
    contemporary issues, addressing
    11, 171–211; finding factor X 23;
    foreign films 23; pragmatic
    approach to defining 31;
    semantic approach to 26,
    27, 31; slasher 19– 39; syntactic
    approach to 26, 27, 31; theories
    on 16–19; as value judgement of
    film 33
genre cinema and the film industry
    9–10, 32–33
German Expressionist cinema,
    62–65; Cabinet of Dr Caligari, The 61,
    63, 68; Nosferatu 61, 63–65, 85,
    176–77, 182; menstruation 112,
    115, 117, 118
ghosts 75, 78, 154, 196–97
Giallo 3, 32, 219n
gimmicks 74–75
Ginger Snaps 112, 113–15
Gothic films 7, 22, 50, 145; and
    Hammer studios 75

Halberstam, Judith 140, 149–50
Halloween: 25, 28f; and cinematic
    gaze 132, 133–36, 138–39;
    virginity 27
Hammer Studios 75, 76–78
Harper, Stephen 178

Haunting, The 154, 163
Hellraiser 82, 83
Hills, Matt 119, 163–64, 165–66
Hitchcock, Alfred 66, 69–70
homosexuality 153, 170, 183–84
horror film: aesthetics of 88–89,
    93; audience definition of 24;
    appeal of 94–166; categories of
    3–7, 10, 21–22; cinematic gaze
    125–40; classifying films as
    14–15; difficulty in defining 1–3,
    19–22; and femininity 140–54;
    film makers 4, 31, 34–35; and
    gender roles 38–39; labelling as
    value judgement 33; and genre
    theories 16–19; German
    Expressionism 62–65; and
    identity, *see* identity; ideologies/
    fears, reflecting of *see* anxieties;
    Italian 79; Japanese 7, 22, 4,
    194–97, 198–99; making of 59–
    93; marketing of 48–51, 186;
    negative views of 12–13;
    popularity of 8–9; violence, as
    encouraging 41; *see also* audience;
    genre; psychoanalysis and entries
    for individual films
horror film theory: cognitive theory
    of emotions 155–66;
    psychoanalysis studies 94–154
Hostel 56, 57–58
House on Haunted Hill, The 74
Howling, The 113

identity: 176–85; cross-gender 133,
    137–40; female identification
    140–54; identifying with victim/
    killer 128–40, 157, 162; *see also*
    other, concept of
Interview with the Vampire 50, 153, 170,
    183–84
Into the Mirror 150
Invasion, The 172, 174, 175
Invasion of the Body Snatchers 171–72,
    174, 175

Jancovich, Mark 15, 42, 43, 75,
    120, 145, 170, 172–73, 174
Japanese horror 7, 22, 48, 194–97,
    198–99
Jews, as race horror 176–77
Jones, Amy: *Slumber Party Massacre*
    25, 35

Kristeva, Julia 112–13, 115, 117,
    118, 150
Ku Klux Klan 178

Lacan, Jacques 107, 115, 131, 150,
    151
lesbianism 153, 154
look of horror cinema 125–40
Lynch, David 44: *Eraserhead* 79, 92,
    199
lynch mobs 177–81

Malèfique 48
marketing 48–51; *Blair Witch Project*
    186–87f
*Masque of the Red Death,?*78–79
McCartney, Jenny 209–10
Méliès, Georges: 60–61, 85
military, conceptions of in horror
    172, 174
mirrors 150–52
monsters 23–30, 99, 105–8,
    156–58, 159–62; *Cloverfield*
    192–94
monstrosity as race/gender/class
    176–85
monstrous-feminine 112, 118–22
mother figure 115–16, 117, 119
Mulvey, Laura 128, 133, 137–38,
    141, 153
music, effect of 68, 69–71, 89
My Bloody Valentine 25
Mystery of the Wax Museum 74

Neale, Stephen 3, 10, 29–30, 46,
    95, 96, 118
Nightbreed 161

Night of the Living Dead 168, 178–79
Nightmare on Elm Street, A 21, 25, 34, 41, 107
Nightwatch 150
Nosferatu 61, 63–65, 85, 176–77, 182

orality 117–18
Other, concept of 107–8, 128, 131, 138, 144, 145, 150, 176 see also identity
Others, The 164–65

Paul, William 123–24, 170
Peeping Tom 150
People Under the Stairs, The 181–82
Phantom of the Opera, The 74, 86, 141–42
Pi 66, 79
Picture of Dorian Gray, The 74
Plague of the Zombies 179
Poltergeist? 68
posters 19, 20f, 48–50, 75, 186
pragmatic approach to genre 31
Prawer, S.S. 44, 45, 54
Psycho 69–70
psychoanalysis of appeal of horror: 99–102; abjection 111–25; conscious/unconscious mind 98–102; studies of 94–102; the uncanny 102–11

Rabid 122
racial interpretation in horror 176–92
repression: 100–101, 104, 106–11, 113; and gender/sexuality 108–9, 112; and women 108–11
Ringu 169, 194–97
Romero, George: 168, 181; Dawn of the Dead 129–32, 168; Day of the Dead 168; Night of the Living Dead 168, 178–79

Saw series 56, 58, 159–60, 163, 194, 200–204

Schneider, Stephen 96, 101–2, 105–6, 155
Scream series 8–9, 42, 70
self, sense of 150–52
semantic/syntactic approaches to genre 26–28, 31
sex 27, 111, 121
sexuality: homosexuality 153–54, 182–85; monstrosity 122, 144; repressed 108–9, 111; sexually transmitted diseases 121, 124; and women 118
sexually transmitted disease 121–22, 124
shadows 30; see also, Cabinet of Dr Caligari, The; Nosferatu
Shaun of the Dead 18–19, 20f
Shaw, Daniel 160–61
Shining, The 80, 92
Shivers 120, 123
Silence of the Lambs, The 15, 27, 33
Silent Night, Deadly Night 22
Sixth Sense, The 164
slasher films: 7, 11, 19–39, 47, 167; A Nightmare on Elm Street 21, 25, 34, 41, 107; cross-gender identity, 133, 137–40; definition of 26–27; feminist approach to 25, 35; Halloween 25, 27, 28f, 132, 133–36, 138–39; identi- fication 132–37; My Bloody Valentine 25; naming of films as 31–33; point of view shot 132–37; and repression 110–11; semantic/ syntactic approach to 26–27, 31; sex in 27; Slumber Party Massacre 25, 35; video nasties 90, 117, 118, 207–8, 220n9; violence against women 132–33, 137, 139, 140–41
Slither 123
Slumber Party Massacre 25; feminist responses to 35
sound 68–73, 86, 141
special effects 35, 80–85, 203–4 see also technological advances

Stam, Robert 16–17, 18, 19, 31
Stepfather, The 109–10, 111
Stern, Lesley 125–26, 128
sublime, the 89–93
supernatural films 7, 48, 154, 194–97
subjectivity 129–40
Suspiria 80, 81–82

technological advances in filmmaking 92–93: camera angles 65–68; colour 73–80; early innovations 60–61; lighting and set design 62–65; sound 68–73, 86; shock cut 85–88; special effects 80–85
technology, as source of anxiety 186–89
Tetsuo 198–99
Texas Chainsaw Massacre, The 87, 88–89, 90–91, 149
Tingler, The 74, 78
torture porn 204, 205–6, 209
Tudor, Andrew 21, 23, 24, 32, 44, 98, 166, 167, 175
Twitchell, James 40, 43–44

uncanny, the 102–11, 125–27, 165
unconscious, the 98–102

vampires 161: Bram Stoker's Dracula 15–16, 50, 194; Dracula 49, 77; homosexuality 182–83; Méliès, Georges 61; Nosferatu 61, 63–65, 85, 176–77, 182; mirror reflection 150–51; sexuality 153; see also Interview with the Vampire
Videodrome 82, 198

video nasties: 90, 117, 118, 220n9; campaign against 207–8
violence, social anxiety about 200–211
virginity 27

Wan, James: Dead Silence 71–73; Saw series 56, 58, 159–60, 163, 194, 200–204
Weaver, J. B. 37–38, 50, 209
Weiss, E. 69
Wells, P. 168, 170, 211
werewolves: 113–15, 156; An American Werewolf in London 70–71, 113; The Howling 113; see also Ginger Snaps
westerns 11, 17
When a Stranger Calls 22
Whitehouse, Mary and video nasties campaign 207–8
White, Patricia 153–54
Williams, Linda 46–47, 82, 84–85, 90, 141–42, 144–45, 152, 153, 154
womb, the 111, 112, 113, 116
women: 48–50, 109, 118–19, 125; changing role of 174; repression of 108–11; as victims 118–19; violence against 132–33, 137, 139, 140–41; see also slasher films
Wood, Robin 36, 97, 106–11, 155, 166, 167–68

Yotsuya Kaidan 196–97

Zillman, Dolf 37–38, 50, 209
Žižek, Slavoj 151
zombies 11–12, 129–32, 156, 168

Related titles from Routledge

Cinema Studies: The Key Concepts
Second Edition

Susan Hayward

This is the essential guide for anyone interested in film. Now in its second edition, the text has been completely revised and expanded to meet the needs of today's students and film enthusiasts. Some 150 key genres, movements, theories and production terms are explained and analyzed with depth and clarity. Entries include:

- Auteur Theory
- Blaxploitation
- British New Wave
- Feminist Film Theory
- Intertextuality
- Method Acting
- Pornography
- Third World Cinema
- Vampire movies

A bibliography of essential writings in cinema studies completes an authoritative yet accessible guide to what is at once a fascinating area of study and arguably the greatest art form of modern times.

ISBN13: 978-0-415-22739-1 (hbk)
ISBN13: 978-0-415-22740-7 (pbk)

Available at all good bookshops
For ordering and further information please visit:
www.routledge.com

Related titles from Routledge

Horror, the Film Reader

Edited by Mark Jancovich

Horror, the Film Reader brings together key articles to provide a comprehensive resource for students of horror cinema. Mark Jancovich's introduction traces the development of horror film from *The Cabinet of Dr. Caligari* to *The Blair Witch Project*, and outlines the main critical debates. Combining classic and recent articles, each section explores a central issue of horror film, and features an editor's introduction outlining the context of debates. Sections include:

- Theorising horror
- Gender, sexuality and the horror film
- Producing horrors
- Consuming fears

Contributors include: Harry M. Benshoff, Rhona Berenstein, Noël Carroll, Brigid Cherry, Carol J. Clover, Barbara Creed, Paul O'Flinn, Joan Hawkins, Peter Hutchings, Mark Jancovich, Andrew Tudor, Linda Williams and Robin Wood.

ISBN13: 978-0-415-23561-7 (hbk)
ISBN13: 978-0-415-23562-4 (pbk)

Available at all good bookshops
For ordering and further information please visit:
www.routledge.com

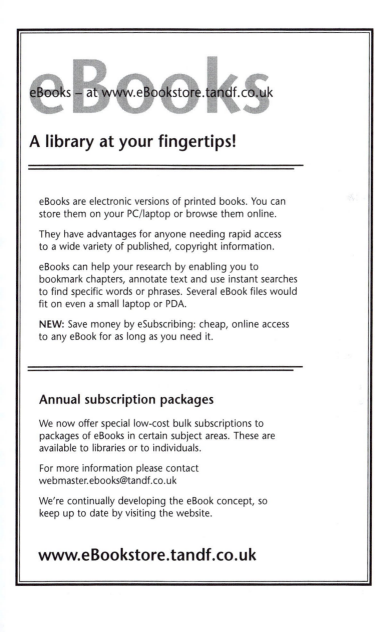